# Aromatherapy

## A practical guide to
## essential oils and aromassage

JAN BALKAM

D1079839

Blitz Editions

Published by Blitz Editions
an imprint of Bookmart Ltd
Registered Number 2372865
Trading as Bookmart Ltd
Desford Road
Enderby
Leicester LE9 5AD

This book created by Amazon Publishing Ltd
Editor: Jayne Booth
Design: Cooper Wilson Ltd
Cover photography: John Freeman
Printed and bound in Great Britain by
BPC Hazell Books Ltd
A member of
The British Printing Company Ltd

ISBN 1-85605-231-1

### SAFETY NOTE

Throughout the book *asterisks refer to important safety information placed in boxes below the marked text. Please read these notes carefully.

### AUTHOR'S NOTE

All recommendations contained in this book are believed by the author to be effective if properly administered and if the correct, good-quality oils are used. However, the author has no control over the essential oils used by others or the manner in which they are used, and the author cannot guarantee the effectiveness of their use or be held in any way liable.

The author is not a qualified medical practitioner and her views and advice are not intended to be a substitute for consulting a qualified medical practitioner.

# Contents

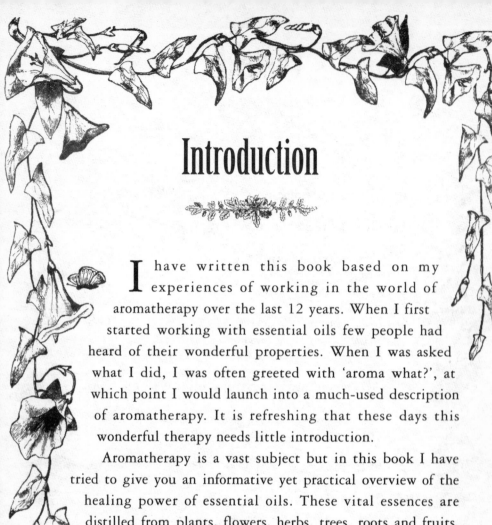

# Introduction

I have written this book based on my experiences of working in the world of aromatherapy over the last 12 years. When I first started working with essential oils few people had heard of their wonderful properties. When I was asked what I did, I was often greeted with 'aroma what?', at which point I would launch into a much-used description of aromatherapy. It is refreshing that these days this wonderful therapy needs little introduction.

Aromatherapy is a vast subject but in this book I have tried to give you an informative yet practical overview of the healing power of essential oils. These vital essences are distilled from plants, flowers, herbs, trees, roots and fruits, and each have different therapeutic properties. Their remarkable quality is that as well as benefiting the physical body, they can also affect you on a mental and emotional level too. In this book you will find out more about what aromatherapy is, a little of its history and what aromatherapy can do for

you. Several methods of using essential oils are covered along with suggested recipes and treatments for the relief of many common ailments which you may experience at different stages of your life. There are step-by-step massage techniques for all the family, and instructions on how to blend your own massage oils. Besides the sensual aspect of aromatherapy you can also learn how to fragrance your environment using the healing and mood-enhancing properties of essential oils. Although I have suggested some recipes, there is also plenty of scope for you to create your own perfumes, skin-care preparations and aromatic bath blends.

Throughout the book safety information and other important notes are presented in boxes and marked with an *asterisk, so please read these sections carefully. If used correctly essential oils can be very healing, but they are natural chemicals and should always be treated with care. If you wish to use essential oils therapeutically be sure not to buy synthetic copies or adulterated oils (certain oils often are). Always buy from a reputable supplier (see Useful Addresses at the back of the book). Where possible buy essential oils which come from wild or organically grown plants.

I hope this book does much to stimulate your curiosity and interest so that you may learn more and incorporate aromatherapy into your everyday life.

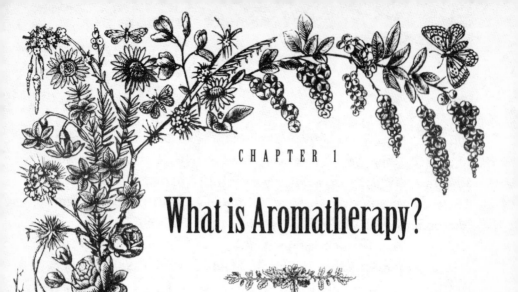

## CHAPTER 1

# What is Aromatherapy?

Aromatherapy is a system of healing which involves the use of pure essential oils. These fragrant oils are distilled from various parts of plants, flowers, herbs and trees, each of which have different therapeutic properties. If you would like to experience a simplified version of aromatherapy, crush some fresh rosemary leaves between your fingers and inhale the penetrating and stimulating scent.

There are hundreds of aromatic oils originating from countries such as India, China, Australia and the Americas to name but a few. However, essential oils are much more than sweet smells; they are also concentrated, natural chemicals. These oils are volatile (they evaporate readily) and consist of powerful constituents and should therefore be treated with care and used in very small amounts. Most essential oils have a water-like consistency, although some like sandalwood, vetiver and myrrh are very viscous (thick). Colours can range from virtually colourless to light green (bergamot), red-brown (patchouli) and inky blue (German camomile).

The oils are derived from different parts of the plant. For instance, lavender oil is distilled from the flowering tops of the plant – and it is one

of the most useful essences for aromatherapy. Among other things this versatile oil is good for burns, headaches, insomnia and it aids relaxation. Eucalyptus oil comes from the leaves of the tree and has decongestant and powerful antiseptic properties making it invaluable when treating catarrh, colds and other infectious conditions.

The benefits of aromatherapy can be enjoyed in a variety of ways. A qualified aromatherapist generally uses the medium of massage and may blend you essences for you to use between treatments. However, you can use essential oils at home in this way or as room fragrancers, perfumes, for skin or hair care in health-giving baths, or to treat many common ailments. Because of their high concentration they must be diluted in a 'fatty' base oil like sweet almond before they can be applied to the skin. Some essential oils blend well together and others make less fragrant blending companions! However, when two or more 'compatible' essential oils are blended together they can enhance each other's qualities creating a more potent effect than if they were used individually. This is called synergy. It is important to realise that this is not accomplished by using large quantities of different oils, instead a subtle blend of just two essences can, in many instances, be more effective. Often a few drops are all that is needed to have a powerful effect on both body and mind.

Other complementary therapies can be used in conjunction with aromatherapy, for example cranial osteopathy, shiatsu, herbalism, dietary therapy and many others. However, if you are taking homeopathic remedies, do talk to your homeopath before using aromatherapy for yourself. I know homeopaths who advise their patients against aromatherapy while taking homeopathic remedies. However, others advise simply not to use essential oils close to the time when you take the homeopathic remedy, so seek your own practitioner's advice on this subject.

## How to choose an essential oil

Select an essential oil that suits not just your physical but also your mental and emotional needs. It is also very important that the aroma is pleasing to

you, as scents have a powerful effect on many levels. An essence which doesn't appeal to you is less likely to have an enhancing effect upon your mood and sense of well-being. There is often a range of oils to choose from which treats the same condition so be guided by your own preferences and intuition. For details of the main qualities of 32 essential oils and tips on successfully blending them, see Chapters 3 and 5.

## HOW DOES AROMATHERAPY WORK?

Aromatherapy, as its name suggests, works partly through our sense of smell. However, the essences also enter the body through skin absorption. In these ways essential oils can affect not just the physical body but the emotional levels too.

As we inhale an essential oil the tiny molecules are drawn into the lungs where some are transported into the bloodstream through the alveoli (small air sacs in the lungs). This is what happens when you take an aromatic bath although here some of the oil on the surface of the water is also absorbed through your skin. Another way for essential oils to enter the body is through an aromatherapy massage. Essential oils diluted in a base oil are readily absorbed by the skin, penetrating through the deep layers of tissue to capillaries (tiny blood vessels) where they pass into the bloodstream. From here they are transported via tissue fluids around the body, influencing various organs or systems according to their individual properties (see Chapter 3). Eventually they are passed out of the body through the skin, lungs and urine. Though essential oils can take as little as 30 minutes to be absorbed (depending upon the person) their wonderful effect can last for many hours after the treatment.

Our sense of smell is still not entirely understood although scientific research is continuing all the time. Aromas are inhaled into the upper nasal cavity (at the top of the nose) where olfactory receptor cells are located under a thin layer of mucus. Fine hairs (cilia) cover the end of each cell and project through the mucus. The latest theory is that different aromatic molecules may fit into different places on the receptors which

cover these hairs according to their shapes. When an inhaled aromatic molecule fits into the 'right' receptor a 'message' or recognition is sent through the olfactory nerve directly into the limbic system in the brain. This causes an immediate response of like or dislike as well as being able to smell the odour. The limbic system deals with our instinctive responses – emotions, sex drive and memory – and is closely related to the part of the brain concerned with the sense of smell. This system links to yet another part of the brain which affects the pituitary gland. This gland has important functions and influences the balance of hormones within the body.

Besides affecting the nervous and hormonal systems, different aromas can also trigger immediate positive or negative feelings. Certain scents may even remind us of people, places and situations in the past. For example, I have a friend who loves ylang-ylang oil as it evokes happy memories of his childhood in Malaysia. Equally if an aroma reminds you of an unpleasant situation or you instinctively dislike it choose another essential oil to suit your needs – your intuition knows best. The versatile nature of essential oils enables them to be used to improve your general sense of well-being as well as to treat a wide range of more physical common ailments.

## A BRIEF HISTORY OF AROMATHERAPY

Aromatherapy is not new, in fact most of the ancient civilisations used essential oils in some form. There is evidence in the Bible of oils being used for anointing, and ancient Indian and Chinese texts detail their medical uses. The ancient Egyptians were very concerned with beauty and oils were widely used; there are even tomb paintings showing foot and body massages. Skilled high priests and physicians blended aromatic oils together with herbs and animal fat to make healing ointments. Fragrant cosmetics, temple incenses and perfumes were some of the other uses for the essential oils and resins like myrrh and frankincense. They also used essences like cedarwood, frankincense, juniper and myrrh in the mummification process.

Cleopatra apparently bathed several times each day and particularly favoured the essences of orange blossom, cedarwood and rose. In her palace she was constantly surrounded by wafting incenses and, like other wealthy Egyptians, she perfumed her body with fragrant oils. Egyptian men and women of this period loved adorning themselves and it was common practice for them to wear different perfumes on various parts of their bodies. At times they would also wear garlands of scented, fresh flowers. These fragrant blooms, like the oils, were highly valued and often given as token offerings to the gods.

The Romans also knew the secrets of aromatic oils and were particularly keen on rose oil, which was sometimes used to make wine as well as for more sensual pleasures. They turned the love of bathing and scenting themselves into a virtual art form, and were massaged with aromatic body oils in their steaming baths. The Greek civilisation produced great 'holistic' physicians who also recognised the healing power of plants. One great physician, Hippocrates, is known as the father of medicine. His observations lead him to recommend aromatic baths and massage to maintain good health. Another, Dioscorides, collated and wrote down his knowledge of medicinal plants in a vast 'Materia Medica'.

However, it is the tenth-century Arab physician 'Avicenna' who is credited with the discovery of steam distillation, a process used to obtain essential oils still used today. Rose was the first essential oil to be produced in this way, and floral waters were made as a by-product of this method. The distilled oils were very concentrated and potent and although oils were blended for healing, many essences, including rose were used as perfumes. Soldiers returning from the Crusades brought back these scents from Arabia which proved very popular with both European men and women. In the West they copied the exotic perfumes and began to use plants like lavender, marjoram and basil to create their own blends. In the seventeenth century, the famous astrologer and physician Nicholas Culpeper wrote his 'herball'. This book contained details about many different plants, 'herbal' oils and their uses. The findings of the Greek physician Dioscorides and Arab physicians are also referred to by Culpeper on numerous occasions.

Throughout history during epidemics, woods like juniper and pine have been burned and essences have been worn in pomanders for their fragrant and antiseptic properties. In medieval Europe, outbreaks of plague were combated in various ways. However, it is reported that the glove makers (who impregnated gloves with aromatics) and the perfumers mostly escaped death, perhaps because they absorbed the 'cocktail' of aromas which surrounded them through their skin as well as constantly inhaled them. During the seventeenth and eighteenth centuries perfume became very popular with those who could afford it. People tended not to bathe much but instead masked body odours with sweet-smelling scents. In France, the extent of this popularity could be seen at Louis XV's royal court which was known as the 'perfumed court'. He adored scent and ordered that a new perfume be created for him everyday. The King's mistress, Madame de Pompadour, didn't disappoint him; in pursuit of the ultimate perfume she spent vast sums of money on essential oils and resins. (Throughout Chapter 3 I have described many past uses, myths and origins of specific essential oils.)

From the early part of the nineteenth century, traditional remedies declined because of the new advances in drug therapy. However, by the early twentieth century it was apparent that these drugs could cause unwanted side-effects. However, the knowledge of 'medicinal' plants had somehow survived and scientists began to research them more closely. One person who was fascinated (initially by the potential cosmetic uses) of vital plant essences was René Maurice Gattefossé. He was a French cosmetic chemist in his family's perfume business and the antiseptic and healing powers of essential oils were confirmed to him in a rather unpleasant manner. One day while experimenting in his laboratory there was an explosion and his arm was badly burned. He immediately plunged it into a vat of lavender oil and it healed extremely quickly, to his amazement, with no trace of scarring. In the 1920s, Gattefossé coined the word *Aromathérapie* and by 1928 he had published a book of the same name. Meanwhile in Italy Drs Cajola and Gatti were also conducting research into the effects of plant essences on the mental and emotional levels as well as physical conditions. Research continued on a small scale until the Second World War began.

However, it was Dr Jean Valnet who brought the power of aromatherapy to the attention of both medical colleagues and ordinary people. Valnet was a French army surgeon who had been interested in the healing power of plants since childhood. During the Second World War, Dr Valnet used essential oils to treat battle wounds and later went on to use the oils with psychiatric patients. He researched and wrote many articles and was a major force in rekindling interest in aromatherapy. In 1964 he published a book entitled *Aromathérapie* (the English translation is called *The Practice of Aromatherapy* ) which is a classic work. Dr Valnet formulated his own range of products, lectured widely and is still writing today.

Also in 1964, the Austrian biochemist Margaret Maury's book *Le Capital Jeunesse* was translated into English as *The Secret Of Life And Youth*. Madame Maury took an holistic approach to the subject of her research, monitoring amongst other things how each essence affected a person's overall well-being. She was really ahead of her time with interests in many forms of natural healing and meditation, ranging from acupuncture to Zen! In France, Madame Maury also exhaustively researched the effect of essential oils on the nervous system and especially their cosmetic and rejuvenating qualities. In fact, her research work into essential oils and cosmetology was honoured in 1962 and 1967 when she received two international prizes. She opened several European clinics and combined aromatherapy with massage techniques. Through her enthusiasm, writing and teaching she did much to establish aromatherapy in the post-war years. Indeed I believe she really helped in many ways to lay the foundations for today's holistic aromatherapists. Up until the early 1970s most essential oil research was taking place in France, Italy and Germany. However, in 1977 Robert Tisserand published a book entitled *The Art of Aromatherapy* and has since worked to popularise the therapy in English-speaking countries.

## THE PRESENT AND THE FUTURE

In the last 10 years or so aromatherapy has become increasingly popular and thankfully more and more people are now hearing of the healing power of

essential oils. To cope with the increased interest various schools, associations and essential oil companies were founded in the UK. Growing numbers of people wanted to know more about aromatherapy or even train as practitioners using these vital plant essences. Over the years this has lead to different ways of practising aromatherapy. There are medical (also known as clinical), holistic and aesthetic approaches to the therapy.

In recent years some French medical doctors have trained to a high standard in medical herbalism and prescribe essential oils alongside herbal medicines for the treatment of some serious illnesses. This is medical aromatherapy and represents a small percentage overall of the way aromatherapy is currently used. In the UK some qualified aromatherapists have been using essential oils externally in hospitals or hospices alongside medical teams. Nurses and midwives are beginning to study aromatherapy, making it even more accessible for patients and pregnant women.

Qualified aromatherapists practise from clinics, their homes, hospitals or hospices, and tend to treat minor or common ailments and relieve symptoms of stress (see Chapter 14). Many of these use an holistic approach to healing which means that they consider the mind, body, emotions, spirit and environmental factors and not just the symptoms before deciding on the treatment. This gives patients the opportunity to be touched and to experience fragrant, uplifting or calming aromas in a potentially very stressful environment. Generally, these aromatherapists use massage with essential oils as a healing tool and may give their patients blends of oils to use in various ways (such as inhalations) at home between treatments. In more recent times some UK hospitals have used stimulating or relaxing essential oils as environmental fragrances with positive results. And aromatherapists or nurses who have trained in aromatherapy may provide massage with essential oils and other palliative care for patients. As this continues we will hopefully see a further bridging of the gap, allowing complementary and orthodox practitioners to work side by side.

Aromatherapy is also used aesthetically with many beauty therapists now completing training courses in essential oils. They are likely to work

with massage but are also experts in other beauty therapy techniques. Essential oils give good results in skin care and are, of course, delightfully scented as well as healing. Commercially the potential of aromatherapy is being recognised too and business is booming. International cosmetic and fragrance companies continue to increase their use of plant oils in quality skin-care products. Other companies are realising the health and 'mood' influencing potential of environmental fragrancing through air-conditioning systems, with Japan and the USA at the leading edge of this developing market. Many consumer products are already being fragranced, nearly always using synthetics (mainly for economic reasons) which do not have the same therapeutic effect as essential oils. Hopefully in the future we may accept more 'essentially' fragranced products and environments like hospitals, hotels and other public places as a matter of course.

Essential oils are once more being used as home remedies for minor ailments. Instead of reaching for the aspirin bottle to relieve a tension headache, people are increasingly reaching for lavender oil. Sprinkle 2 drops of lavender oil onto a tissue and inhale deeply. It has a pleasant smell, relieves your headache, makes you feel good and induces relaxation – what a combination!

> *Aromatherapy can be used successfully in a number of ways as long as some basic safety information is followed (see Chapter 2).*

## WHAT CAN AROMATHERAPY DO FOR YOU?

Aromatherapy can enrich your life in many ways. The unusual versatility of essential oils makes it possible to use them for many purposes in everyday life. Pure essential oils have different therapeutic properties making them effective healing agents for a wide range of common physical ailments. For example, all essential oils are antibacterial to a greater or lesser degree, although tea tree, eucalyptus and lemon oil are particularly powerful. Some essences induce a relaxing effect such as lavender, marjoram and camomile, whereas sweet basil and rosemary are both stimulat-

ing. However, essential oils also have a profound effect on the mental and emotional levels too. Some essences are uplifting emotionally such as bergamot, jasmine and clary sage. Others, like sandalwood, orange blossom and rose oil, have been credited with having aphrodisiac qualities for thousands of years.

Aromatherapy has much to offer whether you have only a little time to benefit from the qualities of essential oils or whether you decide to explore the subject more deeply. The easiest way to use aromatherapy is by sprinkling a few drops (literally) of an essential oil into a bath. This way you can be relaxed, refreshed and invigorated, or use the healing properties of perhaps lavender or tea tree oil to help keep your immune system strong.

Alternatively by adding essential oils to a vaporiser you can influence not just your own health and mood but those of others too. Again the possibilities are endless as you blend different essential oils (usually I would recommend between one and three) to induce the desired effect. Some examples of what can be attained would be relaxing, sensual, uplifting or even mentally stimulating environments. In the 1980s, the practical potential for this method was recognised by several companies in Japan and the United States which diffused various essential oils through their air-conditioning systems. This increased productivity by helping employees maintain a high level of mental alertness, leading to fewer errors at work.

For years French hospitals used antibacterial and antiviral essential oils to reduce the risk of infection. In more recent times hospitals in the UK have been using essences as environmental fragrancers with positive results. While working at a London hospice I not only worked directly with patients, but also used blends of essential oils to fragrance the wards and patients' rooms. The positive effects of the aromas were so marked that I was regularly asked by nurses and doctors to use the essences in their offices. This proved very successful for everybody and generally had an uplifting and energising effect in what could be at times a rather sterile, bleak environment.

Your own skin perfumes and aromatic skin-care preparations can all be made from essential oils and a few other basic ingredients. Each of these blended

products has the added bonus of being your unique creation, made from natural ingredients as well as having a beneficial effect on the health of your skin. Some essences, like orange blossom and frankincense oil, are credited with rejuvenating properties. Hair and scalp problems can also be treated, and by adding a few drops of an appropriate essence to a shampoo or your final rinsing water you can instantly create a subtle fragrance for your hair.

*Aromatherapy can be used in many ways, as you will see in Chapter 2. Although some of these methods are quick and easy to use it must be remembered that pure essential oils are concentrated plant chemicals and must be used with care. If used in excess some are skin irritants (black pepper and others) or can cause discolouration of the skin if it is oiled and then exposed to the sun or ultraviolet light (bergamot and others). Others can promote menstruation (clary sage, sweet marjoram and others) or have relatively high toxicity (sweet fennel and others) so are not suitable for pregnant women, babies and young children or other 'vulnerable' people. There are also a handful of oils which should be avoided by people with epilepsy, high or very low blood pressure. So always check the suitability of an essential oil by referring to safety information and the 'Caution' notes in Chapters 2 and 3. However, the above-mentioned essences, if used correctly, can be very useful in the appropriate circumstances.*

*Only pure essential oils will give the therapeutic effects described in this book so be sure not to buy synthetic copies or diluted essences if you wish to use them for healing purposes.*

However, the healing art of massage remains one of the most luxurious, effective and health-giving ways of using essential oils. Pure essential oils are very powerful and before they can be used on the skin they must be diluted in a good-quality, 'fatty' base oil such as sweet almond oil. Choose an oil or selection of oils which appeals to you and is compatible not only with your physical but also your mental and emotional needs. For easy reference I have outlined which oils blend well together in Chapter 3 but also be guided by your own preferences and intuition. There are endless permutations of 'blends' to be made with essential oils as an extra drop of one essence can change the overall aroma and effect of a therapeutic massage blend.

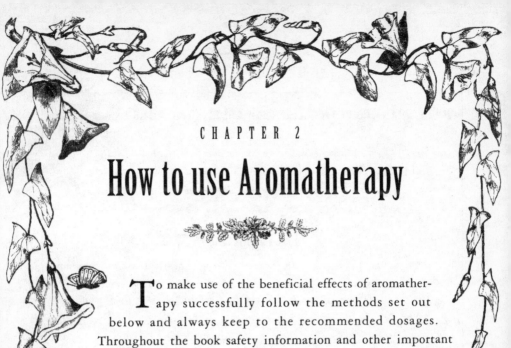

## CHAPTER 2

# How to use Aromatherapy

To make use of the beneficial effects of aromatherapy successfully follow the methods set out below and always keep to the recommended dosages. Throughout the book safety information and other important notes are marked with an *asterisk and presented below in a box, so please read these sections carefully.

When selecting an essential oil choose one whose aroma is pleasing to you, and is compatible not only with your physical condition but also with your mental and emotional needs. Chapter 3 gives details of 32 different essences and lists which oils blend well together. These listings are meant as guidelines for you, so have fun creating blends by letting your own preferences and intuition be your guide. Initially it is best to use only one or two different essential oils then later, when you know each essence very well, a maximum of four may be blended.

Reputable companies sell essential oils with plugs inserted into the tops of the bottles which allow the oils to be dispensed easily in drops. For easy reference here are some helpful guidelines concerning liquid measures of essential oils and base oils.

**20 drops of essential oil = 1ml**
**1 teaspoon = 5ml**
**1 dessertspoon = 10ml**
**1 tablespoon = 15ml**

## RECOMMENDED DOSAGES OF ESSENTIAL OILS

*For massage blends I recommend that* adults and teenagers *use a
2.5 per cent dilution, for example, 25 drops of essential oil diluted in
a 50ml bottle of base oil like sweet almond. For the bath add between 3 drops of
an essential oil and 10 drops in total if using a selection of essences.*

### LOWER DOSAGES

*If a massage blend is to be used on the* face, *or for people with* sensitive skin, pregnant
women *or* children over six years of age *use a 1.25 per cent dilution or even less. For
example, use 12 drops of essential oil in total in a 50ml bottle of a base oil like sweet
almond. For the bath mix between 2 drops of an essential oil or 5 drops in total (if using
a selection of oils) with 2 teaspoons of base oil. Add this prediluted blend to the bath
water and mix well.*

*In massage blends for* babies up to one year old *use 1 or 2 drops only of a suitable
essential oil in a 50ml bottle of base oil like sweet almond. From* one year to five years
of age *use 2 or 3 drops in total of essential oil in 50ml of base oil. For a bath if* less
than one year old *mix just 1 drop of a suitable essential oil with 3 teaspoons of base oil,
add to the bath water and mix well. in baths for young children from* one year to five
years old *mix 2 or 3 drops maximum of essential oil and again, add it to a base oil.
For all other methods the amounts (or less) recommended above should be used according to
the age and condition of the adult, child or baby you are treating.*

## HOW TO STORE ESSENTIAL OILS

Keep your essential oils in dark, glass bottles with secure screw tops. Store
them in a cool, dry and dark place away from direct sunlight. Essential
oils can keep for over two years like this except for most citrus oils
which only retain their therapeutic value for six to eight months
maximum.

## When and how
## to carry out a skin patch test

*When planning to use an essential oil for the first time use a patch test
to check for any allergic reaction to an essence. This is especially important
when using oils on people with sensitive skin or the facial area. Simply mix 2
drops of the essential oil in 5ml (1 teaspoon) of a base oil and apply a little to the inside
of your elbow. Leave for 12 hours and then check the area. Lavender and tea tree oil have
a wide range of uses in aromatherapy and may be used neat, 1 drop on cuts or spots, for
example. Although rare, some cases of skin irritation have been reported when using tea
tree, so for a patch test use 1 drop of neat essential oil on the inside of your elbow, cover
with a plaster and again check the area after 12 hours. If the skin becomes red or
irritated bathe it immediately with cool water and apply some 'fatty' base oil like sweet
almond. You may then choose to use an extremely low dilution of the oil or decide to avoid
it altogether and choose another which suits your needs.*

*Although very rare, there are some people who cannot tolerate essential oils even in extremely
low dilution (1 to 3 drops in 50ml of base oil) when applied to the skin. If this applies to
you or you tend to have many allergies, aromatherapy (even in other forms) may not be appropriate for you either. It would be wise to seek further advice from a qualified aromatherapist.*

## How to use essential oils

### Baths

This method is the easiest way to enjoy the many pleasurable and health-
giving effects of aromatherapy. Use between 3 drops of an essential oil and
10 drops if you are using a selection of oils in a bath. Add the drops just
before you step into the bath and swirl the
surface of the water around. If you add them
before this most of the oil will evaporate so
you won't receive their full benefit
through your skin.

*For babies and children
see recommended lower
dosages on page 18.*

Always predilute for babies and children, and I suggest you do the same for pregnant women and people with sensitive skin.

Essential oils cannot be diluted in water just dispersed, so always swirl the water well to ensure the essences are evenly distributed across the surface of the water. Soak in the bath for at least 15 minutes inhaling the wonderful aromas. An aromatic *foot bath* can also be made by adding between 3 and 6 drops of essential oil to a large bowl of warm water.

### SITZ BATHS

This method is especially useful for cases of cystitis, thrush or for post-natal discomfort. Add between 2 and 4 drops of essential oil to a large bowl of water or to a shallow bath and swirl the surface of the water around to disperse the droplets evenly on the surface before sitting down. Alternatively the aromatic water can just be used to rinse the affected area thoroughly.

### COMPRESSES

Hot compresses are useful for certain arthritic conditions or during childbirth, whereas cold compresses can reduce inflammation in cases of burns or sprains. Fill a medium-sized bowl with water and add between 3 and 6 drops of essential oil, then swirl the water so the oil disperses evenly across the surface. Next gently place a clean cloth on the surface of the water so it 'picks up' the essential oil, then apply it to the affected area.

A hot compress should be comfortably warm and not so hot it scalds the skin. When preparing a cold compress add ice cubes to the water if possible.

*For children add only 2 drops.*

### DOUCHES

This method can be useful for vaginal thrush but should not be used too often — up to twice a day for three days maximum is fine. Fill a sterile, litre bottle with 500ml of warm, preboiled water and add between 2 and 4 drops of a suitable

*Always check with your doctor to see if this method is appropriate for your diagnosed condition and never douche when pregnant.*

essential oil, replace the lid and shake well. Then add another 500ml of water prepared in the same way, shake again to disperse the droplets of oil even more and then pour into the douche or enema pot.

> *Essential oils should not be taken internally so do not swallow any of the mixture.*
>
> *For safety reasons I advise against children using this method.*

## GARGLES

For sore throats an aromatic *gargle is ideal. Boil some water and leave to stand until warm, pour into a glass and add 2 drops of a suitable essential oil. Mix very well and use this as a gargle.

## INHALATIONS

Essential oils can be inhaled directly by sprinkling between 1 and 3 drops of your chosen essence onto a tissue and inhaling deeply at regular intervals. This can be useful in cases of anxiety or nausea. You also inhale various aromas when essences are used as room or environmental fragrancers. The oils can also be used therapeutically in a *steam inhalation to help relieve congestion and to combat respiratory tract infections. Use between 2 drops of an oil and 6 drops in total (if using a selection of oils) in

> *For children use 1 to 3 drops only and always close the eyes when inhaling.*
>
> *The steam inhalation method should never be used by asthmatics, as it aggravates their condition and can cause choking.*

a large bowl or basin of preboiled water. Drape a large towel over your head to create a mini steam room, close your eyes and inhale deeply. Breathe in fresh air at regular intervals, but in doing so try not to let too much of the steam escape. Continue with this method for about five minutes.

## MASSAGE

Essential oils are very powerful and must always be diluted appropriately in a good-quality base oil before being applied to the skin. The only exception to this rule is applying 1 drop of lavender or tea tree oil, for example, to a cut or

spot. (A patch test should be carried out to check for sensitivity if using an oil for the first time.) Use up to a 2.5 per cent dilution for an adult – this equates to 12.5 drops in 25ml of base oil. Add the drops of essential oil to a bottle of base oil, replace the cap and gently shake several times until well blended. Alternatively for a back massage pour 10 to 15ml of base oil into a saucer or bowl, add 5 to 7 drops of essential oil and mix well using your finger or a teaspoon.

Chapter 5 contains information on different base oils and useful tips for successfully mixing, storing and prolonging the shelf life of your own massage blends.

> *For babies' and children's massage oils see recommended dosages on page 18.*

## MOUTHWASHES

This method can be useful to combat mouth ulcers or bad breath. Add 25 drops of essential oil to a bottle containing 100ml of vodka. Shake well before using and add 3 teaspoons of the *mouthwash to a glass of warm water.

> *Essential oils should not be taken internally, so do not swallow any of the mouthwash. For this reason I do not advise this method for young children.*

## INSECT REPELLENTS

To repel insects use any of the methods listed under room fragrancers. Generally I find the spray container method most useful. Alternatively sprinkle a few drops of essential oil onto damp cotton wool or kitchen towel and fix or wipe these around door jambs, steps, window frames and the edges of your bed, etc. See the listing for insect bites in Chapter 4 for details of useful essences.

## OINTMENTS AND CREAMS

Essential oils can be added to commercially prepared aqueous creams and gels which can be bought from good chemists. This is particularly useful when dealing with common ailments where a vegetable base oil blend would not be as effective as a gel or rich cream. Add 2 drops of essential oil to 1 teaspoon of *gel* and mix well. To 30ml of *cream* add 25 drops of

essential oil and mix very well. If you would prefer to make a *homemade ointment* use the following recipe. This will make about 25ml of quite firm ointment which will liquefy on contact with warm skin.

◆ Heat some water in a saucepan and place a Pyrex bowl into the pan.
◆ Add 5gm of shredded, unbleached beeswax and 20ml of sweet almond oil to the bowl.
◆ Stir over a low heat until all traces of the beeswax have melted and mixed with the almond oil.
◆ Take the bowl out of the saucepan and, as the blend begins to cool, thoroughly mix in up to 20 drops of your chosen essential oils and pour into a sterile container.

### PERFUMES

Perfumes made from pure essential oils don't just have delightful scents they can also induce a calming, sensual, uplifting or invigorating effect. Create a unique, long-lasting fragrance by adding up to 6 drops of your chosen essential oil or blend with 10ml of jojoba, a liquid wax. For recipes see Chapter 8.

### ROOM FRAGRANCERS

To create aromatic environments instantly use any of the following methods. Depending upon the size of the room or environment you'd like to fragrance, add between 5 and 10 drops of essential oil to a *vaporiser.* Alternatively sprinkle the same amount of oil in a *bowl of hot water,* and the aroma will diffuse quickly throughout the room. Or add the essential oil to a *spray container.* I use an indoor plant spray filled with approximately 100ml of water. Add the essential oil and shake well before spraying. However, if essential oil is kept in plastic for any length of time it causes the plastic it to deteriorate, so a ceramic sprayer would be a wiser investment.

> *When employing any of these methods ensure that whatever you use is put in a safe place out of the reach of children and pets.*

## SAFETY CHECKLIST

*Essential oils are very powerful and should always be used in small amounts and before being used on the skin should be diluted appropriately in a base oil (see recommended dosages and Chapter 5 for base oils).*

*Never use essential oils near or in the eyes.*

*Never take essential oils internally. Some, like eucalyptus, are toxic if used in this way, so keep all essences out of children's reach. If either of the latter occurs accidentally seek urgent medical assistance.*

*Before using an essential oil always check its suitability for you and read any safety information in this chapter and any 'Caution' notes listed under specific essential oils in Chapter 3.*

*Keep to the recommended dosages for adults, children, babies, those with sensitive skin and pregnant women. Chapters 6 and 7 list recommended essential oils for pregnant women and babies and young children.*

*Pure essential oils are needed to give therapeutic effects, so only buy products from a reputable supplier (see Useful Addresses on page 255).*

### SKIN-CARE PREPARATIONS

Aromatic facial oils are made in the same way as body massage oils, except they should contain less essential oil because they are used on delicate facial skin. Use up to a 1.25 per cent dilution, this equates to just over 6 drops of essential oil in 25ml of base oil. If you have very sensitive skin, halve the recommended amount of essential oil to 3 drops in 25ml of base oil. Choose both essential and base oils according to your skin type. Refer to Chapter 9 for further skin-care details and how to prepare and use facial oils, face masks, floral waters and homemade aromatic waters, a facial 'steam' and exfoliating scrubs.

Most essential oils can be used effectively by most people, although there are some exceptions.

## SKIN IRRITATION

Some oils may irritate the skin so must only be used in a dilution of up to 1 per cent in a base oil or 3 drops maximum in a bath. Always carry out a patch test to check for allergic reaction if using an oil for the first time. Skin irritation may be caused by the following essential oils, so always use them in a 1 per cent (or less) dilution of base oil for massage and only add up to 3 drops in a bath. These oils are not suitable for highly sensitive skins, babies and children. They are: basil, black pepper, cinnamon leaf, clove bud, eucalyptus, fennel, lemon, lemon verbena, peppermint, pine. (Although very rare some people with sensitive skin have reacted to the use of jasmine and tea tree essential oils.)

## SKIN DISCOLOURATION

The following oils are phototoxic, which means they cause discolouration of the skin – even if diluted essences are used – if the skin is then exposed to the sun or ultraviolet light. They are: bergamot, cumin, lemon, lemon verbena, lime, orange.

## PREGNANCY

Some essential oils promote menstruation or have quite high toxicity levels so are not suitable for pregnant women, babies, children or other 'vulnerable' people. The following oils should be avoided during pregnancy: angelica, basil, carrot seed, cedarwood, clary sage, clove bud, cinnamon leaf, citronella, cypress, fennel, hyssop, jasmine, juniper, lovage, marjoram, melissa, myrrh, origanum, parsley, peppermint, rose, rosemary, sage, tarragon, thyme. See Chapter 6 for further details.

*If there is a history or high risk of miscarriage also avoid camomile (Roman) and lavender oil for the first three months.*

*After 20 weeks only the following essential oils may be used moderately and with care: cypress, jasmine and rose oil. See Chapter 6 for further details.*

## OTHER 'VULNERABLE' PEOPLE

There is also a handful of oils which should be avoided by people suffering from epilepsy (as they could potentially cause an attack) and a few are not suitable for people with high blood pressure or very low blood pressure. However, in Chapters 4, 6 and 7 I have recommended alternative recipes where appropriate for these groups of people. If you suffer from any of these diseases, *avoid* using the essential oils listed below.

**Epilepsy**
*Avoid* fennel, hyssop, sage.

**High blood pressure**
*Avoid* hyssop, rosemary, sage, thyme.

**Very low blood pressure**
*Avoid* marjoram.

*The following essential oils should be used moderately, in a 1 per cent or less dilution and* with care *because of their powerful action or potentially high toxicity. They are: black pepper, carrot seed, clove bud, eucalyptus, fennel, juniper, myrrh.*

*Some essential oils are dangerous and must* never *be used. Most are not easily obtainable but in case you come across them you should never use the following: almond (bitter), arnica, boldo leaf, calamus, horseradish, jaborandi leaf, mugwort, mustard, pennyroyal, rue, sassafras, savin, southernwood, tansy, thuja, wintergreen, wormseed, wormwood.*

*If you cannot find information about a certain oil or are unsure whether it is suitable for yourself or those you care for,* do not use it. *Consult a qualified aromatherapist for professional advice.*

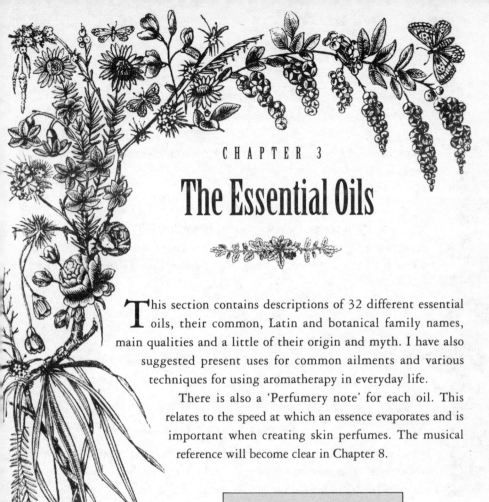

## CHAPTER 3

# The Essential Oils

This section contains descriptions of 32 different essential oils, their common, Latin and botanical family names, main qualities and a little of their origin and myth. I have also suggested present uses for common ailments and various techniques for using aromatherapy in everyday life.

There is also a 'Perfumery note' for each oil. This relates to the speed at which an essence evaporates and is important when creating skin perfumes. The musical reference will become clear in Chapter 8.

> *Important safety information is highlighted in boxes. Before using a new oil be certain to read these details. Other helpful information can be found in Chapter 2.*

# BASIL (SWEET)
*Ocimum basilicum*

**Family:** labiatae. ♦ **Perfumery note:** top. ♦ **Aroma:** clear and spicy, reminiscent of aniseed.

There are many varieties of basil but the one favoured for aromatherapy is French basil, sometimes known as true sweet basil. The oil is obtained through steam distillation of the herb's flowering tops and leaves.

**Blends well with:** bergamot, clary sage, frankincense, geranium, lemon, mandarin, neroli, orange, peppermint, petitgrain.

### MAIN QUALITIES

Antidepressant, antiseptic, antispasmodic, expectorant, insect repellent.

**Helps to:** clear and stimulate the mind; promote menstruation, reduce fevers; strengthen the stomach and nervous system; increase sweating and generally invigorates mind and body.

### TALES FROM THE PAST

Basil is derived from the Latin word *basilisca,* meaning royal, and since ancient times this herb has been respected for its excellent qualities. For centuries basil has figured strongly in magical and religious ceremonies. Hindus believed it protected people from spirits and revered it by growing the plant in their homes and making daily offerings of flowers to it. The Greeks believed basil to be the antidote to the venom of the 'basilisk', a fabulous reptile whose breath or even glance was said to be fatal! In the seventeenth century, Nicholas Culpeper tells us, 'Being applied to the place bitten by venomous beasts, or stung by a wasp or hornet, it speedily draws the poison to it. Every like draws like.'

### PRESENT USES

I find basil to be the best antidote to mental fatigue, it awakens and refreshes the mind almost at once. The aroma is very penetrating and helps to bring clarity of mind and generally stimulate the whole nervous system. It has a strengthening

*Not suitable in pregnancy, for babies or young children.*

*Basil may irritate sensitive skin, so use in low dilution only – 1 per cent in a massage oil and 3 drops in a bath.*

effect on the respiratory tract and really helps in cases of bad colds and flu when, for whatever reason, you just can't put your life on hold.

Basil promotes healing and eases aches and pains in overtired muscles when used in a massage oil. It has a notable effect in cases of rheumatism and arthritis as it stimulates the circulation and detoxification process.

On the emotional side, basil acts as an antidepressant, enlivening both mind and body, and leaving you with a feeling of renewed strength and vitality.

### CAN BENEFIT

♦ Bronchitis, colds, fever, flu. ♦ Depression, fatigue, lethargy, mental exhaustion, nervous tension. ♦ Fainting. ♦ Flatulence. ♦ Insect bites and stings.

### HOW TO USE

Bath, inhalation, insect repellent, massage, room fragrancer.

# BERGAMOT

*Citrus bergamia*

**Family**: rutaceae. ♦ **Perfumery note**: top. ♦ **Aroma**: light citrus with a hint of floral.

The bergamot tree grows up to 16 feet high and is closely related to the lemon and bitter orange tree. The essential oil is obtained by expressing (literally squeezing) the rind of its green fruits which resemble slightly oval-shaped oranges. Although there is a herb called bergamot which is native to North America it is no relation to the tree *citrus bergamia*.

**Blends well with**: basil, Roman and German camomile, carrot seed, cedarwood,

clary sage, cypress, eucalyptus, frankincense, geranium, grapefruit, jasmine, juniper, lavender, lemon, mandarin, marjoram, myrrh, myrtle, neroli, orange, patchouli, petitgrain, pine, rose, rosemary, ylang-ylang.

## MAIN QUALITIES

Antibacterial, antidepressant, anti-inflammatory, antiseptic, deodorant, expectorant.

**Helps to:** promote new cell growth and heal wounds; relieve pain; reduce fever; stimulate the immune system; generally calms the nervous system and is emotionally uplifting.

## TALES FROM THE PAST

Bergamot is named after the northern Italian town of Bergamo, in which its oil was first sold. However, it is said that Christopher Columbus brought the first tree to Italy from the Canary Islands and since then it has flourished on the southern tip of the country. Here the local people used bergamot for fevers although its full healing potential has only been discovered relatively recently. It has long been used in perfumery and was one of the ingredients of the original *eau de Cologne*. It also provides Earl Grey tea with its distinctive aroma.

## PRESENT USES

Bergamot is a delightful, uplifting fragrance yet it actually has a sedative effect upon the body. Its sheer versatility has made it one of my favourites over the years and I have yet to find someone who dislikes the aroma of bergamot. This bright green essence works as a top note in many of the finest perfumes and aftershaves, and often perfects homemade blends too!

*Do not use bergamot oil on skin which is to be exposed to the sun or ultraviolet light as it causes skin discolouration and sensitivity. However, it is now possible to obtain a 'bergaptene-free' oil suitable for skin care and home use. Its label should be marked accordingly or with the letters FCF which shows that the offending compounds have been reduced appropriately and will not cause phototoxicity.*

*Not suitable for babies or young children.*

Its antiseptic and toning properties are effective when used for various skin conditions including acne, cold sores, oily skin and psoriasis. When blended with geranium or rose oil, bergamot exerts a particularly powerful antidepressant and destressing effect. Besides combating anxiety and depression, scientific research in Italy has proved bergamot's strong antiseptic and antiviral properties especially when used for urinary or respiratory system infections. It also has many uses in pregnancy (see Chapter 6).

### CAN BENEFIT

♦ Acne, boils, cold sores, oily skin, psoriasis, shingles, spots, ulcers.
♦ Anxiety, depression, fatigue, insomnia, nervous tension, stress-related ailments. ♦ Appetite disorders, flatulence. ♦ Colds, coughs, fever, flu.
♦ Greasy hair, head lice. ♦ Urinary tract infections, pruritus (itching).

### HOW TO USE

Bath, compress, hair care, inhalation, massage, mouthwash, perfume, room fragrancer, skin-care preparations.

# BLACK PEPPER

*Piper nigrum*

**Family:** piperaceae. ♦ **Perfumery note:** top. ♦ **Aroma:** pungent and spicy, like fresh peppercorns.

This shrub, native to the East can grow up to 20 feet in the wild. The essential oil is extracted by steam distillation of the unripened dried fruit known commonly as black peppercorn.
**Blends well with:** carrot seed, frankincense, grapefruit, lavender, lemon, marjoram, mandarin, myrtle, orange, patchouli, rosemary, sandalwood, vetiver.

### MAIN QUALITIES

Antibacterial, antiseptic, antispasmodic, antiviral, aphrodisiac.

**Helps to:** relieve pain; expel gas and aid digestion; promote fluid loss by stimulating urination; reduce fever; lower blood pressure; produce warmth and redness when applied to the skin; strengthens the spleen and stomach and is generally stimulating.

### TALES FROM THE PAST

Even in the fifth century, the Romans knew the digestive properties of black pepper, and Gibbon tells us, 'Pepper was a favourite ingredient of the most expensive Roman cookery.' The Romans prized this spice so highly that it was sometimes used in lieu of money to pay rent or taxes. In his seventeenth-century herbal, the astrologer-physician Nicholas Culpeper said of black pepper, 'It dissolves wind in the stomach or bowels, provokes urine, helps the cough and other diseases of the breast, and is an ingredient in the great antidotes.' Black pepper was exported to Europe from India and the East from the Middle Ages onwards for its culinary virtues. It is still used widely today.

### PRESENT USES

Black pepper oil is very strong and can easily overpower a blend of other essential oils, so use in tiny amounts if you wish to enhance a blend or perfume with a spicy 'note'. This essence is fabulous when treating chills, colds or flu, because it has the effect of warming the body right through while (if used sparingly) reducing any fever that may be present. Combined with lavender, marjoram or rosemary in a massage oil it works well for rheumatic aches and pains by stimulating circulation and aiding elimination of waste products from the body. I've often used this blend for football and hockey players who have to brave cold weather in the winter by applying it to the legs before a match. Black pepper can also guard against griping indigestion pains and is one of the oils known to reduce high blood pressure.

*Black pepper is a skin irritant so use in low dilution only – 1 per cent in a massage oil or 3 drops in a bath.*

### CAN BENEFIT

♦ Aches and pains (muscles), arthritis, rheumatism, slack muscles,

*Not suitable for babies or young children and should be used in moderation and with care.*

sprains. ♦ Chilblains. ♦ Chills, colds, fever, flu. ♦ Constipation, diarrhoea, flatulence, griping pains, indigestion. ♦ Exhaustion, lethargy. ♦ Low blood pressure, poor circulation, cellulite.

## HOW TO USE

Bath, massage, room fragrancer.

# CAMOMILE (GERMAN) and CAMOMILE (ROMAN)

*Matricaria chamomilla*          *Anthemis nobilis*

**Family:** compositae. ♦ **Perfumery note:** middle. ♦ **Aroma:** musty, strong and herbaceous (German); fairly sweet with a hint of apple (Roman).

There are many types of camomile but the two favoured in aromatherapy are German and Roman camomile. Both are members of the daisy family and their oils are obtained through steam distillation of the flowers. The oils are not easily confused because German camomile is a deep blue colour whereas Roman camomile is a pale, soft blue which turns yellow with age. There is another plant, called camomile (Maroc) ormenis oil, which is a distant relative of the above but does not share the scope of their therapeutic value.

**Blends well with:** *German camomile:* bergamot, clary sage, geranium, lemon, mandarin, marjoram, neroli, orange, patchouli, rose, ylang-ylang.

*Roman camomile:* bergamot, clary sage, frankincense, geranium, jasmine, lavender, myrrh, neroli, rose, sandalwood, tea tree.

## MAIN QUALITIES

Both German and Roman camomile share many of the same properties. However, German camomile is more effective when dealing with inflammatory and immune system conditions because it has a high azulene content (azulene is a chemical which is anti-inflammatory). Camomile is antibacterial, antidepressant, anti-inflammatory, antiseptic, antispasmodic.

**Helps to:** expel gas; strengthen the stomach,

liver and spleen; promote new cell growth; encourage fluid loss by stimulating urination; promote menstruation; reduce fever; increase sweating; generally has a very calming effect on the nervous system and is soothing emotionally.

## TALES FROM THE PAST

Known for its versatility through the centuries, camomile is perhaps one of the best-known medicinal herbs. The ancient Greek name for the herb translates as 'apple of the Earth' because of its soft, sweet aroma. In England during the Middle Ages, camomile was planted along pathways so that the herb would release its soothing scent as people trod on it . The plant actually thrives when this happens. It is interesting to note that the Queen still has a camomile lawn at Buckingham Palace today. Traditionally, fair-haired people have used camomile flower water as a finishing rinse to help maintain their blond locks.

## PRESENT USES

The uses of camomile are many and varied. It is invaluable in skin care especially where there is inflammation, for example, in cases of acne, eczema or psoriasis. Dry or sensitive skin also benefits from the oil's antiseptic qualities. German camomile is particularly good for the above conditions and is excellent for boosting the immune system because of its high content of azulene, which also gives this variety its deep blue colouring. Both types of camomile have an antispasmodic and calming effect on the digestive system, soothing away tummy aches and helping with nervous tension which can upset the stomach and intestines.

Camomile mildly promotes *menstruation and its pain-killing and soothing qualities help with menstrual cramps and ease premenstrual symptoms. This essence is especially useful for children, allaying fear and anxiety as well as fighting off coughs, colds and other infectious illnesses. Finally, a blend of camomile and lavender make insomniacs' dreams come true!

> *Camomile is a very mild emmenagogue (i.e. it promotes menstruation) so avoid in early pregnancy if there is a history or serious risk of miscarriage.*

### CAN BENEFIT

♦ Acne, bruises, burns, chickenpox, dry/sensitive or inflamed skin, eczema, nappy rash, normal skin, pruritus (itching), psoriasis, thread veins. ♦ Asthma, colds, coughs, sinusitis. ♦ Colitis, stomach cramps, tummy aches. ♦ Dry hair. ♦ Fever. ♦ Headache, earache, migraine, toothache. ♦ High blood pressure. ♦ Muscular aches and pains. ♦ Period pain, premenstrual syndrome, scanty periods. ♦ Sleeplessness, anxiety, fear, nervous tension, restlessness.

### HOW TO USE

Bath, compress, hair care, inhalation, massage, perfume, room fragrancer, skin-care preparations.

# CARROT SEED
*Daucus carota*

**Family:** umbelliferae. ♦ **Perfumery note:** middle. ♦ **Aroma:** earthy, warm and spicy.

Carrot seed oil is obtained through steam distillation of the dried seeds of the wild carrot. This plant grows up to 3 feet high and has small white and deep purple flowers. An oil is also obtained from the well-known cultivated garden carrot (*Daucus carota subspecies sativus*).
**Blends well with:** bergamot, black pepper, cedarwood, geranium, lavender, lemon, mandarin, neroli, orange, sandalwood.

### MAIN QUALITIES

Antiseptic, detoxifying.
**Helps to:** expel gas promote new cell growth; encourage fluid loss by promoting urination; regulate hormones; stimulate and strengthen the liver, kidneys and lymphatic system; contract small blood vessels, generally tones the body and is excellent for skin care.

## TALES FROM THE PAST

The carrot's warming and stimulating properties have been recognised since ancient times. Culpeper notes in his seventeenth-century herbal that carrot seed, 'helpeth the colic, the stone in the kidneys and the rising of the mother', and if applied externally with honey it was said to cleanse cancerous ulcers and weeping sores. A soup made from garden carrots was said to ease the pain of stomach ulcers and restore vitality. The plant was often used to combat gout as it aids the elimination of uric acid (the chemical that builds up in the body and causes gout). It was also used to help in cases of jaundice, diarrhoea and worms. The garden carrot became especially popular with cooks in Elizabethan times and is still used very widely today. Carrot juice is also often recommended by many dietary therapists for the diets of people with cancer.

## PRESENT USES

Carrot seed is a useful detoxifying oil and is an excellent skin-care oil. It is stimulating and helpful if the body feels congested or if there is a build up of toxins. Carrot seed oil has a cleansing effect upon the liver, kidneys and lymphatic system and best results are achieved through receiving regular massage which will promote the elimination of toxins and excess fluids. This oil helps in cases of indigestion or flatulence, and it also has diuretic properties (it aids urination) which help relieve cystitis and fluid retention.

However, it is in skin care that carrot oil comes into its own. A few drops in a face cream or oil clears and tones the complexion, leaving dull and tired-looking skin glowing with vitality.

## CAN BENEFIT

♦ Boils, congested skin, dry skin, eczema, mature skin, rashes, spots, thread veins, ulcers, wrinkles. ♦ Dry hair. ♦ Flatulence, indigestion, liver congestion. ♦ Fluid retention. ♦ Scanty periods, period pain, premenstrual syndrome.
♦ Urinary tract infections.

> *Carrot seed oil promotes menstruation and is not suitable in pregnancy, for babies or young children.*
>
> *This oil should be used in moderation only.*

## How to Use

Bath, hair care, massage, skin-care preparations.

# CEDARWOOD (Atlas)

*Cedrus atlantica*

**Family:** pinaceae. ♦ **Perfumery note:** base. ♦ **Aroma:** subtle, warm and woody.

This beautiful tree from North Africa can grow to over 100 feet high. The oil is obtained through steam distillation of the wood. I would highly recommend Atlas cedarwood for therapeutic use. However, there are a few other oils commonly known as 'cedarwood' which are, in fact, from the cupressaceae family and are chemically quite different to Atlas cedarwood.

**Blends well with:** bergamot, carrot seed, clary sage, cypress, eucalyptus, frankincense, geranium, juniper, lavender, marjoram, myrrh, myrtle, neroli, pine, patchouli, petitgrain, rose, rosemary, sandalwood, ylang-ylang.

## Main Qualities

Antiseptic, aphrodisiac, astringent, expectorant, insect repellent.
**Helps to:** stimulate new cell growth; encourage fluid loss by promoting urination; generally has a very calming effect upon the nervous system and brings about relaxation.

## Tales from the Past

This oil is also known as libanol, probably because the trees are thought to originate from the great cedars of Lebanon. These giants of history were used to build many famous temples, not least King Solomon's which according to the Bible employed over 100,000 men just to cut and transport the logs. The spirited Egyptian Queen Hatshepsut also adorned her temple with cedar. Wars were

fought to conquer lands where the cedars grew because the wood and oil were valuable commodities and were used medicinally as well as for perfumery, cosmetics, insect repellents and temple incenses. Sarcophagi were often made from cedarwood, which naturally repels insects and is very durable, and traces of the oil have been found by scientists in mummies' remains. The ancient Greeks and Chinese also held cedarwood sacred and used it in spiritual ceremonies.

### PRESENT USES

This woody oil is highly antiseptic and is a mild astringent making it ideal for treating acne, eczema or dermatitis. Catarrh or respiratory conditions like asthma respond very well to cedarwood's expectorant yet soothing action. It is particularly useful when treating chronic complaints, for example, bronchitis, coughs, rheumatic pain or nervous tension. Cystitis is also relieved by using the oil in a sitz bath or compress.

Today the oil provides the perfumery industry with an excellent fixative and is used widely to perfume soaps, toiletries and especially aftershaves. Generally, cedarwood relaxes and calms both body and mind, and has a soothing effect on the spirit, being ideal for meditation or 'centering' oneself.

*Not suitable in pregnancy.*

### CAN BENEFIT

♦ Acne, dermatitis, eczema, oily skin. ♦ Anxiety and nervous tension, stress-related ailments. ♦ Arthritis, rheumatism. ♦ Asthma, bronchitis, catarrh, coughs. ♦ Cystitis. ♦ Dandruff, greasy hair.

### HOW TO USE

Bath, compress, hair care, inhalation, massage, insect repellent, perfume, room fragrancer, skin-care preparations.

# CLARY SAGE

*Salvia sclarea*

**Family:** labiatae. ♦ **Perfumery note:** middle/base. ♦ **Aroma:** herbaceous, nutty with a hint of floral.

The essential oil is obtained through steam distillation of the flowering tops and leaves of the plant. Clary sage should not be confused with common sage (*salvia officinalis*), which is a close relative but has a high toxicity level and should only be used by a qualified aromatherapist.
**Blends well with:** basil, bergamot, camomile, cedarwood, cypress, frankincense, geranium, grapefruit, jasmine, lavender, lemon, mandarin, marjoram, neroli, orange, patchouli, petitgrain, rose, rosemary, sandalwood, vetiver, ylang-ylang.

## MAIN QUALITIES

Antibacterial, antidepressant, antiseptic, antispasmodic, aphrodisiac, deodorant.
**Helps to:** expel gas; relieve pain; promote menstruation; lower blood pressure; strengthen the stomach and uterus; calm the nervous system; generally has a relaxing, warming and uplifting effect on the emotions.

## TALES FROM THE PAST

The name clary probably derives from *clarus* which is Latin for clear. The herb was brought to Britain in 1562 and was widely used to clear foreign bodies from the eyes, earning it the common name of 'clear eye'. Nicholas Culpeper writes in his seventeenth-century herbal, 'It also draweth forth splinters, thorns or other things got into the flesh.' Apparently in Germany, some merchants used clary and elderflowers to add to their wine so that it would taste like the more expensive muscatel! The drink induced dangerous levels of intoxication and severe hangovers and to this day clary sage is still known in Germany as *Muskateller salbei* or muscatel sage. A similar wine also became popular in sixteenth-century England. It was called 'clary' and was made

from even less savoury ingredients: clary sage, honey, ginger and pepper!

## PRESENT USES

This oil is one of the best antidepressant oils as it uplifts spirits, quells anxiety attacks and generally reduces nervous tension. Clary is very effective against period pain and can be used locally in a massage oil or warm compress. By using a little oil regularly, unpleasant premenstrual and menopausal symptoms can be eased enormously. Clary is often used when women are in labour, either in a massage oil, compress or room freshener (see Chapter 6).

Clary also helps when treating digestive disorders especially griping pain. Generally, if you feel uptight clary will help to unwind you. The oil's action on the nervous system is very relaxing, almost hypnotic, and it imparts a positive, sometimes even euphoric effect upon the mind. The oil is used commercially as a perfume fixative and for adding scent to vermouth.

> *Clary sage promotes menstruation so is not suitable in pregnancy. However, it is very useful for labour pain.*
>
> *It is advisable not to drink alcohol or drive just after using this oil as it can induce sleepiness.*

## CAN BENEFIT

♦ Absence of periods, labour pain, period pain, premenstrual syndrome and menopausal symptoms. ♦ Anxiety, epression, frigidity, impotence, nervous tension, stress-related ailments. ♦ Asthma. ♦ Flatulence, stomach and intestinal spasms. ♦ High blood pressure. ♦ Mature skin, overhydrated skin. ♦ Muscular aches and pains, cramps.

## HOW TO USE

Bath, compress, massage, perfume, room fragrancer, skin-care preparations.

# CYPRESS

*Cupressus sempervirens*

**Family:** cupressaceae. ♦ **Perfumery note:** middle. ♦ **Aroma:** clear, yet woody with a hint of spice.

The cypress is an evergreen tree which can grow up to a height of 85 feet and has a definite conical shape. The essential oil is obtained through steam distillation of the needles and twigs. Although there are several types of cypress, the one favoured for aromatherapy is *cupressus sempervirens*.

**Blends well with:** bergamot, cedarwood, clary sage, eucalyptus, frankincense, geranium, grapefruit, juniper, lavender, lemon, mandarin, marjoram, myrrh, myrtle, neroli, orange, peppermint, petitgrain, pine, rosemary, sandalwood.

## MAIN QUALITIES

Antiseptic, antispasmodic, astringent, deodorant, detoxifying, insect repellent.

**Helps to:** decrease perspiration; stimulate fluid loss by promoting urination; stop bleeding; contract the small blood vessels; generally relaxes while refreshing mind and body.

## TALES FROM THE PAST

The Mediterranean countries are full of these beautiful trees. However, they are traditionally planted in cemeteries and sprigs are used at funerals as a symbol of mourning. There is evidence that the Babylonians were importing cypress 4,000 years ago. The Romans and Greeks assigned this tree to death and the afterlife, perhaps signifying that death is merely a process of transformation. Its Latin name means 'ever living' as the cypress stays green all year round. The medicinal qualities of cypress were espoused by Hippocrates who believed it healed uterine problems and haemorrhoids. Centuries later Culpeper states that the leaves, 'prevent the bleeding of the gums, and fasten loose teeth'.

## PRESENT USES

Cypress has powerful astringent, detoxifying and diuretic qualities which can be useful for treating a variety of complaints. Fluid retention, cellulitis, haemorrhoids, oily or overhydrated skin and thread veins can all be helped by these properties. For relief from aching, heavy legs caused by varicose veins or fluid retention, try combining geranium, juniper or lavender with cypress in a massage oil and apply to the legs using light strokes. *Never* massage over varicose veins, always above, i.e. nearest to your heart. Rheumatic problems and overtired muscles benefit greatly from this oil, as do menopausal symptoms such as heavy menstrual flow. Because of its strong antiseptic and antispasmodic effect, cypress is useful in cases of asthma, colds and especially spasmodic coughs. Cypress is a fantastic deodorant – its fragrance was compared to ambergris and is employed as such in the perfumery trade where it continues to be a ingredient in many perfumes and men's aftershaves

> *Not suitable in early pregnancy.*
> *Use moderately only after*
> *20 weeks.*

### CAN BENEFIT

♦ Anxiety, nervous tension and stress-related ailments. ♦ Asthma, colds, coughs, whooping cough. ♦ Bruises, minor wounds. ♦ Cellulitis, fluid retention, poor circulation, varicose veins. ♦ Dandruff. ♦ Diarrhoea. ♦ Excessive perspiration. ♦ Gingivitis (gum infections). ♦ Haemorrhoids. ♦ Heavy menstrual flow, menopausal symptoms. ♦ Muscular cramp, overtired muscles, rheumatism. ♦ Oily skin, overhydrated skin. ♦ Thread veins.

### HOW TO USE

Bath, compress, inhalation, massage, insect repellent, perfume, room fragrancer, skin-care preparations.

# EUCALYPTUS
*Eucalyptus globulus*

**Family:** myrtaceae. ◆ **Perfumery note:** top. ◆ **Aroma:** clearing, sharp, like camphor.

This Australian tree can grow to a height of 380 feet. The essence is obtained through steam distillation of its oil-rich leaves and twigs. There are over 300 varieties of eucalyptus worldwide but only a few are used in aromatherapy. The most common is the one above but *eucalyptus radiata*, *dives* and *citriodora* are becoming more popular. The latter is used in perfumery for its fresh, lemony scent.
**Blends well with:** bergamot, cedarwood, cypress, grapefruit, lavender, lemon, juniper, mandarin, marjoram, myrtle, orange, peppermint, petitgrain, pine, rosemary, sandalwood, tea tree.

## MAIN QUALITIES

Antibacterial, antiseptic, antiviral, decongestant, deodorant, disinfectant, expectorant, insect repellent.
**Helps to:** stimulate fluid loss by promoting urination; reduce fever; produce warmth and redness when used on the skin; heal wounds; boost the immune system; generally stimulates and has a cooling, refreshing effect on mind and body.

## TALES FROM THE PAST

Eucalyptus originates from Australia where most of the forests consist of this tree. Over time it was successfully introduced to other regions, namely Africa, the Mediterranean and China. Eucalyptus was planted in marshy areas where malaria and other infectious diseases were prevalent, with very positive results. The tree roots absorbed much of the excess water from the soil and the leaves' well-known scent permeated the air, transforming previously 'bug-stricken' neighbourhoods into healthy oases. The tree is still sometimes known as the 'fever tree' or 'blue gum tree'; the Aboriginal word for it is *kino*. The Aborigines bound eucalyptus leaves around serious wounds to cleanse them, prevent infec-

tion and promote swift healing. For years pharmaceutical companies have recognised the powerful healing properties of eucalyptus, and it still forms the basis of many medicines and ointments used today.

## PRESENT USES

Eucalyptus is a great winter remedy, its antiviral, antibacterial and expectorant properties making it ideal for treating coughs, colds and flu, bronchitis, sinusitis and catarrhal conditions. The eminent French doctor, Jean Valnet, illustrated the oil's powerful action by reporting that a dilution of 2 per cent eucalyptus used in a spray kills 70 per cent of airborne staphylococci (a type of bacterium). Use with lemon or lavender oil as a regular room freshener to beat 'bugs'. The oil exerts a clearing, stimulating effect upon the mind, and in small amounts cools and refreshes the body. It is ideal for hot climates. Eucalyptus also stimulates the immune system which helps the body stay free from infectious illnesses.

*Not suitable for babies or young children.*

*Eucalyptus may irritate sensitive skin so use in low dilution only – 1 per cent in a massage oil or 3 drops in a bath.*

*This oil should be used moderately and with care.*

*Please note: if taken internally eucalyptus is toxic and has proved fatal even in low doses so keep out of children's reach.*

The oil in a bath is helpful for cystitis and its cooling quality is of great value when fever is present. Its pain-killing and antiviral properties have proved useful for cold sores and shingles and it promotes the healing of wounds. Like geranium and juniper, eucalyptus helps lower blood sugar levels so may be helpful to diabetics; further advice can be sought from a qualified aromatherapist. When combined with lavender, marjoram or rosemary in a massage oil, it brings warm relief to aching muscles, sprains and rheumatic pains.

## CAN BENEFIT

♦ Arthritis, muscular aches and pains, sprains. ♦ Asthma, bronchitis, catarrh,

chest infections, colds, coughs, flu, sinusitis. ♦ Boils, chilblains, cold sores, shingles, skin infections, skin ulcers, wounds. ♦ Chickenpox, fever. ♦ Diarrhoea. ♦ Headaches. ♦ High blood sugar. ♦ Low blood pressure, poor circulation.

### HOW TO USE

Bath, compress, insect repellent, massage, room fragrancer, steam inhalation.

# FENNEL
*Foeniculum vulgare*

**Family:** umbelliferae. ♦ **Perfumery note:** middle/top. ♦ **Aroma:** herbaceous, light and sweet, reminiscent of aniseed.

The plant has fine leaves, topped with clusters of small yellow flowers. The essential oil is obtained by steam distillation of the pulverised seeds. Sweet fennel (fennel variety *dulce*), also known as Roman or French fennel, is the variety favoured for aromatherapy use. However, this should not be confused with bitter fennel (fennel variety *amara*) as this is a toxic oil and should never be used.
**Blends well with:** geranium, grapefruit, lavender, lemon, mandarin, orange, rose, sandalwood.

### MAIN QUALITIES

Antiseptic, antispasmodic, detoxifying.
**Helps to:** expel gas; encourage fluid loss by promoting urination; stimulate menstruation; strengthen the stomach; generally helpful to the digestion.

### TALES FROM THE PAST

The name fennel comes from the Latin *foenum* meaning 'hay'. However, records

show that the ancient Egyptians used it as a paste for diseases of the eye. This belief in fennel's medicinal properties was shared by the Greeks who also harnessed its purifying qualities to help overcome obesity. Many ancient civilisations used the herb as an antidote to snake venom. Hippocrates espoused its ability to increase the flow of milk in nursing mothers and Pliny ascribed over 20 medicinal uses to fennel. In the Middle Ages, fennel was believed to ward off evil spirits and bad luck, so it was customary to hang generous sprigs of the herb over the entrance to and from the rafters of homes. Fennel tea is said to settle the stomach, alleviate nausea, promote the flow of milk in nursing women and calm digestive problems. This also seems to work for horses — it is traditional Romany practice to feed colicky horses fennel and dandelion leaves. Many proprietary medicines contain fennel, mainly cough mixtures and, of course, babies' gripe water.

## PRESENT USES

Fennel is an excellent detoxifying oil and because it relieves fluid retention it is often used in anti-cellulite blends. It is essentially a 'balancing' oil, bringing harmony and normalising various systems of the body. It has a particular affinity with the digestive process, alleviating painful griping sensations, nausea, flatulence and constipation. Another quality fennel is said to possess is that of an appetite suppressant, but this is rather confusing as some herbals state that drinking fennel tea actually increases the appetite! One thing is certain, if used in massage treatments, combined with geranium, grapefruit or juniper the body will eliminate unwanted fluid and toxins, banishing unsightly cellulite. Because of its effect on the kidneys this treatment should not be overused and should ideally be undertaken in conjunction

*Not at all suitable for babies, children under seven years of age, epileptics or during pregnancy.*

*This oil may irritate sensitive skin so use in low dilution only — 1 per cent in a massage oil or 3 drops in a bath.*

*Generally fennel should be used in moderation and with care.*

*Bitter fennel (fennel variety* amara) *is toxic and should* never *be used.*

with a qualified aromatherapist who can give appropriate holistic advice, such as diet and lifestyle changes. Fennel's diuretic quality not only aids a sluggish lymphatic system but can also be useful in urinary tract infections and may help with kidney stones. A plant hormone is present in fennel which seems to mimic the effect of oestrogen, so it also helps to regulate irregular periods and harmonise fluctuating hormonal levels during menopause. Sweet fennel oil can be useful when wishing to add an unusual, anise-like quality to a scent.

### CAN BENEFIT

♦ Bruises. ♦ Cellulitis, oedema (fluid retention), sluggish lymphatic system. ♦ Colitis, constipation, flatulence, griping pains, indigestion, nausea. ♦ Mature skin. ♦ Period pain, scanty periods, menopausal or hormonal imbalances. ♦ Poor muscle tone, rheumatism. ♦ Urinary tract infections.

### HOW TO USE

Bath, compress, massage, perfume, room fragrancer, skin-care preparations.

# FRANKINCENSE

*Boswellia carteri*

**Family:** burseraceae. ♦ **Perfumery note:** middle/base. ♦ **Aroma:** woody, spicy with a slight pine-like top note.

Frankincense is a hardy shrub which can grow in the most barren of soil. It originates from the Middle East but today the oil is also exported from North Africa, China and western India. The bark is cut and exudes a resin which is collected and then steam distilled to extract the essential oil. Frankincense is also known as olibanum a name which dates from its links with Lebanon.

**Blends well with:** basil, bergamot, black pepper, camomile, cedarwood, clary sage, cypress, geranium, grapefruit, juniper, lavender, lemon, mandarin, myrrh, neroli, orange, patchouli, petitgrain, pine, rose, rosemary, sandalwood.

## MAIN QUALITIES

Anti-inflammatory, antiseptic, astringent, expectorant.

**Helps to:** promote the formation of new cells and scar tissue; heal wounds; encourage fluid loss by stimulating urination; strengthen the uterus; sedate the nervous system; generally has a balancing, deeply calming effect on an emotional and spiritual level.

## TALES FROM THE PAST

Since antiquity frankincense has been highly prized and used in spiritual rites in temples from China to Egypt. Gold, myrrh and frankincense were given as gifts to the infant Jesus, and according to the Bible frankincense was also used widely at religious ceremonies and for anointing purposes. The ancient Egyptians used it with myrrh, juniper berries, cinnamon, mint, sweet flag and raisins to make *kyphi*, a popular form of temple incense which doubled as a wine additive! The Egyptians and Hebrews put frankincense to many uses and paid great sums of money to obtain it from the Phoenicians. With myrrh they would mould it into balls of incense to fumigate and sweeten the air in their homes. Frankincense was also chewed to freshen the breath and used widely in rejuvenating creams and face masks. Past medicinal uses were for the treatment of toothache, respiratory and digestive disorders and syphilis. Today olibanum is still used as an incense by the Catholic church, Buddhists and other religions.

## PRESENT USES

Frankincense has a strong de-stressing effect upon the whole psyche. Whether it is used as a room fragrancer, perfume or in a massage oil or bath, this beautiful essence has the effect of calming breathing and the nervous system while uplifting the spirits. It is ideal to use for meditation, or to melt away worrying thoughts or nervous tension.

Frankincense is a fantastic skin-care oil for mature or prematurely ageing skin, especially when blended with rose or carrot seed oil. It also has a toning effect which dry, normal or combination skin can benefit from when used in a cream or oil. The oil's properties of promoting cell regeneration and healing

wounds make it an ideal choice for sores, wounds and scars. Its effect upon the respiratory system is very healing for bronchitis, chronic coughs, colds and catarrh, and it can help people with asthma where they are holding onto tension or negative emotions which worsens their condition.

Frankincense's astringent quality helps where there is heavy menstrual flow and urinary tract infections can benefit because of its diuretic action. In pregnancy I've used frankincense with great success to allay anxiety, to help relax and deepen breathing in labour and to combat stretch marks and engorged breasts (see Chapter 6). This is a useful essence for depression or where there is stress-related illness.

### CAN BENEFIT

♦ Anxiety, depression, nervous tension, stress-related illness. ♦ Asthma, bronchitis, catarrh, colds, coughs. ♦ Combination skin, dry skin, mature skin, normal skin, prematurely ageing skin, scars, stretch marks, sores, wounds. ♦ Engorged breasts, labour pain, excessive menstruation, premenstrual symptoms. ♦ Rheumatism.

### HOW TO USE

Bath, compress, massage, perfume, room fragrancer, skin-care preparations, steam inhalation.

# GERANIUM
*Pelargonium graveolens*

**Family:** geraniaceae. ♦ **Perfumery note:** middle. ♦ **Aroma:** delicate floral, sweet and rose-like.

The essential oil is steam distilled from the flowers, leaves and stalks of this attractive plant. There are over 700 varieties of pelargonium but the most

common types favoured for aromatherapy are *pelargonium graveolens* and *pelargonium odorantissimum*.

**Blends well with:** basil, bergamot, cedarwood, cypress, fennel, frankincense, grapefruit, jasmine, juniper, lavender, lemon, mandarin, myrrh, myrtle, neroli, orange, patchouli, petitgrain, rose, rosemary, sandalwood, ylang-ylang – in fact most oils.

## MAIN QUALITIES

Antidepressant, anti-inflammatory, antiseptic, astringent, deodorant, insect repellent.

**Helps to:** stimulate new cell growth; encourage fluid loss by promoting urination; stop bleeding; regulate hormonal levels; stimulate and tone; generally has a harmonising effect on the emotions.

## TALES FROM THE PAST

The ancients valued this plant highly and used it to heal fractures, internal bleeding, wounds and even apparently to treat cancers. Originally from the Cape area of Africa, geraniums, or more correctly pelargoniums, were introduced to Europe in the seventeenth century where their popularity soon spread. In his herbal of this time Nicholas Culpeper explained the uses of a common British variety, Herb Robert: 'It is under the dominion of Venus and is commended against the stone, and to stay blood, where or however flowing; it speedily heals all green wounds, and is effectual in old ulcers in the privy parts or elsewhere. All geraniums are vulneraries, but this herb more particularly so, only rather more detersive and diuretic, which quality is discovered by its strong, soapy smell.'

Geranium oil is sometimes referred to as geranium bourbon as it was widely cultivated on the Ile de Bourbon, now called Réunion Island. The oil is still produced here and is noted for its superior quality in perfumery work. France, Morocco, Egypt and China are also major exporters.

## PRESENT USES

This oil has a delightful floral quality which blends well with most oils to create truly beautiful fragrances. I find geranium's best quality to be its balancing

effect on both body and mind, making it an ideal choice when treating stress-related disorders. In fact, geranium has so many positive effects upon common ailments I would not leave home without it!

Most skin conditions can benefit from the use of geranium as it has a normalising effect on the production of sebum (the skin's natural oil). Dry, oily, congested, combination, dehydrated and overhydrated skins can be helped, as can cases of acne and dry eczema. Cuts, sores, chilblains and burns also respond well to the antiseptic and healing properties of this oil.

The hormone regulating action of geranium is of great use when treating premenstrual and menopausal problems, and besides being emotionally uplifting, it can also relieve fluid retention. This oil's astringent and anti-inflammatory properties soothe painful piles, help to stop diarrhoea and ease gastro-enteritis. Sore throats, colds and flu can be helped, as can rheumatic pain, especially when combined with frankincense and lavender oil for massage. Besides being an excellent anti-cellulite oil, geranium has a pronounced effect in cases of varicose veins and circulation problems, and is particularly helpful in late pregnancy. It also has an effect of balancing extremes of blood sugar levels which may be of use in cases of diabetes (further information should be sought from a qualified aromatherapist). Though some people find geranium gently stimulating, in my experience, if used sparingly, it generally encourages physical relaxation and brings harmony to mind, body and emotions.

### CAN BENEFIT

♦ Acne, all skin types, bruises, burns, chilblains, dehydrated skin, eczema (dry), wounds. ♦ Anxiety, depression, nervous tension, stress-related illnesses. ♦ Cellulitis, circulation problems, fluid retention, varicose veins. ♦ Colds, flu, sore throats. ♦ Diarrhoea, gastro-enteritis, haemorrhoids, high blood sugar. ♦ Engorged breasts, mastitis, menopausal problems, premenstrual syndrome. ♦ Greasy hair, head lice. ♦ Rheumatism.

### HOW TO USE

Bath, compress, hair care, insect repellent, massage, perfume, room fragrancer, skin-care preparations.

# GRAPEFRUIT
*Citrus paradisi*

**Family:** rutaceae. ♦ **Perfumery note:** top. ♦ **Aroma:** citrus sharp, sweet and fresh.

This handsome tree can grow up to a height of 40 feet. It has dark-green shiny, oval-shaped leaves and bears large yellow fruits. The essential oil is obtained by cold expression, (literally squeezing) of the rind of the fruit. Please note that grapefruit oil only retains its therapeutic value for a maximum of six months even if stored and used in ideal conditions.
**Blends well with:** bergamot, black pepper, clary sage, cypress, eucalyptus, fennel, frankincense, geranium, jasmine, juniper, lavender, myrrh, neroli, patchouli, pine, rosemary, ylang-ylang.

## MAIN QUALITIES

Antibacterial, antidepressant, antiseptic, astringent, detoxifying.
**Helps to:** stimulate fluid loss by promoting urination; has stimulant and tonic actions; generally revives and refreshes on an emotional level.

## TALES FROM THE PAST

The grapefruit is believed to have evolved from the pomelo (*citrus grandis*), a tree originally native to Asia. The fruit was larger than the grapefruit we know today and its sour yet refreshing flesh was very popular in India. A Captain Shaddock is said to have brought the species from China and introduced it to the West Indies; where the fruit was thereafter known as 'shaddock fruit'. In 1809, the seeds found their way with Spanish settlers from Jamaica to the United States, but the plant was not commercially grown until 1880. Its action of protecting against infectious illnesses because of its high vitamin C content has been known for years. By the early 1900s, the fruit had become popular and the canning of segments and juice began in Florida. Cultivation spread to Texas and California, which along with Israel is where most oil is produced today.

## PRESENT USES

Grapefruit's antiseptic and astringent properties make it beneficial for acne or oily skin, and if used sparingly in a facial oil it helps purify and tone dry or normal skin which is congested. Poor muscle tone can be improved through massage as can a sluggish digestive system. This citrus oil has an affinity with the liver, gall bladder and kidneys, exerting a stimulating and detoxifying effect. For this reason it has been recommended when suffering after indulging in too much food or alcohol, and it can also be of use in cases of drug withdrawal. Because of its high limonene (one of the chemicals found in citrus oils) content it has proved useful in breaking down small kidney or gall stones. Being a lymphatic stimulant and able to ease fluid retention, grapefruit is helpful when cellulite or obesity is a problem. However, diet and lifestyle changes are needed too, such as eating fresh fruit and vegetables, cutting out stimulants like coffee, salt and alcohol and instead drinking plenty of spring water. Exercise is a must – one brisk walk for 20 minutes each day combined with dry skin brushing will go a long way towards regaining a healthy body and mind. However, every individual has unique requirements so a visit to a qualified aromatherapist will provide you with further specific information.

Grapefruit's uplifting effect on the emotions also helps in cases of depression. Used in a bath, for massage or as a refreshing room fragrancer, it converts negative emotions, and revives and energises tired minds.

## CAN BENEFIT

♦ Acne, congested skin, oily skin. ♦ Anxiety, depression, mental exhaustion, nervous tension, stress-related ailments. ♦ Build up of toxicity, drug withdrawal. ♦ Digestive problems, hangovers, liver and gall bladder problems. ♦ Fluid retention, cellulitis. ♦ Poor muscle tone, muscle fatigue.

## HOW TO USE

Bath, compress, massage, room fragrancer, skin-care preparations.

# JASMINE
*Jasminum officinale*

**Family:** oleaceae. ♦ **Perfumery note:** middle. ♦ **Aroma:**
rich, 'heady' and floral, just like fresh jasmine flowers.

This climbing shrub can grow to a height of approximately 25 feet.
The oil comes from the small, white flowers. There are several varieties of
jasmine from around the world. The oils from *jasminum officinale* and *jasminum
grandiflorum* are favoured for use in aromatherapy. Like rose, jasmine is gathered
before dawn when the oil yield is at its peak – literally thousands of flowers are
needed to make even the smallest amount of essential oil. A good-quality oil
should be a deep orange-brown colour and of quite a thick consistency. North
Africa, Italy, India, Turkey and China are all major producers, but it is the
French oil which is generally considered superior.
**Blends well with:** bergamot, clary sage, geranium, grapefruit, lemon,
mandarin, myrtle, neroli, orange, patchouli, petitgrain, rose, sandalwood, ylang-
ylang and most others.

## MAIN QUALITIES

Antidepressant, anti-inflammatory, antispasmodic, antiseptic, aphrodisiac,
expectorant.
**Helps to:** expel gas; calm the nervous system; strengthen the uterus; generally
has an uplifting even euphoric effect on the emotions and can be helpful with
sexual problems.

## TALES FROM THE PAST

For thousands of years this luxurious fragrance has been known for its aphrodisiac qualities, and because of this the flowers and oil have been major ingredients in love potions and sensual perfumes. The Hindus used the flowers to
make sweet-smelling garlands for honoured guests and at Ghazipur a
conditioning hair oil was made consisting of jasmine and
sesame oil. The women of Borneo and the
Philippines also traditionally placed jasmine

blossoms into their well-oiled hair for the attractive scent as well as to display the beauty of the flowers. This plant was held sacred to the followers of Indra, an ancient Indo-Iranian god, and to devotees of Vishnu who used the flowers as votive offerings at religious ceremonies.

In old English the name for jasmine was jessamine and the astrologer and physician Culpeper tells us that 'the oil made by infusion of the flowers, is used for perfumes. It disperses crude humours, and is good for cold and cattarhous constitutions, but not for the hot.' This beautiful fragrance is accurately described in the language of flowers – jasmine means happiness, amiability and elegance.

## Present Uses

Jasmine is one of the most pleasing and powerfully scented oils used in aromatherapy today. In my opinion it is the 'king' of the antidepressant oils as it not only calms nerves but seems to impart confidence, joy and new-found positivity. This is an ideal oil for anybody suffering from heartbreak, grief, anger or stress-related ailments. Jasmine 'warms' and uplifts the emotions, giving a person some breathing space from dark moods or anxieties. It is particularly useful in these circumstances when combined with bergamot or rose. Its aphrodisiac effects are enhanced when blended with clary sage, myrtle, patchouli, rose, sandalwood or ylang-ylang. Jasmine is said to be useful for prostate gland problems and generally strengthens the male sexual organs. For women, the oil is useful for strengthening the uterus and is particularly helpful for women in labour and, if needed, for post-natal depression.

A useful skin-care oil, jasmine is especially good for hot, dry, mature or wrinkled skin. It is interesting to note that jasmine oil is a vital constituent in many of the world's finest perfumes and colognes, not least Chanel No. 5. Over the years, chemists have tried in vain to capture the exquisite fragrance of jasmine – they are unsuccessful perhaps because the oil consists of over 100 finely balanced natural chemical constituents. So beware of bottles labelled as jasmine yet selling for only a few pounds; they are almost definitely synthetic or greatly diluted, inferior-quality oils. A

true jasmine oil is expensive but totally worth the investment as tiny amounts are needed when making your own perfumes, cosmetics and massage blends. If just 1 drop is applied to the wrists this exotic fragrance will last for hours, instilling good feelings in the wearer whereas the synthetic brand produces none of these effects. It is now possible to buy the pure oil in a base of jojoba (a liquid wax

*Not suitable for babies, young children or in early pregnancy – use moderately only after 20 weeks.*

*Although rare, some people with sensitive skin have experienced a degree of irritation from this oil, so test yourself for an allergic reaction by carrying out a simple patch test (see Chapter 2 for details of how to carry out a test). If redness or sensitivity occurs dilute the oil to 1 per cent or avoid it altogether.*

which has a very long shelf life) which is an excellent way to enjoy this luxurious essence at a reasonable price. Using exotic jasmine on a bleak day is like putting a drop of sunshine into your life.

## CAN BENEFIT

♦ Anger, anxiety, apathy, depression, frigidity, impotence, nervous tension, stress-related illness. ♦ Catarrhal conditions, coughs (other oils can be substituted). ♦ Enlarged prostate gland. ♦ Menstrual problems, period pain, labour, premenstrual syndrome. ♦ Most skin types especially dry and mature skin, wrinkles.

## HOW TO USE

Bath, compress, massage, perfume, room fragrancer, skin-care preparations.

# JUNIPER

*Juniperus communis*

**Family:** cupressaceae. ♦ **Perfumery note:** middle. ♦ **Aroma:** refreshing, yet woody with a slight turpentine-like scent.

This tree is usually anywhere between 6 and 15 feet high and has fine needle-like leaves and bears small berries which, although green in its first year, turn to blue-black in successive years. It is from the same family as the cypress tree and shares a similar aroma and qualities. Juniper berry oil is obtained through steam distillation of the berries, whereas juniper oil is extracted from the needle-like leaves and twigs. The essential oil obtained from the berries is considered of superior therapeutic quality to that of the leaves and twigs.
**Blends well with:** bergamot, cedarwood, cypress, eucalyptus, frankincense, geranium, grapefruit, lavender, lemon, mandarin, marjoram, myrrh, neroli, orange, petitgrain, pine, rosemary, sandalwood, tea tree.

## MAIN QUALITIES

Antibacterial, antirheumatic, antiseptic, astringent, detoxifying.
**Helps to:** expel gas; stimulate fluid loss by promoting urination; promote menstruation; strengthen the nervous system; produce warmth and redness when applied to the skin; increase perspiration; generally has a tonic, purifying effect on the body and is emotionally refreshing.

## TALES FROM THE PAST

The ancient Egyptians used juniper to ease asthmatic symptoms and used it with frankincense as a popular headache cure. The Egyptians placed great importance on physical appearance and juniper was a core ingredient in hair dye which was then rubbed into grey hair to blacken it. The berries were also used for dyeing fabric. In Tibet, juniper wood and berries were used for their medicinal properties as well as in

cleansing temple incenses. Other nations traditionally used juniper for fumigation purposes and it was burned in public places in towns as well as in houses as protection from the plague and other contagious diseases. Much later, in nineteenth-century Paris, it was used to combat another epidemic, this time smallpox. The French recognised its disinfectant quality by burning juniper along with rosemary and thyme in hospital wards to decrease airborne infections. Juniper is used widely in cooking and gives gin its familiar bouquet.

## PRESENT USES

Juniper has excellent purifying properties which can be especially helpful for cases of obesity, cellulite and fluid retention as well as rheumatism where a build up of toxins may be aggravating the condition. This often colourless oil has a sharp, clean aroma which helps clear up coughs, colds, flu and sinusitis. Vaporised in a sick room it will act as a disinfectant, helping to protect carers from catching the illnesses they are treating. Juniper also has a stimulating effect on the circulation, relieving varicose veins and haemorrhoids. Its toning effect on aching, overtired muscles is great too.

The cleansing quality is evident again when juniper is used to treat acne, overhydrated skin, boils and weeping eczema. Like eucalyptus and geranium, juniper lowers blood sugar levels and may be of help to diabetics (further information can be sought from a qualified aromatherapist). It also relieves flatulence and indigestion. Juniper oil encourages menstruation so is not suitable for pregnancy. However, it is useful for painful and scanty periods. The uncomfortable, bloated feeling and fatigue that some women feel before their period can be alleviated by using this oil in a bath or massage blend as it is energising and relieves fluid retention. Its power-ful antiseptic and diuretic actions (it encour-ages urination) make juniper ideal for cystitis and, as juniper promotes the elimination of uric acid and other impurities from the body,

> *Not suitable in pregnancy, for babies or young children.*
>
> *Generally this oil should be used in moderation and with care.*

it is helpful in cases if gout. This oil not only cleanses and stimulates the body but also has a similar clearing effect upon the mind, emotions and spirit.

### CAN BENEFIT

♦ Acne, boils, eczema (weeping), oily skin (as a toner), overhydrated skin. Arthritis, cramp, gout, rheumatism, muscles which lack tone, overtired muscles, varicose veins. ♦ Cellulite, fluid retention, obesity, poor circulation, toxicity. ♦ Colds, coughs, flu, sinusitis. ♦ Dandruff. ♦ Diarrhoea, indigestion, flatulence, haemorrhoids, high blood sugar. ♦ Mental exhaustion, sluggish, under-motivated states of mind. ♦ Painful and scanty periods, premenstrual tension. ♦ Urinary tract infections.

### HOW TO USE

Bath, compress, hair care, inhalation, massage, room fragrancer, skin-care preparations.

# LAVENDER
*Lavendula angustifolia*

**Family:** labiatae. ♦ **Perfumery note:** top/middle. ♦ **Aroma:** fresh, floral, sweet with herbaceous undertones.

Several varieties of this well-known plant are grown worldwide, but it is *lavendula angustifolia* which is favoured for use in aromatherapy. This type of lavender is also known as *lavendula vera*, 'true' lavender or *lavendula officinale*. It grows well at altitudes of about 3,000 feet and has beautiful lavender-coloured flowering tops. It is from these that the essential oil is steam distilled. Sometimes the oil from lavendin (a hybrid) is used in aromatherapy, but this has a sharper aroma and is considered to be therapeutically inferior to 'true' lavender oil.

**Blends well with:** bergamot, black pepper, camomile, cedarwood, clary sage, cypress, eucalyptus, fennel, frankincense, geranium, grapefruit, juniper, lemon,

mandarin, marjoram, myrtle, neroli, orange, patchouli, peppermint, pine, rose, rosemary, tea tree, ylang-ylang – in fact most other oils.

## MAIN QUALITIES

Antibacterial, antidepressant, antifungal, anti-inflammatory, antiseptic, antiviral, deodorant, insect repellent.

**Helps to:** relieve pain; stimulate new cell growth; encourage fluid loss by promoting urination; stimulate menstruation; lower blood pressure; boost the immune system; increase sweating; strengthen and relax the nervous system; tone muscles; generally calms emotions and can induce sleep.

## TALES FROM THE PAST

Lavender has been used for centuries because of its amazing versatility. The Egyptians grew lavender in their walled gardens, using the dried flowers to make body oils and to perfume clothes. The Romans used it for bathing and coined the name lavender from *lavare* which means 'to wash'. They also used it as an antidote to snake venom. Only the wealthiest Roman women could afford the lavender which they used as a breath freshener and in perfumes with lilies and myrrh. It was also used as an insect repellent and as a preventative treatment against head lice.

In fourteenth-century Europe, lavender's popularity spread – already believed to be an aphrodisiac and a protector from evil spirits, miraculous rejuvenation was added to the list of its qualities. It was a principal ingredient in Hungary Water, a cosmetic which apparently allowed Queen Elizabeth of Hungary to stay irresistibly attractive into her seventies. Lavender was a favourite of the English Queen Elizabeth I. She is said to have drunk it as a tea to relieve migraine attacks. Later it was incorporated into *eau de Cologne* and proved a favourite not only with Empress Josephine but also with Napoleon. Although lavender water is still popular today it was most fashionable in the latter part of the nineteenth century. Victorian women tucked small lavender bags under their pillows to ensure restful sleep and received lavender in bouquets as love tokens from courting men. The great healing properties of lavender oil were rediscovered almost by accident earlier in this century by a French chemist named Gattefossé. He plunged his

burning arms into a vat of lavender oil after an explosion in his laboratory and they healed very quickly, to his amazement, and with no trace of scarring.

## PRESENT USES

This fresh, sweetly fragrant essence is unquestionably one of the most therapeutic oils used in aromatherapy, treating everything from burns, headaches and high blood pressure to chickenpox, cystitis and nervous tension. Lavender has a balancing effect on the skin's natural oil, sebum, and its strong antiseptic effect successfully treats many skin conditions – acne, burns, dermatitis and eczema to name but a few. It is a relatively mild oil, safe for a variety of children's ailments (see Chapter 7) and a useful oil in pregnancy (see Chapter 6).

Its antispasmodic, antiviral actions and ability to boost the immune system come into play when treating irritating coughs, colds, sinusitis, flu and swollen lymph nodes. Lavender can help relieve nausea and headaches and is a classic remedy for migraine especially if used at the onset of an attack. Rheumatic pain, sprains and overtired muscles all benefit greatly from lavender's soothing quality, especially when blended with rosemary or marjoram. Its first aid uses are numerous and it is the only oil except for tea tree that I would recommend to use neat on the skin (1 drop on a cut, for example). Lavender helps to cleanse the body by stimulating the lymphatic system and promoting the elimination of waste products. It eases flatulence, gastro-enteritis, and indigestion. This oil alone or combined with camomile will help you sleep as they both have a sedating effect on the nervous system. Lavender is a 'warm', comforting oil whose pleasing scent melts away nervous tension, anxiety and lifts depression. The healing qualities of this oil are remarkable and it blends well with most other oils.

> *Lavender is a very mild emmenagogue (it promotes menstruation) so avoid in early pregnancy if there is a history or serious risk of miscarriage.*

## CAN BENEFIT

♦ Acne, all skin types, athlete's foot, boils, burns, bruises, cuts, eczema, grazes, inflamed skin, insect stings and bites, itching, minor wounds, psoriasis, rashes

(nappy), ringworm, scalds, scars, sores, spots, sunburn, stretch
marks, ulcers. ♦ Anxiety, depression, hysteria, insomnia,
nervous tension, stress-related ailments. ♦ Arthritis, aches
and pains (muscles), cramp, gout, sciatica, sprains.
♦ Asthma, bronchitis, colds, coughs (tickly), croup, flu, laryngitis, sinusitis, sore throats, whooping cough. ♦ Cellulite, high blood
pressure, palpitations, poor circulation, varicose veins. ♦ Chickenpox,
measles, immune system deficiency. ♦ Colitis, constipation, diarrhoea, flatulence, gall bladder problems, indigestion, nausea, tummy ache. ♦ Dandruff,
head lice. ♦ Earache, headache, migraine. ♦ Engorged breasts, labour pain,
leukorrhoea (thick, white vaginal discharge), period pain, premenstrual
syndrome, thrush. ♦ Urinary tract infections.

### HOW TO USE

Bath, compress, douche, hair care, insect repellent, massage, neat (1 drop only),
perfume, room fragrancer, skin-care preparations.

# LEMON
### Citrus limonum

**Family:** rutaceae. ♦ **Perfumery note:** top. ♦ **Aroma:** fresh, sharp and slightly
sweet citrus aroma.

This hardy tree grows up to a height of 16 feet and bears not only the well-
known fruit but beautifully scented flowers. The essential oil is obtained by cold
expression (literally squeezing) of the peel of the fruit. Originally native to Asia,
lemon is now found throughout the Mediterranean area as well as being
cultivated in vast quantities in Israel and the Americas. Bergamot is closely
related to this attractive tree. Please note that lemon, like most citrus
oils, only retains its therapeutic properties for a maximum of six to
eight months, even if stored and used in ideal
conditions.

**Blends well with:** basil, bergamot, black pepper, camomile, carrot seed, clary sage, cypress, eucalyptus, fennel, frankincense, geranium, jasmine, juniper, lavender, mandarin, marjoram, myrtle, neroli, orange, patchouli, petitgrain, pine, rosemary, sandalwood, tea tree, ylang-ylang and most other oils.

## MAIN QUALITIES

Antibacterial, antifungal, antiseptic, astringent, detoxifying, insect repellent.
**Helps to:** heal wounds; stimulate fluid loss by promoting urination; reduce fever; lower blood pressure; boost the immune system; strengthen the stomach and liver; tone the skin; energises while refreshing and reviving on an emotional level.

## TALES FROM THE PAST

This fruit is widely believed to help maintain good health generally. Although native to Asia, the ancient Egyptians obtained lemon and used it to prevent food poisoning and epidemics. The lemon was brought to Europe in the Middle Ages by the Crusaders, where it spread rapidly into Greece, Italy, Sicily, Spain and Portugal. Its high vitamin C content was valued by English sailors as a preventative measure against scurvy on long voyages. So successful was this remedy that until early in this century the British Navy required that enough lemon juice be carried on its ships if the voyage lasted more than 10 days.

Externally, lemon has a mild bleaching effect on the skin and so it has been used for years to whiten the hands and fade freckles. This fruit is used widely in medicines, confectionery, and in food and drink flavourings.

## PRESENT USES

This refreshing oil has many uses but is essentially a purifier with strong antiseptic and astringent properties. Lemon oil reduces congestion in the skin and has a toning and stimulating effect on the circulation and lymphatic system. These qualities make it valuable for treating oily skin, acne, cellulite or varicose veins. It can also be used for these complaints in pregnancy (see Chapter 6) as well as providing a clean, fresh scent to vaporise if morning sickness becomes a problem.

Lemon oil stimulates the immune system which helps combat infectious illness and it has proved helpful in dissolving small kidney stones. It has been shown that it takes lemon oil between five and 20 minutes to neutralise the bacilli (micro-organisms which cause bacterial infections) of typhoid, diphtheria and TB. When vaporised it takes the essence less than an hour to neutralise the typhus germ and between one and three hours to have the effect on the germ which causes pneumonia. This strong antibacterial action makes it a valuable sick room freshener.

The juice of lemons also tones both liver and spleen and eases arthritic pain and gout. Although the acidity and sharp taste of lemon are well known, once ingested it promotes an alkaline reaction in the stomach, relieving gastric problems associated with acidity. Honey and lemon in hot water is a comforting treatment for colds and sore throats.

If you need to purify suspect drinking water while travelling, boil it then add the juice of a lemon per litre of water and the lemon will act as a disinfectant. The oil is also an effective insect repellent.

Since the 1980s, some Japanese companies have diffused lemon oil in the working environment of their employees, reporting a heightened sense of mental clarity and fewer errors. Lemon refreshes and invigorates, making it indispensable for lethargic and depressed states of mind and body.

*Do not use lemon oil on skin which is to be exposed to the sun or ultraviolet light as it is phototoxic (it can cause skin discolouration).*

*Lemon oil is a skin irritant so use in a low dilution only – 1 per cent in a massage oil or 3 drops in a bath.*

*Not suitable for babies or young children.*

### CAN BENEFIT

♦ Acne, chilblains, cuts, gum infections, insect bites, mouth ulcers, oily skin, spots, over-hydrated skin, warts. ♦ Asthma, catarrh, colds, coughs, flu, sinusitis, sore throats. ♦ Cellulite, gout, poor circulation, varicose veins. ♦ Depression, lethargy, nervous tension, stress-related ailments.
♦ Flatulence, gall bladder and liver problems, hangovers, heartburn,

indigestion, nausea. ♦ Greasy hair. ♦ Kidney stones (small).

## How to Use

Bath, compress, hair care, insect repellent, massage, mouthwash, perfume, room fragrancer, skin-care preparations, steam inhalation.

# MANDARIN

*Citrus nobilis*

**Family:** rutaceae. ♦ **Perfumery note:** top. ♦ **Aroma:** delicate, fresh, sweet, citrus scent.

This attractive tree, which can grow to about 16 feet in height, also has aromatic flowers and shiny leaves. It originates from China but is now cultivated widely throughout the Mediterranean, Brazil and North America. Mandarin (*citrus nobilis* or *citrus madurensis*) is sometimes known as tangerine (*citrus reticulata*), a close relative, but the oils like the fruits are different. The oil comes from the rind of a small, flattened variety of Chinese orange and is obtained by cold expression (literally squeezed). Please note that this oil, like most citrus essences, only retains its therapeutic value for a maximum of six to eight months, even if stored and used in ideal conditions.

**Blends well with:** basil, bergamot, black pepper, camomile, carrot seed, clary sage, cypress, eucalyptus, fennel, frankincense, geranium, jasmine, juniper, lavender, lemon, myrrh, myrtle, neroli, orange, patchouli, peppermint, petitgrain, pine, rose, rosemary, tea tree, sandalwood, ylang-ylang.

## Main Qualities

Antiseptic, antidepressant, antispasmodic, detoxifying.

**Helps to:** stimulate fluid loss by promoting urination; aid digestion; relax the nervous system and intestines acting as a mild laxative; stimulate the lymphatic

system; tone the stomach and liver; generally has a gently sedative and uplifting action emotionally.

## TALES FROM THE PAST

Being native to China and the Far East, it is said that mandarin is so named because the fruits were given as gifts to the rulers at that time, the Mandarins. It was brought to Europe in the early nineteenth century where it thrived throughout the Mediterranean region. It was not until the middle of the century that the mandarin was exported to the Americas, which is where it is widely cultivated today.

The French recognise mandarin oil as *the* children's remedy and use it to relieve hiccups, gas or wind and stomach upsets. The oil is used in toiletries, perfumery, confectionery and to flavour liqueurs.

## PRESENT USES

Mandarin has a delightful, orangey aroma which uplifts the spirits yet also acts as a gentle sedative upon the nervous system. It is a relatively mild oil and is safe to use in pregnancy and for children's ailments like tummy ache, hiccups and for gas or wind pains. The relative mildness of mandarin makes it useful for other people who may need gentle care, like older or convalescing people.

In pregnancy it is a gift as there are many oils which should be avoided at this time, usually when you most need them! Lavender, neroli and mandarin make a soothing tummy rub for indigestion while simultaneously combating stretch marks, and mandarin with geranium, ylang-ylang or frankincense will help reduce high blood pressure (see Chapter 6).

Children generally love mandarin and mixed with geranium it becomes a 'special party' perfume. To ensure they have a restful sleep after the fun add 1 drop each of lavender and mandarin to a night bath.

The oil has a particularly positive effect on stomach and digestive problems especially if they are of a nervous origin. Mandarin calms the stomach, relieves constipation and is a refreshing, energising aroma for those recovering from recent illness or exhaustion.

Skin-care products are enhanced by the addition of mandarin which helps to

tone the skin gently and works especially well on congested, oily or overhydrated skin types. This fresh oil can also alleviate mild cases of fluid retention and improve circulation, therefore combating cellulite and encouraging the elimination of waste products from the body.

On the emotional plane mandarin relaxes anxious, restless states of mind, having a cheering yet relaxing effect upon the whole psyche.

## CAN BENEFIT

♦ Acne, congested skin, gum and mouth infections, oily skin, overhydrated skin, stretch marks. ♦ Anxiety, depression, fear, lack of confidence, insomnia, stress-related illness. ♦ Cellulite, fluid retention, poor circulation. ♦ Constipation, flatulence, griping pains, heartburn, hiccups, indigestion, nausea, tummy ache. ♦ Cramps. ♦ Premenstrual syndrome.

## HOW TO USE

Bath, compress, massage, perfume, room fragrancer, skin-care preparations.

# MARJORAM (SWEET)
*Origanum marjorana*

**Family:** labiatae. ♦ **Perfumery note:** middle. ♦ **Aroma:** warm, penetrating, herbaceous and spicy.

This well-known herb grows to about 2 feet high and has highly aromatic leaves and small white flowers arranged in clusters. The plant specified above is also known as *marjorana hortensis* or knotted marjoram. The essential oil is obtained by steam distillation of the leaves and flowering tops. This oil should not be confused with the so-called Spanish 'marjoram' (*thymus mastichina*), which is actually a species of thyme and should only be used by qualified aromatherapists.
**Blends well with:** bergamot, black pepper, camomile, cedarwood, clary

sage, cypress, eucalyptus, juniper, lavender, mandarin, orange, patchouli, peppermint, petitgrain, pine, rosemary, tea tree.

## MAIN QUALITIES

Anaphrodisiac, antibacterial, antifungal, antiseptic, antispasmodic, antiviral, expectorant.

**Helps to:** expel gas; stimulate fluid loss by promoting urination; promote menstruation; lower blood pressure; strengthen the stomach and relax spasms; produce warmth and redness when applied to the skin; promote healing of wounds; calm and strengthen the nervous system; expand small blood vessels; generally induces deep relaxation and calms the emotions.

## TALES FROM THE PAST

Marjoram's name comes from the Greek meaning 'joy of the mountain', apparently alluding to the beautiful carpet the herbs created as they grew on mountainsides. The ancient Greeks used marjoram as an antidote to narcotic poisoning, headaches and convulsions as well as for flatulence and gastric problems. Both Roman and Greek tradition dictated that newly-weds should be crowned with wreaths woven from the herb for good fortune and long life.

Centuries later, it was favoured by Louis XIV of France who ordered his clothes and apartments to be scented daily with marjoram and nutmeg. It seems that before the introduction of more exotic Eastern perfumes marjoram was very fashionable in Europe. Although the exact recipe was a closely guarded secret, Queen Elizabeth of Hungary's rejuvenating Hungary Water was known to contain marjoram. Today the herb is used widely for culinary purposes, especially in Italian dishes, and in the manufacture of perfumes and toiletries.

## PRESENT USES

Marjoram has a distinctive herby yet spicy aroma. It is warming, relaxing and has pain-killing properties. These qualities are of great value for stiff joints, overtired muscles, sprains and strains. I have used marjoram combined with lavender and geranium in the treatment of injured athletes with very positive

results. This oil stimulates the circulation and dilates the arteries making it useful in cases of arthritis (for dispersing and eliminating toxins) and for reducing high blood pressure.

Headaches, migraine attacks and nervous tensions are relieved through using marjoram as a compress, room fragrancer or massage oil. The oil's powerful antispasmodic and strengthening actions can also alleviate symptoms of flatulence, indigestion, diarrhoea and griping intestinal pains. It is important to note that this oil is an anaphrodisiac – it *decreases* sexual desire so shouldn't be confused with an aphrodisiac which stimulates it!

Colds, coughs, bronchitis and aching flu symptoms can all be relieved by using marjoram either in a steam inhalation or bath. Blend a relaxing bath or potent room freshener to keep infections at bay using marjoram and pine or lavender or tea tree.

Marjoram can also help to relax asthmatics, clear sinusitis and ease period pain. In the emotional sphere marjoram is a powerful sedative and is sometimes recommended for people who are hyperactive, anxious types. The oil exerts not only a physically warming effect but an emotional one too, comforting and calming people who have experienced shock or have recently lost someone they love. Marjoram is an ideal oil to use for extreme physical or mental tension and works particularly well with lavender, camomile or bergamot.

*Not suitable in pregnancy, for babies, young children or people with very low blood pressure.*

*Not to be confused with Spanish 'marjoram' (thymus mastichina) which is from the thyme family and should only be used by qualified aromatherapists.*

## CAN BENEFIT

♦ Anxiety, depression, insomnia, restlessness, stress-related illness.
♦ Arthritis, aching muscles, cramp, rheumatic pain, sprains, stiff joints, strains, overtired muscles. ♦ Asthma, bronchitis, colds, coughs, flu, sinusitis.
♦ Bruises, chilblains. ♦ Constipation, diarrhoea, indigestion, flatulence, griping pains. ♦ Excessive sexual desire. ♦ Headaches, migraines. ♦ High blood pressure, poor circulation. ♦ Irregular periods, period pain.

### How to Use

Bath, compress, inhalation, massage, room freshener, vaporiser.

# MYRRH

*Commiphora myrhha*

**Family:** burseraceae. ♦ **Perfumery note:** middle/base. ♦ **Aroma:** subtle, balsamic, warm, almost 'smoky'.

This small tree, native to north-east Africa, is very hardy and can survive in virtually barren conditions. It exudes a sticky, golden resin when cuts are made into the bark which then hardens into reddish–brown pieces or 'tears'. These are then collected and steam distilled to provide the essential oil of myrrh. Sometimes the 'oil' may revert to a gum-like consistency making it difficult to use. If this happens, pour a little into a bottle and stand it in a bowl of warm water for five minutes and this will encourage it to liquefy.

**Blends well with:** bergamot, camomile, cedarwood, cypress, frankincense, geranium, grapefruit, juniper, lavender, lemon, mandarin, neroli, orange, patchouli, peppermint, petitgrain, pine, rose, sandalwood, vetiver.

### Main Qualities

Anticatarrhal, antifungal, anti-inflammatory, antiseptic, astringent, expectorant.
**Helps to:** promote menstruation; energise the respiratory and digestive tracts; tone the skin; strengthen the uterus; promote healing of wounds; generally comforting and restful for distressed emotions.

### Tales from the Past

This gum or oil has been in constant use for over 3,000 years. The name myrrh derives from the Greek for 'gum carrier' which describes the protective action of the tree when the bark is cut. The Greeks valued myrrh for its long-lasting aroma which improved with age, and it became a very popular perfume called

'megaleion' when blended with oils of cinnamon and saffron. The ancient Egyptians used this gum in *kyphi*, a temple incense which sometimes doubled as a wine additive! They also utilised myrrh in rejuvenating cosmetics, for fumigation and in the mummification process.

Many of the ancient peoples recognised the healing power of this oil and used myrrh to cleanse battle wounds and ulcers. On a more sensual note, the Queen of Sheba was said to have entranced King Solomon with the scent of oils of myrrh and frankincense. It was highly prized by the ancients and along with gold and frankincense, myrrh was brought as a gift to the infant Jesus. The Bible also tells us that Moses used the oil for sacred anointings. Myrrh continued to be used widely and even today chemists still stock tincture of myrrh which can be used for mouth ulcers or infections. Commercially it is used in other medicines, mouthwashes and often in toothpaste.

## PRESENT USES

Myrrh has a very healing effect on the respiratory system and is a useful skin-care oil, especially for mature or prematurely ageing skin. Chapped lips or hands and rough or cracked skin can be treated by adding myrrh to a nourishing base cream with lavender or camomile which are also helpful 'healers'. Myrrh's antiseptic, anti-inflammatory and antifungal qualities are of particular value when treating mouth ulcers or gum infections, and other skin problems like cuts, athletes' foot, ringworm, and weeping eczema and sores.

Used in a massage oil for chest and throat infections, myrrh helps heal coughs, colds and clears catarrh as it is a powerful expectorant. This oil is useful when scanty periods are a problem but because of this action it should be avoided in pregnancy. Generally myrrh is a strengthening, healing oil which makes for a useful middle/base note when creating homemade perfumes and cosmetics.

> *Not suitable for use in pregnancy.*
>
> *Generally this oil should be used in moderation.*

## CAN BENEFIT

♦ Boils, athletes' foot, cuts, chapped skin,

cracked or rough skin, eczema (weeping), gum and mouth infections, mature skin, ringworm, sores, ulcers, wrinkles. ♦ Catarrh, chest infections, colds, coughs, throat infections. ♦ Diarrhoea, flatulence. ♦ Scanty periods.

### HOW TO USE

Bath, massage, mouthwash, perfume, room fragrancer, skin-care preparations.

# MYRTLE

*Myrtus communis*

**Family:** myrtaceae. ♦ **Perfumery note:** middle. ♦ **Aroma:** warm, slightly camphor-like, spicy.

Myrtle is a large shrub from North Africa which bears fragrant, white flowers and later bluish-coloured berries. The essential oil is obtained through steam distillation of the shrub's leaves and twigs. It is still produced in its native North Africa but also in Austria, Russia and many Mediterranean countries. Myrtle is from the same family as tea tree and eucalyptus but has a much more delicate aroma than its relatives.

**Blends well with:** bergamot, black pepper, cedarwood, cypress, eucalyptus, geranium, jasmine, lavender, lemon, mandarin, neroli, orange, patchouli, petitgrain, pine, rose, rosemary, sandalwood, tea tree, ylang-ylang.

### MAIN QUALITIES

Antibacterial, anticatarrhal, antifungal, antiseptic, aphrodisiac, astringent, expectorant.

**Helps to:** ease coughing; gently sedate nervous system; generally beneficial for urinary and lung ailments; emotionally it has a harmonising effect.

## TALES FROM THE PAST

Legend has it that a beautiful goddess was born from the ocean near Cyprus. Her name was Aphrodite. It is said that she then plucked a branch of myrtle leaves to hide her nakedness and from that time the myrtle has been an emblem of purity and love. Perhaps this explains why it was so popular in love potions through the ages and that traditionally brides carried myrtle in their bouquets. This small tree has been around for a long time; the Bible mentions the 'myrtle and the oyle tree' as being planted in the wilderness, and the ancient Egyptians were known to favour it. They used it with herbs as an incense and it was an ingredient in a fragrant hair ointment along with gazelle dung!

Medicinally, myrtle was used in many ways – for treating urinary infections, skin disorders, coughs, mucus problems, swellings and muscular stiffness to name but a few. In the seventeenth century Nicholas Culpeper tells us, 'The leaves sometimes but chiefly the berries are used. They are both of them drying and binding, good for diarrhoea and dysentery.'

## PRESENT USES

This oil has a slightly sweet yet spicy aroma and is reminiscent of a subtle camphor-like odour. Emotionally this essence is very nurturing, bringing harmony and clarity of mind. It is a great anti-stress oil as it also acts as a mild relaxant to the nervous system. Myrtle is an effective antiseptic and toner for all skin types, but shows best results for acne, oily or congested or overhydrated skins.

This oil has a strong expectorant action that is effective when treating colds, coughs and especially catarrhal problems. It is useful when treating children as they usually find its mild scent pleasing. Bronchitis and flu can be relieved by using myrtle in a massage oil for the chest, and sinusitis can be helped by a steam inhalation or simply vaporising some oil in the bedroom at night. It also helps relieve urinary tract infections like cystitis. Simply have a sitz bath or use a warm compress with myrtle and lavender to alleviate the pain. When mixed with a neutral gel myrtle's astringent action is useful for haemorrhoids and if

used in a massage oil it can relieve diarrhoea. A sensual body massage with myrtle is a delight. Try blending it with jasmine, patchouli, rose sandalwood or ylang-ylang to discover its aphrodisiac qualities.

*There is one important point to remember: When treating any digestive problem with massage, always work gently in a clockwise direction.*

### CAN BENEFIT

♦ Acne, all skin types, but especially oily, congested or overhydrated skin, minor wounds. ♦ Anxiety, frigidity, lack of confidence, impotence, nervous tension, stress-related ailments. ♦ Bronchitis, catarrh, colds, coughs, flu, sinusitis.
♦ Diarrhoea, haemorrhoids. ♦ Urinary tract infections.

### HOW TO USE

Bath, compress, massage, perfume, room fragrancer, skin-care preparations, steam inhalation.

# NEROLI

*Citrus aurantium* (variety *amara*)

**Family:** rutaceae. ♦ **Perfumery note:** middle. ♦ **Aroma:** floral, bitter-sweet, a beautiful (non-citrus) scent.

The bitter orange, *citrus vulgaris* or *bigaradia* and Seville orange are all names for the tree specified above. Neroli or orange blossom oil is derived from the fragrant, white flowers of this tree which was originally native to China but now grows across the Mediterranean region. Sometimes the sweet orange (*citrus sinensis*) is used to obtain neroli Portugal oil but it is the former type that is considered superior for aromatherapy. It takes 1 tonne of hand-picked blossoms to yield approximately 1kg of oil.
**Blends well with:** basil, bergamot, camomile, carrot seed, cedarwood, clary sage, cypress, frankincense, geranium, grapefruit, jasmine, juniper,

lavender, lemon, mandarin, myrrh, myrtle, orange, patchouli, petitgrain, rose, sandalwood, vetiver, ylang-ylang.

## MAIN QUALITIES

Antibacterial, antidepressant, antiseptic, antispasmodic, aphrodisiac, deodorant. **Helps to:** expel gas; stimulate new cell growth; sedate the nervous system; tone the skin; generally has a deeply relaxing and soothing effect on the emotions.

## TALES FROM THE PAST

A duchess who was married to the Prince of Nerola in Italy is credited with giving neroli its name. She was of French origin and loved the perfume of orange blossoms so much that she scented her bath water, gloves and other clothes with them. This practice was widely imitated by other aristocrats and soon orange blossom scent was fashionable and in demand. Long before this, another woman in Egypt had discovered the secret attraction of neroli. It is said that Cleopatra used orange blossom, honey and cinnamon in a heady, exotic body oil before she seduced Julius Caesar.

For centuries, it became customary in Europe for brides to wear or carry orange blossoms as a symbol of purity and loveliness. The blossoms' scent was said to calm nerves and bring joy to the couple on their wedding night. In sixteenth-century Europe, neroli was blended with angelica, ambergris, myrtle and rose to become 'Angel Water' a popular tonic for the skin. Napoleon, Emperor of France, adored the scent of violets and neroli in his favourite Cologne and used it lavishly even on campaigns! This oil, along with bergamot, lavender and rosemary, was also one of the ingredients in the original eau de Cologne. Today it is still used in perfumery as a fixative and to impart its beautiful, delicate notes to many different types of fragrance.

## PRESENT USES

This exquisite flower oil may be compared to rose and jasmine, not in fragrance but because they are the most costly and luxurious scents in aromatherapy. All three blend beautifully together, and if you feel like treating yourself a tiny

amount is all you need to create a very special perfume or massage blend. Neroli does not have a citrus smell as one would imagine coming from the bitter orange tree; instead it is rich, delicate and floral yet contains a slightly bitter undertone.

Neroli induces deep relaxation and its calming action on the heart makes it useful in cases of nervous palpitations and apprehensive feelings like butterflies in the tummy. The oil also has a remarkably calming effect on a psychological level and is good in cases of fear, shock and chronic stress. It is an effective antidepressant, soothing anxiety, hysteria and nervous tension generally. A tiny amount of neroli is an excellent choice for examination nerves as it can help to reduce nervousness.

This oil is reputed to be an aphrodisiac, probably because of its ability to take the 'edge' off nerves, thereby reducing self-doubt and increasing self-confidence. Neroli oil helps to lift premenstrual and menopausal symptoms like mood swings, helping to bring harmony where there may be anger or tears, etc. Not only is it a valuable oil for the emotions, but it also works well on the physical body. Neroli is effective in skin care—its antiseptic, toning action is good for all skin types especially where there is dryness, sensitivity, broken veins or scarring.

The oil is useful in pregnancy to combat stretch marks (see Chapter 6), to allay anxiety and to soothe and uplift emotions. Neroli's antispasmodic effect eases indigestion, diarrhoea and nervous churning feelings in the stomach or intestinal area. It remains one of the best oils with which to treat stress-related ailments. Oil of neroli gently envelops the senses bringing tranquillity and leaves you feeling rebalanced and refreshed.

### CAN BENEFIT

♦ Acne, eczema, scars, stretch marks, thread veins, tones all skin types, especially dry, mature or sensitive skin, wrinkles. ♦ Anxiety, depression, frigidity, hysteria, impotence, insomnia, irritability, nervous tension, restlessness, shock, stress-related ailments. ♦ Colitis, diarrhoea, indigestion, intestinal spasms. ♦ Menopausal problems, premenstrual syndrome.

### HOW TO USE

Bath, massage, perfume, room fragrancer, skin-care preparations.

# ORANGE
*Citrus aurantium*

**Family:** rutaceae. ♦ **Perfumery note:** top. ♦ **Aroma:** refreshing, sweet, citrus scent like fresh oranges.

There are two types of orange tree: the sweet orange (*citrus aurantium* variety *dulcis*) and the bitter orange (*citrus aurantium* variety *amara*). Essential oil is obtained from both of them through the cold expression (literally squeezing) or distillation of the rind of their fruits. The aroma description above is that of the sweet orange; the bitter variety has a richer, more subtle scent. The latter also provides us with neroli oil from its fragrant blossoms and petitgrain oil from its leaves. Although native to China and the Middle East, these beautiful trees grow widely in Brazil, the Mediterranean and the USA. Orange oil, like most citrus essences, only retains its therapeutic value for a maximum of six to eight months even when stored and used in ideal conditions.

**Blends well with:** basil, bergamot, black pepper, camomile, carrot seed, clary sage, cypress, eucalyptus, fennel, frankincense, geranium, jasmine, juniper, lavender, lemon, mandarin, marjoram, myrrh, myrtle, neroli, patchouli, petitgrain, pine, rose, rosemary, sandalwood, tea tree, vetiver and ylang-ylang.

## MAIN QUALITIES

Antibacterial, antidepressant, antifungal, antiseptic, antispasmodic, detoxifying.

**Helps to:** expel gas; stimulate fluid loss by promoting urination; lower blood pressure; strengthen the stomach and digestion; sedate the nervous system; generally uplifting and refreshing yet calming on an emotional level.

## TALES FROM THE PAST

In Greek mythology a dragon and nymphs guarded a sacred island garden where golden apples grew. These 'apples' were probably oranges as the nymphs were

known as the Hesperides and this is a botanical name for the orange family. Over 4,000 years ago the orange was being used by the Indians and Chinese for cosmetic as well as medicinal uses.

Oranges were taken to the West Indies by Columbus and by 1565 was imported to Florida by the Spanish. Back in Europe during outbreaks of the plague, pomanders made from oranges stuck with cloves were carried by the wealthy as protection from the disease. Queen Elizabeth I was said to wear one constantly, fixed to a long chain around her neck. In 1769, the tree was taken to the west of America and successfully culti-vated by Franciscan monks, and California as well as Florida are the world's major producers today.

The edible fruit containing high levels of vitamins comes from the sweet orange tree, whereas the bitter orange fruit is inedible. Both oils are used for perfumery and cosmetic manufacture as well as flavouring food and liqueurs like Curaçao.

## PRESENT USES

Orange oil has a delightfully fresh and invigorating aroma which blends well with many essences. When used in small amounts for skin care it has a refreshing, toning effect good for all skin types and its slightly astrin-gent action works especially well for acne and oily skin.

Children usually love orange's aroma as it is one that they recog-nise. The oil is very relaxing and makes a calming bedtime bath.

Orange can make delicious blends when combined with other oils; with lemon and bergamot it is cooling and refreshing yet when mixed with black pepper, frankincense or clary sage it develops a warmer quality. The fruit is traditionally associated with boosting the immune system, fighting off infectious illnesses and generally imparting zest and good health. The oil is endowed with the same qualities and is invaluable in cases of coughs, colds, flu, bronchitis and chills where it may be used in a bath, steam inhalation or vaporiser. Orange oil helps to relieve digestive problems – it alleviates both constipation and chronic diarrhoea, eases flatulence and spasms, and generally calms symptoms of indigestion.

As it promotes the elimination of toxins from the body, orange is a helpful

addition to an anti-cellulite oil as it eases fluid retention. It is interesting that the French sometimes refer to cellulite as *peau d'orange* or 'orange-peel skin'. On an emotional level the effect of orange is uplifting, warming and ideal for treating stress-related ailments. This well-known scent seems to impart memories of warm sunshine and vitality making it a useful tonic for convalescents or people who need fresh energy or zest in their lives.

> *Do not use orange oil on skin which is to be exposed to the sun or ultraviolet light as it is phototoxic (it can cause skin discolouration).*

### CAN BENEFIT

♦ Acne, congested and oily skin, gum and mouth infections, tones all skin types. ♦ Anxiety, depression, insomnia, nervous tension, stress-related disorders. ♦ Bronchitis, chills, colds, coughs, flu. ♦ Cellulite. ♦ Constipation, diarrhoea, flatulence, indigestion, nausea, spasmodic pain.

### HOW TO USE

Bath, compress, massage, mouthwash, perfume, room fragrancer, skin-care preparations, steam inhalation.

# PATCHOULI

*Pogostemon cablin*

**Family:** labiatae. ♦ **Perfumery note:** base. ♦ **Aroma:** warm, musty an earthy, heavy scent.

This plant grows to about 3 feet high and has broad, furry leaves and white flowers with a hint of purple. The plant is native to Indonesia but oil is now produced in Sumatra, India, the Philippines and South America. The essence is obtained through the steam distillation of the plant's dried leaves. Patchouli essential oil is a rich, red-brown colour and has a thick consistency.
**Blends well with:** bergamot, black pepper, camomile (German), cedar-

wood, clary sage, frankincense, geranium, grapefruit, jasmine, lavender, lemon, mandarin, marjoram, myrrh, myrtle, neroli, orange, petitgrain, rose, sandalwood, vetiver, ylang-ylang.

## MAIN QUALITIES

Antibacterial, antidepressant, antifungal, anti-inflammatory, antiseptic, aphrodisiac, insect repellent.

**Helps to:** aid digestion; stimulate fluid loss by promoting urination; reduce fever; strengthen the nervous system; generally uplifts and balances emotional energy.

## TALES FROM THE PAST

The Arabs, Chinese and Japanese used patchouli as a protection against infectious diseases. It was also used as an antidote for snake and insect bites, for headaches, wounds and diarrhoea. In nineteenth-century India, the long-lasting scent was used to impregnate shawls for export and on long voyages overseas, the strong aroma keeping moths and other insects at bay. In fact, in the last century patchouli became very fashionable in Europe and was often blended with rose to form the well-known 'patchouli' perfume. Its popularity was revived in the 1960s when it was worn by hippies and was associated with peace and free love. This oil has always been used by perfumers as a natural fixative in Oriental fragrances and is still used widely in the manufacture of cosmetics and toiletries.

## PRESENT USES

Patchouli has a slightly spicy, exotic fragrance with a long-lasting base note. Like black pepper only a small amount is needed in any blend otherwise it may dominate, masking other more subtle aromas. Patchouli blends especially well with rose, sandalwood, lavender, vetiver and flower oils. It is an aphrodisiac and can have a deeply relaxing or conversely an energising effect depending on the amount used. However, it is always emotionally uplifting. Try blending it with myrtle and sensual sandalwood or ylang-ylang and rose. Although it can attract on a sexual level it can repel on another, being one of the most valuable insect repellents and a must if travelling in hot countries.

Therapeutically, patchouli oil heals cracked or chapped skin and in this way has similar properties to myrrh. Its antifungal and antiseptic qualities are effective for ringworm, athlete's foot, weeping eczema, dermatitis and dandruff. As a general skin-care oil it works well for oily, overhydrated, mature skin and even wrinkles! As this oil promotes the elimination of toxins from the body, it can be useful for general congestion, cellulite and fluid retention. Patchouli is also helpful for the psychological premenstrual symptoms, soothing frustrations, relaxing nervous tension and cheering the spirits. Generally this is a great oil for treating stress-related ailments, mental exhaustion and insomnia.

### Can Benefit

♦ Acne, athlete's foot, chapped or cracked skin, eczema (weeping), mature, overhydrated skin, ringworm, weeping sores, wrinkles. ♦ Anger, anxiety, confusion, depression, frigidity, frustration, impotence, insomnia, mental exhaustion, nervous tension, stress-related ailments. ♦ Dandruff. ♦ Fluid retention. ♦ Premenstrual syndrome.

### How to Use

Bath, hair care, insect repellent, massage, perfume, room fragrancer, skin-care preparations.

# Peppermint

*Mentha piperita*

**Family:** labiatae. ♦ **Perfumery note:** top. ♦ **Aroma:** cool, refreshing, a strong, penetrating menthol scent.

There are many varieties of mint but the one generally used in aromatherapy is peppermint (*mentha piperita*) which is a hybrid of water-

mint and spearmint. This herb grows to a height of about 3 feet. The essential oil is obtained through steam distillation of the leaves and flowering tops. Believed to be native to southern Europe, this well-known herb is now cultivated worldwide. The USA is the leading producer of the oil although the oil from England is widely considered to be of superior quality.

**Blends well with:** basil, cypress, eucalyptus, lavender, mandarin, marjoram, myrrh, pine, rosemary, tea tree.

### MAIN QUALITIES

Anti-inflammatory, antiseptic, antispasmodic, antiviral, astringent, deodorant, expectorant, insect repellent.

**Helps to:** expel gas; stimulate the mind; aid digestion; relieve pain; reduce fever; stimulate fluid loss by promoting urination; strengthen the liver; produce warmth and redness when applied to the skin; increase sweating; contract small blood vessels; generally cooling, with a stimulating and refreshing effect on mind and body.

### TALES FROM THE PAST

The ancient Egyptians, Chinese and Japanese all cultivated mint for its culinary and medicinal value. The Romans did the same and loved to flavour both food and wine with the herb, as well as eating the odd leaf between courses! In Greek mythology, Pluto is said to have seduced a beautiful nymph named Mentha. However, when his wife discovered this she jealously trod Menthe into the ground. Pluto then turned her into a sweetly smelling herb so as to remind him always of his great love for her. Mint was a prime ingredient in refreshing perfumes in ancient Greece. Athletes also used it to anoint their muscles before competitions. However, Greek soldiers were not allowed to eat mint as it was reputed to have aphrodisiac and therefore 'anti-combat' properties!

Today peppermint tea is made from dried mint leaves and the herb is found in many proprietary medicines especially for digestive complaints. Peppermint is used for flavouring and fragrancing on a vast scale, enhancing everything from food, drinks and toothpaste to toiletries. For me, mint is aptly described in the language of herbs as it is said to represent 'eternal refreshment'.

## PRESENT USES

Peppermint has a powerful, fresh, menthol aroma which is long lasting. Only a tiny amount is needed when mixing a massage oil and just 1 drop in a vaporiser will send its clearing fragrance spinning around the room. The intense aroma of this herb may overwhelm other more subtle oils in blends so only use tiny amounts. Most people are not averse to its smell but as it is very strong make sure it is dilute before using it on the skin.

Peppermint has been shown to neutralise the bacillus (micro-organism) which causes TB and kills staphylococcus (a bacterium) in a few hours. These qualities can be of great help when tackling colds, coughs, flu and other infectious illnesses. If fever is present a cooling compress may be applied and by vaporising the oil cases of sinusitis can be eased. When used with lavender or marjoram in a massage oil, peppermint stimulates the circulation, warming and easing tight, aching muscles. Conversely, it has an excellent cooling and deodorising effect – just 1 drop in a foot bath refreshes hot, swollen feet. Peppermint also has an effective insect repellent quality and it is said to deter animals like deer, rodents and cats too.

Peppermint oil is the best remedy I know for digestive problems. This oil has amazing antispasmodic and healing actions which can relieve nausea, indigestion, flatulence, diarrhoea and constipation. It is equally effective when treating headaches or migraine attacks and even fainting.

Physically it has an invigorating effect, alleviating symptoms of stress or tiredness, and on a psychological level peppermint brings clarity and fresh insight. This is essentially a cleansing, fresh, aromatic oil which quickly revives, stimulates and sharpens the mind and body.

> *Peppermint is a skin irritant so use it in low dilution only – 1 per cent in a local massage oil or 3 drops in a bath. Not suitable in pregnancy, for babies or young children.*

## CAN BENEFIT

♦ Asthma, catarrh, colds, coughs, flu, sinusitis. ♦ Bad breath, constipation, diarrhoea, flatulence, indigestion, nausea, spasmodic pain, travel sickness.
♦ Bruises, cold sores, excessive perspiration, gum and mouth infections.

- ◆ Confusion, fainting, lethargy, mental tiredness, stress-related ailments.
- ◆ Fever.  ◆ Headaches, migraine.  ◆ Low blood pressure, poor circulation.
- ◆ Muscular aches and pains.

### HOW TO USE

Bath, compress, insect repellent, massage, mouthwash, room fragrancer, skin-care preparations, steam inhalation.

# PETITGRAIN

*Citrus aurantium* (variety *amara*)

**Family:** rutaceae.  ◆ **Perfumery note:** top/middle.  ◆ **Aroma:** bitter-sweet, woody with a hint of floral.

Petitgrain essential oil is obtained by steam distillation of the leaves and twigs of the bitter orange tree. This hardy tree is also known as *citrus vulgaris* or *bigaradia* or Seville orange, and neroli oil is derived from its fragrant blossoms and bitter orange from the rind of its fruit. Other petit-grain oils are sometimes distilled from bergamot, mandarin and lemon but the oil specified above is the oil favoured for use in aromatherapy. Although native to China and the Middle East, this beautiful tree now also grows throughout the Mediterranean, Brazil and the USA.

**Blends well with:** basil, bergamot, cedarwood, cypress, clary sage, eucalyptus, frankincense, geranium, jasmine, juniper, lavender, lemon, mandarin, marjoram, myrrh, myrtle, neroli, orange, patchouli, rose, rosemary, sandalwood, ylang-ylang and most other oils.

### MAIN QUALITIES

Antidepressant, antiseptic, antispasmodic, deodorant.

**Helps to:** strengthen the nervous system; stimulate the digestive system; generally has a calming yet refreshing effect on an emotional level.

## TALES FROM THE PAST

The name is centuries old and derives from a time when an oil was distilled from the unripe fruits. As the fruits had not grown to full size they were known in French as *petits grains* or 'little grains'. However, this method proved very uneconomical and now only the leaves and twigs are used to produce this fragrant oil. Currently it is used widely in the manufacture of bath oils, cosmetics, soaps and is a major component in good-quality *eau de Cologne*.

## PRESENT USES

Petitgrain can often be substituted for costly neroli oil as it is quite inexpensive yet shares some of its healing properties and has a lighter but comparable aroma. However, neroli has stronger sedative action and has a significant effect on dry, mature and wrinkled skin whereas petitgrain does not; although its antiseptic and toning qualities are ideal for improving acne, congested or oily skin. Petitgrain is a refreshing oil which can act as a deodorant and gently encourages the elimination of unwanted toxins and fluid retention from the body. Indigestion, especially when of a nervous origin, is relieved through the use of petitgrain.

On an emotional level the oil gently sedates the nervous system yet uplifts the spirits. It is ideal for treating anxiety, depression and stress-related illness. In fact, petitgrain is useful for insomnia and can be used instead of (or combined with) lavender or marjoram as these oils alone are sometimes not to people's taste. Petitgrain is an exceptionally versatile oil as it blends well with almost every essence. When used with stimulating oils it seems to exert a similar effect and the same is true when mixed with relaxing essences. I have used this oil to create luxurious, relaxing massage oils with geranium, jasmine, rose or ylang-ylang, and I have blended it with myrtle and ylang-ylang for a re-energising, uplifting effect. Perfumes benefit from its beautiful scent and a refreshing Cologne water can be easily made by combining petitgrain, lemon, bergamot and/or mandarin.

### CAN BENEFIT

♦ Acne, congested or oily skin, excessive perspiration. ♦ Anxiety, depression, insomnia, nervous tension, stress-related ailments and tiredness. ♦ Cellulite, fluid retention. ♦ Nausea, flatulence, indigestion.

### HOW TO USE

Bath, massage, perfume, room fragrancer, skin-care preparations.

# PINE

*Pinus sylvestris*

**Family:** pinaceae. ♦ **Perfumery note:** top/middle. ♦ **Aroma:** light, fresh and woody.

There are many varieties of pine but the one favoured for aromatherapy is Scot's pine (*pinus sylvestris*). This majestic, evergreen tree grows to a height of approximately 115 feet and is found primarily in northern Europe and the USA. The essence is obtained through distillation of the needles, thus the essential oil is often referred to as pine needle. The tree also gives us edible pine kernels which come from the cones.

**Blends well with:** bergamot, cedarwood, cypress, eucalyptus, frankincense, grapefruit, juniper, lavender, lemon, mandarin, marjoram, myrrh, myrtle, orange, peppermint, rosemary, sandalwood, tea tree, ylang-ylang.

### MAIN QUALITIES

Antibacterial, anti-rheumatic, antiseptic, antispasmodic, deodorant, disinfectant, expectorant, insect repellent.

**Helps to:** stimulate fluid loss by promoting urination; stimulate the circulation; strengthen the nervous system; produce warmth and redness when applied to the skin; treat respiratory and urinary tract infections; generally stimulating with an enlivening effect on the emotions.

## TALES FROM THE PAST

There is recorded evidence in a cookery book dating from 1 AD that the Egyptians used pine kernels liberally as a source of nutrition. Centuries later, Nicholas Culpeper recommended that, 'The kernels are excellent restoratives in consumptions, and after long illness. The best way of giving them is in an emulsion beat up with barley water, which is also very good for heat and urine, and other disorders of the urinary passages.'

On the other side of the world, native American Indians used an extract from pine needles against scurvy, as a disinfectant and to repel insects. Respiratory problems were treated with pine resin and they also chewed a gum made from it to relieve stomach upsets.

In more recent times pine inhalations have been used to fight TB and other chronic lung illnesses. Today its fragrance is mainly in demand for bath oils and other toiletries.

## PRESENT USES

Pine is one of the most popular aromas and is pleasing and familiar to most people inducing thoughts of tranquil, green pine forests. Aromatic fragrances which are evocative of the seasons can be made, for instance, pine blended with frankincense or orange oils creates a wintry, Christmassy atmosphere if used as a room fragrancer.

Besides being a pleasant scent, pine has exceptional healing properties. It stimulates the circulation, is a powerful antiseptic and is helpful in eliminating toxins from the body. These qualities are of great value when treating arthritis, rheumatic pain, cystitis and other urinary tract problems. When blended with lavender, marjoram or rosemary in a massage oil it exerts a local warming effect bringing relief to stiff, overtired muscles. Its disinfectant and decongestant properties are especially useful for colds, coughs, sore throats and flu. Being an expectorant, pine helps clear catarrh and sinusitis especially when used in a

> *If used in large amounts pine is a skin irritant so use in low dilution only – 1 per cent in a massage oil or 3 drops in a bath.*
>
> *Not suitable for babies or young children.*

steam inhalation. Using pine oil as a room freshener or even
blending it with bergamot, lemon or, at night, lavender will
help keep infections at bay. For a revitalising or morning bath
try blending pine with geranium and rosemary or juniper.

Generally pine has a stimulating effect on the mind and
emotions and is valuable in cases of mental exhaustion or stress.

### CAN BENEFIT

♦ Aching, overtired muscles. ♦ Apathy, confusion, mental exhaustion, stress-
related ailments. ♦ Arthritis, rheumatism, poor circulation. ♦ Asthma, catarrh,
chest infections, colds, coughs, flu, sinusitis, sore throats. ♦ Cystitis and other
urinary tract infections. ♦ Excessive perspiration.

### HOW TO USE

Bath, compress, insect repellent, room fragrancer, steam inhalation.

# ROSE

*Rosa damascena* and *Rosa centifolia*

**Family:** rosaceae. ♦ **Perfumery note:** middle/base. ♦ **Aroma:** rich, floral,
sweet, an exquisite scent.

There are many hundreds of varieties of rose worldwide but two fragrant types
are generally used in aromatherapy. Damask rose (*rosa damascena*) is also known
as Bulgarian or Turkish rose, and cabbage rose (*rosa centifolia*) is sometimes called
*rose Maroc* or *rose de mai*. The roses are picked before dawn when the flowers are
oil rich and it can take about 1 tonne of petals to produce just 500g of oil!
Essences are obtained from the petals of both of these shrubs through steam
distillation or by a method using volatile solvents like liquid carbon
dioxide. The former produces an oil known as an 'otto' and the
latter an 'absolute'. Although rather involved,
this knowledge is useful to have when buying

the oil as Bulgarian rose 'otto' is said to be the finest in the world and is therapeutically superior to the fragrant rose Maroc 'absolute'. Rosewater is also produced for the cosmetic and food industries, the best coming from France. Rose oil is produced mainly in Morocco, Bulgaria, Egypt, China, India, France and Russia.

**Blends well with:** bergamot, camomile, cedarwood, clary sage, frankincense, fennel, geranium, jasmine, lavender, mandarin, myrrh, myrtle, neroli, orange, patchouli, petitgrain, sandalwood, vetiver, ylang-ylang and many others.

## MAIN QUALITIES

Antibacterial, antidepressant, anti-inflammatory, antiseptic, aphrodisiac, astringent, detoxifying.

**Helps to:** promote menstruation; strengthen the uterus, heart and liver; contract small blood vessels; lower blood pressure; generally heals distressing emotions, exerting a comforting and even euphoric effect.

## TALES FROM THE PAST

Native to ancient Persia, the rose or 'queen of flowers' has been linked with beauty, love and war through the ages. The Egyptians used rose body oils, and Cleopatra was said to have commanded her bedroom floor be strewn with rose petals over a foot deep before she seduced Julius Caesar. The Romans added roses to wine, soaked their clothes in rosewater and also scattered roses for the scent on the marriage bed. They were used to sweeten the breath and Arab healers believed rose 'jam' could heal lung complaints. The rose was brought to Europe at the time of the Crusades and was used medicinally in decoctions for headaches, sore eyes and throats. In the twentieth century, rosehip syrup was given to soothe coughs and during rationing in the Second World War, rosehips, which are rich in vitamin C, were given to ensure good health.

This flower has inspired writers and artists throughout the ages; the ancient Persian poet, Omar Khyam, likened the rose to a state of divine perfection and Shakespeare's Romeo says of Juliet, 'a rose

by any other name would smell as sweet', perpetuating the flower's romantic reputation.

## PRESENT USES

Rose oil has an exquisite, flowery, sweet yet rich aroma and like jasmine and neroli it can be worn as a luxurious perfume. Although costly it is well worth the investment as only tiny amounts are needed in homemade blends or cosmetics. Rose is exceptional in that it enhances virtually any blend and its versatile, delicious aroma is used in most of the world's finest perfumes. Like jasmine, rose is a popular scent which is often made synthetically, so beware of cheap imitations as they have no therapeutic value and may even cause skin irritation or headaches. True rose otto is very pale yellow with a hint of green and the absolute is a deep reddish-orange and has a quite thick consistency.

Besides having a pleasing aroma, rose possesses many powerful healing properties while also being one of the mildest essential oils. It helps normalise irregular periods and has a general purifying and strengthening effect on the uterus. Rose improves circulation and has a strengthening effect on the liver and the body's digestive system. It is also an effective tonic for all types of skin, having a nurturing effect on mature skin and wrinkles – like neroli it is credited with rejuvenating qualities. It helps to clear congested and overhydrated skin types, soothes dry, sensitive skin and can help to decrease thread veins. Rose oil's anti-inflammatory action can also be of use in the treatment of eczema and other inflamed, irritated skin conditions. Good-quality rosewater provides a gentle way to cleanse and tone the skin and can be dabbed around the eye area to refresh hot, tired eyes. Rose is useful for sleep problems and is particularly good for stress-related ailments.

This essence is well known for its aphrodisiac qualities, so try blending it with sandalwood, jasmine or ylang-ylang and patchouli for a sensual bath or body oil. Rose exerts a powerful healing influence on the emotions, lifting depression and helping to relieve

> *Rose helps to promote menstruation so is not suitable for early pregnancy. Use moderately after 20 weeks only.*

shock, grief, anger, fear and anxiety. Generally rose is very relaxing and comforting, it warms the heart, bringing joy, serenity and even euphoria!

### CAN BENEFIT

♦ All skin types (tones) – dry, inflamed, irritated, sensitive, mature skin – eczema, scars, thread veins, wrinkles. ♦ Anger, anxiety, depression, fear, frigidity, grief, impotence, insomnia, nervous tension, shock, stress-related ailments. ♦ Constipation, liver congestion, hangovers, nausea.
♦ Headaches. ♦ Heavy, irregular or painful periods, labour pain, menopausal problems, premenstrual syndrome, uterine problems.

### HOW TO USE

Bath, compress, massage, perfume, room fragrancer, skin-care preparations.

# ROSEMARY
*Rosmarinus officinalis*

**Family:** labiatae. ♦ **Perfumery note:** top/middle. ♦ **Aroma:** fresh, camphor-like, a herbal scent.

Rosemary is a herb which can grow to a height of approximately 4 feet with fine needle-like leaves and small, blue flowers. The essential oil is obtained through steam distillation of the leaves and flowering tops. Originally native to the Mediterranean, rosemary now grows worldwide. Oil is exported mainly from France, Spain and North Africa.
**Blends well with:** bergamot, black pepper, cedarwood, clary sage, cypress, eucalyptus, frankincense, geranium, grapefruit, juniper, lavender, lemon, mandarin, marjoram, myrtle, orange, peppermint, petitgrain, pine, ylang-ylang.

## MAIN QUALITIES

Antibacterial, antiseptic, antispasmodic, expectorant, insect repellent.

**Helps to:** relieve pain; stimulate the mind; promote new cell growth; encourage fluid loss by promoting urination; stimulate menstruation; raise blood pressure; strengthen the liver and nervous system; stimulate the immune system; produce warmth and redness when applied to the skin; generally stimulates and clears the mind, energising the emotions.

## TALES FROM THE PAST

For centuries rosemary has been used for its culinary and medicinal qualities. The Romans held the herb to be sacred and it was given to newlyweds as well as placed on graves as a symbol of remembrance and friendship. During the plagues, rosemary was one of the fragrant herbs which were used as a protective remedy against the disease. Rosemary was used in 'nosegays' (posies) or strewn upon the floors of houses where it was trodden upon and would impart its purifying scent. The English herbalist Bankes tells us that, 'even to smell the scent of the leaves kept one youngly', and it was also said that if rosemary grew in a garden that the woman there was definitely 'mistress of the house'. Rosemary was also an ingredient in the reputedly rejuvenating cosmetic Hungary Water. Rosemary is still used in the best *eau de Cologne*, as well as in many other toiletyries. It also helps give vermouth its familiar scent.

## PRESENT USES

A rosemary oil bath is an ideal way to start the day. This essence is invigorating, refreshing and stimulating to the mind. Besides being a lovely wake-up oil it has remarkable therapeutic uses too, being generally fortifying and purifying it can help in cases of acne, chilblains and head lice. Used in a final hair rinse, rosemary has an antiseptic and tonic action relieving dandruff, stimulating hair growth and leaving hair beautifully fragrant. It helps to fight the germs which cause colds and flu and when used in a steam inhalation or vaporiser, it relieves nasal congestion, coughs and sinusitis.

Rosemary has a powerful detoxifying action as it stimulates the circulation which in turn encourages the elimination of waste products from the body. Cellulite, varicose veins, fluid retention and low blood pressure all benefit from these actions. The oil's qualities are also helpful when treating sports injuries, sprains, rheumatic pain and gout. Try combining rosemary, lavender, black pepper or marjoram in a massage oil to bring relief to overtired, aching muscles, and for easing arthritic pain try a blend of frankincense, juniper and rosemary.

It is also a useful oil for digestive complaints, alleviating constipation and flatulence when the abdomen is massaged appropriately (see Chapter 5). The oil is very beneficial for headaches, fainting, stress and both mental and physical fatigue. This refreshing essence stimulates and energises the mind and body while imparting a strengthening effect on the emotions.

> *Not suitable in pregnancy or for people suffering from high blood pressure.*

## CAN BENEFIT

♦ Aching, overtired muscles, arthritis, gout, rheumatism, sports injuries, sprains, strains. ♦ Acne, bruises, chilblains. ♦ Apathy, exhaustion (mental and physical), fainting, stress-related ailments. ♦ Catarrhal conditions, colds, coughs, fever, flu, sinusitis. ♦ Cellulite, fluid retention, low blood pressure, poor circulation, varicose veins. ♦ Constipation, flatulence, liver and gall bladder problems. ♦ Dandruff, hair loss, head lice. ♦ Headaches.

## HOW TO USE

Bath, compress, hair care, insect repellent, room fragrancer, skin-care preparations, steam inhalation.

# SANDALWOOD
*Santalum album*

**Family:** santalaceae. ♦ **Perfumery note:** base.
♦ **Aroma:** subtle, warm, woody with a hint of spice.

Sandalwood is a parasitic evergreen tree which is native to Asia. The essential oil is obtained through steam distillation of the heart wood found at the very centre of the tree. In order for it to be economical to process the oil, the trees are left to mature for at least 30 years before felling. Although there are other types of sandalwood, for example, the Australian (*santalum spicatum*), the oil from Mysore in India is believed to be superior therapeutically.

**Blends well with:** black pepper, camomile, carrot seed, cedarwood, clary sage, cypress, eucalyptus, fennel, frankincense, geranium, jasmine, juniper, lavender, lemon, mandarin, myrrh, myrtle, neroli, orange, patchouli, petitgrain, pine, rose, ylang-ylang and most other oils.

## MAIN QUALITIES

Antibacterial, antidepressant, anti-inflammatory, antiseptic, antispasmodic, aphrodisiac, astringent.

**Helps to:** ease coughs; stimulate fluid loss by promoting urination; sedate the nervous system; generally has a relaxing and soothing yet uplifting and harmonising effect on the emotional and spiritual levels.

## TALES FROM THE PAST

Sandalwood was valued by the ancients for its divine scent, and they used it to make many perfumes and cosmetics as well as temple incenses. In fact, many Hindu temples were actually built from the wood of this tree. It was held in high respect by the ancient Moslems who believed that in their afterlife, beautiful, alluring, goddess-like beings called the *Houris* were actually 'made' of sandalwood. In ancient China, sandalwood was used for skin and digestive disorders and to treat cases of gonorrhoea. Ayurvedic medical practitioners still use

sandalwood today for urinary and respiratory tract infections. For years the women of Tahiti have conditioned their hair with a blend of the oils of sandalwood and coconut.

As one of the best natural perfume fixatives, sandalwood is valued today for its long-lasting base note. Its name adorns products ranging from detergents to cosmetics, however, many of these 'sandalwoods' will be synthetic imitations. Indian sandalwood trees are not nearly so plentiful as they were, and although oil production still takes place it is on a much smaller scale.

## PRESENT USES

Sandalwood is a beautiful, subtle and lingering aroma. The true oil is pale gold and has a thick consistency. This woody oil is very useful in skin care as it balances the production of sebum, the skin's natural oil, making it an ideal essence for all skin types. However, its powerful healing properties achieve particularly good results when used in cases of acne, dry and congested or inflamed skin. These qualities also help to heal cuts and wounds and to fade scars and stretch marks.

The oil has been shown to stimulate the production of white blood cells thereby boosting the body's natural defences. Dry coughs and laryngitis respond well to sandalwood's soothing effects and its expectorant and antiseptic actions help to clear catarrh, bronchitis and chest infections. A calming, antispasmodic effect is exerted upon digestive problems, enabling sandalwood to treat nausea, diarrhoea, flatulence and colicky pains.

Because of this sedative action, sandalwood can help reduce high blood pressure and is an ideal choice for treating stress-related disorders. Perhaps where sandalwood is particularly useful is in the treatment of genito-urinary conditions. Its anti-inflammatory, strengthening properties in this area and its ability to eliminate impurities from the body combine successfully to relieve painful infections like cystitis.

For thousands of years sandalwood has been known as an aphrodisiac, so try blending it with ylang-ylang and myrtle or patchouli or with rose to create a sensual and exotic massage or bath oil. Emotionally this oil is relaxing and harmonising and can be

of help for insomnia where camomile or other more herbaceous-type scents are disliked. Whether used for massage, bathing or in a perfume or room freshener, sandalwood soothes away stress and has an uplifting and harmonising effect on a spiritual and emotional plane.

### CAN BENEFIT

♦ Aching muscles. ♦ Acne, cuts, dry, congested, inflamed, oily, mature skin, scars, stretch marks, wounds, wrinkles. ♦ Anxiety, depression, impotence, nervous tension, stress-related ailments. ♦ Bronchitis, catarrh, chest infections, dry coughs, laryngitis. ♦ Cystitis and other urinary tract infections. ♦ Diarrhoea, flatulence, nausea, spasmodic pains. ♦ High blood pressure.

### HOW TO USE

Bath, compress, massage, perfume, room fragrancer, skin-care preparations, steam inhalation.

# TEA TREE

*Melaleuca alternifolia*

**Family:** myrtaceae. ♦ **Perfumery note:** top/middle. ♦ **Aroma:** penetrating, camphor-like, with a hint of spice.

The tea tree is a shrub or small tree which is native to Australia. The essential oil is obtained by distilling its fine needle-like leaves. Although there any many hundreds of varieties of tea tree in Australia, *melaleuca alternifolia* is the only one with outstanding therapeutic properties.

**Blends well with:** camomile, eucalyptus, lavender, lemon, juniper, mandarin, marjoram, myrtle, orange, peppermint, pine.

## MAIN QUALITIES

Antibiotic, antifungal, antiseptic, antiviral, disinfectant, expectorant.
**Helps to:** stimulate new cell growth; reduce fever; boost the immune
system; increase sweating; generally a remarkable healing oil.

## TALES FROM THE PAST

The Aboriginal tribes of Australia believed tea tree to be something of a
cure all and used it especially for preventing infections and healing wounds.
Early settlers to New South Wales soon recognised the healing properties of
tea tree and used it when medical supplies were unavailable in the bush.
However, it was only in the 1920s that scientific research began into this
remarkable oil. By 1925, experiments proved tea tree to be a powerful
antiseptic, 13 times stronger than carbolic acid. After these findings tea
tree research has never looked back! In 1990, controlled experiments were
carried out in Australia comparing tea tree oil against benzoyl peroxide, a
common agent used in the treatment of acne. It was documented that tea
tree compared very favourably and had fewer and harsh side-effects for the
patients. Today because of the oil's antiseptic action it is widely used in
dentistry and is an ingredient in many products from disinfectants and
shampoos to toothpastes.

## PRESENT USES

It is difficult to think of an ailment that this oil does not help! Its
antibacterial, antiviral and antifungal properties mean it can treat a wide
variety of infections and common ailments. Tea tree oil helps all kinds of
skin infections and for me is the best remedy for spots, boils, abscesses,
athlete's foot, ringworm, cold sores, shingles and verrucae. It also has a
very beneficial effect on insect stings or bites, rashes, psoriasis, chickenpox, mouth ulcers, gingivitis (infected gums) and more!

Tea tree helps cut down the risk of airborne infection and is a powerful stimulant for the immune system, strengthening the body and encouraging
general good health. Its antiviral and expectorant actions relieve cold and flu
symptoms and it is also beneficial for treating bronchitis, sinusitis, coughs and
chest infections. It is useful when used against thrush and also has a healing

effect on genital herpes. Tea tree oil helps to reduce fevers and can also alleviate symptoms of cystitis and other urinary tract infections.

Generally tea tree is a remarkable immune system stimulant, its strengths are its sheer versatility and powerful health-protecting qualities. This oil's usefulness cannot be emphasised enough.

*Although rare, some cases of skin irritation have been reported when using tea tree so always keep to the recommended dosage. I have used small amounts of neat oil for many years but it would be wise to test yourself for an allergic reaction or sensitivity by carrying out a skin patch test. If irritation occurs choose between using the oil diluted to 1 per cent or less in a base oil or avoid it altogether and substitute another essential oil.*

### CAN BENEFIT

♦ Acne, athlete's foot, boils, chilblains, cold sores, cuts, congested oily skin, dental abscess, gingivitis (infected gums), insect bites and stings, mouth ulcers, pruritus (itching), psoriasis, rashes (nappy), ringworm, spots, verrucae, warts, minor wounds. ♦ Bronchitis, colds, coughs, flu, sinusitis. ♦ Chickenpox and measles, fevers, herpes, shingles, viral infections. ♦ Dandruff and head lice. ♦ Thrush, leukorrhoea (thick, white vaginal discharge), genital herpes, urinary tract infections.

### HOW TO USE

Bath, compress, gargle, hair care, massage, mouthwash, neat (1 drop only), room fragrancer, skin-care preparations, steam inhalation.

# YLANG-YLANG

*Cananga odorata*

**Family:** anonaceae. ♦ **Perfumery note:** middle. ♦ **Aroma:** rich, sweet and floral, similar to jasmine flowers.

This tree can grow to a height of 60 feet and has beautiful, highly fragrant, yellow flowers. The essential oil is obtained through steam distillation of the

flowers. The tree is native to Asia, notably the Philippines, but today the oil is produced in other tropical countries namely the Commorro Islands and Réunion in the Indian Ocean.

**Blends well with:** bergamot, camomile, cedarwood, clary sage, geranium, grapefruit, jasmine, lavender, lemon, mandarin, myrtle, neroli, orange, patchouli, petitgrain, pine, rose, rosemary, sandalwood, vetiver.

## MAIN QUALITIES

Antidepressant, antiseptic, aphrodisiac.

**Helps to:** balance sebum production; lower blood pressure; sedate the nervous system; generally has an uplifting even euphoric effect on the emotions and can be helpful for sexual problems.

## TALES FROM THE PAST

Ylang-ylang (pronounced eelang-eelang) means 'flower of flowers' and is also called 'perfume tree' because of its drooping, fragrant blooms. The women of Tahiti have used this essence for centuries with sandalwood and coconut oils to condition and scent their hair. In the nineteenth century, a hair oil for men, called macassar, became fashionable which contained ylang-ylang among other ingredients. The slick, oiled image lasted for some time and small cloths or anti-macassars were introduced to the backs of chairs to prevent the hair oil from staining the furniture! Today ylang-ylang is used in superior-quality perfumes, for fragrancing toiletries and as a flavouring agent in food.

## PRESENT USES

This exquisite flower oil can be rather sweet and too heady for some tastes but it is one of my favourites. It is a useful skin-care essence as it normalises the production of sebum, the skin's natural oil, making it beneficial for both dry and oily skin conditions. This essential oil also has a gentle, stimulating and toning effect on the scalp, encouraging the growth of healthy new hair and imparting a delicious scent if used as a conditioner or in a finishing rinse.

Ylang-ylang is safe to use in pregnancy and being emotionally uplifting and destressing, it also lends itself to this special time. It can also reduce high blood pressure and calm nervous palpitations, especially if combined with neroli. For centuries ylang-ylang has been known as an aphrodisiac oil but as it is too sweet for some tastes it may have the opposite effect on your partner, in which case try subtle sandalwood instead, perhaps with myrtle. Ylang-ylang has a rich, floral, exotic aroma which combines beautifully with most oils, especially the flower essences like rose, neroli or jasmine. However, it does lose a little of its characteristic sweetness when blended with citrus oils, for example petitgrain or mandarin, and this produces a wonderful aroma which is very relaxing. The scent of ylang-ylang 'deepens' and becomes more subtle when mixed with the heavier oils of sandalwood, patchouli or vetiver and is ideal for an evening massage or bath for an adult. The oil is so lovely that you can easily wear it as a fragrance by itself too.

Ylang-ylang is a versatile oil on the emotional level. It has a powerful antidepressant effect and sometimes people have experienced a euphoric effect. Stress-related ailments respond well to this oil as do sleep problems, and it can alleviate fear-based emotions, shock and anger. Ylang-ylang strengthens the nervous system and generally imparts feelings of confidence and joy!

## CAN BENEFIT

♦ Acne, dry and oily skins, tones all skin types. ♦ Anger, anxiety, depression, fear-based emotions, frigidity, frustration, impotence, insomnia, irritability, nervous tension, shock, stress-related ailments. ♦ Hair loss. ♦ High blood pressure, palpitations, over-rapid breathing. ♦ Premenstrual syndrome.

## HOW TO USE

Bath, massage, perfume, room fragrancer, skin-care preparations.

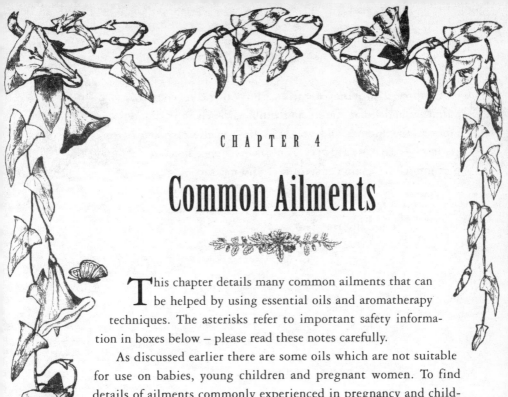

## CHAPTER 4

# Common Ailments

This chapter details many common ailments that can be helped by using essential oils and aromatherapy techniques. The asterisks refer to important safety information in boxes below – please read these notes carefully.

As discussed earlier there are some oils which are not suitable for use on babies, young children and pregnant women. To find details of ailments commonly experienced in pregnancy and childhood and their suggested treatments refer to Chapters 6 and 7.

There is also a small number of oils which should be avoided by people who have epilepsy, or those suffering from high or very low blood pressure and I have given alternative recipes for them where appropriate in this chapter.

The recommended recipes and dosages in this chapter are for adults. Even so, please do not be tempted to use larger amounts than are specified in the recipes. Essential oils can be wonderful healers if used correctly, but never forget they are powerful substances and should be treated with care. Before using a new oil always carry out a skin patch test and read the safety information presented in boxes in Chapters 2 and 3, the latter giving details of 32 different essences.

Finally, it is very satisfying to treat yourself or those you care for using essential oils but if you have the slightest doubt about what you are treating or if symptoms persist, seek medical advice immediately. Also, always consult your doctor before adjusting or stopping any prescribed medication.

Chapter 2 provides details of how to make your own ointments and floral waters and explains patch tests, safety information, dosages and generally how to use essential oils in everyday life. However, for easy reference here are some guidelines again concerning liquid measures.

20 drops = 1ml     1 dessertspoon = 10ml

1 teaspoon = 5ml     1 tablespoon = 15ml

# ABSCESS, DENTAL *see also* BOILS

Use 1 drop of neat tea tree *or* dilute 1 drop of *clove oil in a teaspoon of sweet almond oil and apply directly to the gum using a cotton bud.

Make a hot compress by adding 2 drops of camomile to a small bowl of hot water, swirl the water so the oil disperses evenly. Place a clean cloth on the surface of the water so it picks up the oil and then apply to the affected area. This will help relieve pain and help to draw out the pus.

Also mix 1 drop of camomile and 2 drops of tea tree in a teaspoon of sweet almond oil and apply up to three times a day to the outside of the affected cheek or jaw.

> *Do not swallow essential oils; they should not be taken internally.*
>
> *Clove oil should not be used by pregnant women. Refer to Chapter 6 for suitable essential oils for pregnancy.*

# ACNE

Cleanliness is of the utmost importance when treating acne. Add 3 drops of tea tree *or* lavender to a basin of warm water and splash the face at least twice a day, making sure the oil does not get into your eyes.

Do not use a flannel as it will harbour germs.

Alternatively use a floral water to cleanse and tone the skin. To make an effective astringent fill a sterile bottle with 75ml of orange flower water and 25ml of witch hazel, shake well and gently wipe over affected areas with cotton wool. Add 10 drops of lavender *or* camomile (if inflamed) to this blend if desired. For particularly 'angry' spots, apply 1 drop of tea tree oil using a cotton bud.

An antiseptic facial oil can be made by adding 5 drops of bergamot, 3 drops of geranium and 4 drops of lavender to 25ml of base oil (20ml of apricot kernel and 5ml of jojoba is ideal). To help reduce inflammation substitute 3 drops of camomile for the geranium for a week or so. A more masculine aroma is created by mixing 4 drops of bergamot, 4 drops of Atlas cedarwood and 4 drops of tea tree in the same base oil as above. To help reduce inflammation substitute 3 drops of camomile in place of the bergamot oil for a week or so. Apply the facial oil after cleansing morning and evening, leave on the skin for a minimum of 10 minutes then tissue off any excess. The oil should ideally be left on overnight.

A detoxifying face mask can be easily made by mixing 3 level teaspoons of green clay with 2 or 3 teaspoons of orange flower water and half a teaspoon of cornflower extract (*centaurea cyanus*) in a small bowl. Then add 2 drops of camomile, 1 drop of geranium and 1 drop of lavender and mix well. If you cannot obtain green clay use light kaolin. All these ingredients are readily available from good chemists and healthfood shops.

For an occasional facial steam treatment to open pores and help encourage elimination of impurities from the skin, add 2 drops of lavender oil, 2 drops of lemon and 1 drop of tea tree to a large bowl of boiling water. Pin back your hair from your face and drape a large towel over your head creating a mini steam room. Close your eyes. Breathe fresh air at regular intervals while trying not to let too much steam escape. Afterwards, splash the skin liberally with cold water and then apply your aromatic facial oil.

Try not to touch your face unnecessarily or squeeze the spots as this may lead to further infection and scarring of the skin. Try to be patient;

this condition often benefits from regular body massage and dietary or lifestyle changes, so consult an aromatherapist or other health practitioner for further advice.

> *Some of the above essential oils should not be used by pregnant women, so refer to Chapter 6 for suitable essential oils for pregnancy.*

## ANXIETY AND NERVOUS TENSION

Anxiety and nervous tension cannot only affect a person's mental and emotional health but this state of mind may also cause disease, leading to a wide range of physical symptoms. Headaches, muscular and stomach pain, nausea, constipation, diarrhoea and insomnia can all be symptoms of anxiety. Excessive sweating, rapid breathing as well as restlessness, fatigue and depression are other common symptoms. Further recipes and treatments are listed separately under the following headings: depression; fatigue; headaches; indigestion; insomnia; nausea and stress.

Take regular aromatic baths to ease anxiety and nervous tension. There are many essential oils to choose from depending on the effect you require. Try experimenting yourself – see Chapter 2 for dosages and cautions – but here are some suggestions.

To help relaxation try adding the following oils to a warm bath, then soak for at least 15 minutes inhaling the soothing aromas: 4 drops of clary sage, 3 drops of lavender and 2 drops of *sweet marjoram *or* 2 drops of bergamot, 4 drops of frankincense, 1 drop of petitgrain and 3 drops of sandalwood *or* 3 drops of bergamot, 2 drops of geranium and 3 drops of lavender. For a more woody aroma try: 3 drops of Atlas cedarwood, 3 drops of sandalwood and 2 drops of vetiver. For a revitalising combination try: 3 drops of cypress, 3 drops of pine needle oil and 3 drops of bergamot *or* 3 drops of lemon oil.

The following oils are helpful for reducing anxiety and nervous tension: bergamot, camomile, Atlas cedarwood, clary sage, cypress, frankincense, geranium, jasmine, lavender, lemon, mandarin, sweet marjoram, myrtle, neroli, orange, patchouli, petitgrain, rose, sandalwood, vetiver and ylang-ylang. Sweet basil, cypress, grapefruit, lemon and pine needle have a

refreshing and revitalising effect. I feel the best oils for anxiety and fear are: camomile, jasmine, neroli, rose and ylang-ylang, and for anger or frustration I would choose bergamot, jasmine, neroli and rose.

To help prevent anxiety and release tension held in muscles I recommend regular massage treatments. Use any of the above essential oils or recipes and mix up to 12 drops *in total* of your chosen blend in a base of 25ml sweet almond oil.

Any of the above essential oils can also be used as room fragrancers to create a similar effect in your environment. Simply add between 5 and 10 drops of your chosen oil or blend to a vaporiser, bowl of warm water or a spray container. Alternatively use just a few drops of your favourite oil or blend on a tissue and inhale deeply to help reduce anxiety. A fragrant skin perfume created from your chosen essences can also help to combat anxious feelings.

> *Some of the above oils should not be used by pregnant women, so refer to Chapter 6 for suitable essential oils for pregnancy.*
>
> *If suffering from very low blood pressure avoid marjoram oil.*

Anxiety, nervous tension and many stress-related conditions can often benefit from changes to diet and lifestyle and even counselling. Consult an aromatherapist or other health practitioner for further advice.

## ARTHRITIS, GOUT AND RHEUMATISM

This is a wide subject encompassing many common ailments. There are different types of arthritis – osteoarthritis, rheumatoid arthritis and gout are the most well known. However, the term 'rheumatism' is also used to describe complaints where there is inflammation and pain in ligaments and muscles surrounding joints such as fibrositis. All of these conditions have different causes, ranging from injuries and 'wear and tear' to auto-immune system problems. However, they present similar symptoms such as stiffness, pain, sometimes inflammation and generally a restriction of mobility in one or more joints of the body.

## ARTHRITIS AND RHEUMATISM

Make a warm compress by adding 2 drops of lavender *or* camomile and 2 drops of juniper *or* \*rosemary to a small bowl of water. Swirl the water so the oil disperses evenly. Place a clean cloth on the surface of the water so it picks up the oil, then apply to the affected area. This can help to relieve pain and swelling. Follow this with a cool compress and then gently move the affected area.

Take regular aromatic baths using essential oils which encourage the body to eliminate toxins, such as cypress, grapefruit, juniper and \*sweet fennel. For an uplifting yet detoxifying bath add: 4 drops of cypress, 3 drops of grapefruit and 3 drops of juniper.

For the despondency, irritability and frustration which often accompanies arthritis or rheumatic pain, use either one or a selection of the following oils in a bath: bergamot, camomile, clary sage, geranium, jasmine, neroli, petitgrain, rose and ylang-ylang. Add to a bath between 3 drops of an oil and 10 drops *in total* if using a selection of oils. These oils can also be used as room fragrancers to create a similar effect in your environment. Add 5 to 10 drops of your chosen oil or blend to a vaporiser, bowl of warm water or spray container.

The following massage oil is helpful when used locally on stiff joints such as the fingers, wrists, ankles and knees and for muscular pain. To make the massage oil, mix 5 drops of frankincense, 6 drops of juniper, 6 drops of lavender and 8 drops of rosemary in 50ml of sweet almond oil.

When giving a full body massage, use gentle pressure always towards the heart (see Chapter 5). It is also important to remember that inflamed joints should *never* be massaged, although it may be comforting to have the oil stroked over these areas using a feather-light touch.

### GOUT

For acute gout apply a cold compress to the painful joint using 2 drops of lavender and 2 drops of rosemary and gently stroke the above massage oil around the affected area. Besides massage, gentle yet regular exercise or movement, however slight, is of great benefit to this condition.

Dietary and lifestyle changes can often benefit these ailments, so consult an aromatherapist or other health practitioner for further advice.

> *Some of the above oils should not be used by pregnant women, so refer to Chapter 6 for suitable essential oils for pregnancy.*
>
> *Fennel oil should be avoided if you suffer from epilepsy so choose another of this listed oils which encourage elimination.*
>
> *Rosemary oil should be avoided if you have high blood pressure, in which case use sweet marjoram instead.*
>
> *Always seek a medical diagnosis and advice concerning these conditions.*

## ASTHMA

This ailment affects every individual differently with possible causes ranging from food allergies, damp or cold air, changes in pollution levels, to *sensitivity to substances like dust, feathers, fur, mites, and chemicals found in household and cosmetic products. However, colds, lung infections along with physical exertion, anxiety and nervous tension also account for much suffering. An asthma attack can happen suddenly, causing great distress to both patient and loved ones, who can do little but remain calm and provide loving support at this stressful time.

If you are not sensitive to the oils, during an attack sprinkle 3 drops of camomile and 3 drops of frankincense on a tissue and inhale.

Between attacks regular massage is an ideal way to reduce the anxiety and stress which so often lead to an attack. Massage the chest, ribcage and upper back, paying special attention to the area between the shoulder blades on either side of the spine. Try the following blend: mix 4 drops of camomile, 4 drops of frankincense and 4 drops of lavender in 25ml of sweet almond oil.

To help generally with relaxation and to uplift the spirits essential oils may be used as room fragrancers. Add 5 to 10 drops of the following oil or selection of oils to a vaporiser, bowl of warm water or a spray container: bergamot, camomile, Atlas cedarwood, clary sage, frankincense, geranium, lavender, myrtle, *sweet marjoram, neroli, rose and sandalwood. Peppermint is also useful when a 'clearing' and stimulating effect is required.

The above oil or blend of oils may also be used for relaxing aromatic baths. Add to a warm bath between 3 drops of an oil and 10 drops *in total* if using a selection.

It is not uncommon for asthmatics to suffer from bouts of bronchitis, and if this is the case also refer to the listing under bronchitis.

Identifying allergens, receiving regular massage, and changes to diet and lifestyle can benefit this condition. Consult an aromatherapist or other health professional for further advice on these subjects.

*Many asthmatics are sensitive to a wide range of allergens and, for some people, this can include essential oils, so always make sure that a patch test is carried out before using any oils.*

*A steam inhalation should never be used for asthmatics as this method aggravates the condition and can cause choking.*

*Always consult a doctor if an attack is severe.*

*Marjoram should be avoided by people with very low blood pressure.*

*Some of the above oils are not suitable for pregnant women or young children. See Chapters 6 and 7 for suitable oils.*

## ATHLETE'S FOOT

To combat athlete's foot wash the feet every day in a foot bath to which 3 drops of lavender and 3 drops of tea tree have been added. It is very important to dry the feet thoroughly as fungal infections thrive in warm and moist conditions.

You can apply 2 drops of neat tea tree directly between the toes on a cotton bud. However, the following suggestion is somewhat gentler if the

skin is broken. Mix 2 drops of lavender and 2 drops of tea tree in 5ml (1 teaspoon) of aqueous cream and if the skin is badly cracked add 1 drop of patchouli to the blend. Apply the foot cream regularly with a cotton bud, especially after bathing.

## BAD BREATH *see* HALITOSIS

## BOILS

Bathe the affected area twice a day using 2 drops of lavender and 2 drops of camomile in a small bowl of warm water. A hot compress made by adding 2 drops of lavender and 2 drops of tea tree to a small bowl of water will help draw the pus out (see page 102).

## BRONCHITIS

Massage the following blend all over the chest, neck and upper back area: mix 4 drops of Atlas cedarwood, 4 drops of eucalyptus and 4 drops of frankincense in 25ml of sweet almond oil.

To help relieve congestion in the chest and the dry cough use the following oils in a *steam inhalation twice a day until symptoms decrease. Add 3 drops of eucalyptus and 3 drops of lavender to a bowl of hot water, close your eyes and for a few minutes inhale the vapours deeply. A few drops of your chosen oil or selection of oils may also be sprinkled onto a tissue and inhaled.

A disinfectant room fragrance is very useful for this condition. Use the following essences: eucalyptus, lavender, lemon, peppermint, pine and tea tree. Simply add between 5 and 10 drops of your oil or blend to a vaporiser, bowl of warm water or a spray container. Here are some ideas for different blends: 5 drops of lavender with 5 drops of pine *or* 4 drops of eucalyptus with 6 drops of lemon *or* 6 drops of lemon and 4 drops of peppermint *or* 5 drops of lavender and 5 drops of tea tree. Try experimenting yourself – there are many differ-ent aromas to be made among these oils and they are all powerful disinfec-

Steam inhalations should never
be used by asthmatics as this
method aggravates the condition
and can cause choking.

Some of the above oils should not
be used by pregnant women, so
refer to Chapter 6 for suitable
essential oils for pregnancy.

tants. To help reduce the risk of secondary infection it is useful to continue using the essences as room fresheners until strength is regained.

For chronic bronchitis, Atlas cedarwood, eucalyptus, lavender, myrtle and sandalwood are all helpful used in a bath or for massage. Apply the following blend to the chest, throat and upper back areas. Mix 4 drops each of Atlas cedarwood, sandalwood and lavender *or* myrtle in 25ml of sweet almond oil.

It is not uncommon to find *asthmatics suffering from bronchitis, and if this is the case also refer to the listing under asthma.

## BRUISES

Add 2 drops of camomile and 2 drops of lavender to a bowl of ice-cold water. Swirl the water so the oil disperses evenly. Place a clean cloth on the surface of the water so it picks up the oil and then apply the compress to the injured area. Use 2 drops of camomile and 1 drop of lavender in 5ml of sweet almond oil to help with any inflammation.

Arnica homeopathic remedy or
ointment (not the essential oil) is
excellent for shock and bruising.

## BURNS AND SCALDS

Immediately run cold water onto the site of the burn for at least 10 minutes. If this is difficult then immerse the affected area in ice-cold water or apply an ice-cold compress for the same amount of time. Make the compress by placing ice cubes in a bowl of cold water, add 4 drops of lavender and use a sterile cloth to pick up the oil from the surface of the water, and then apply to the injured area.

For very minor burns, apply 2 drops of lavender oil directly to the burn. The application of lavender oil can be repeated up to four times a day. To dress the burn, add 5 drops of neat lavender to a sterile gauze dressing and gently cover the area. Or mix 5 drops of neat lavendar in 1 teaspoon (5ml) of a gel base. Reapply lavender oil up to four times a day.

### SUNBURN

To help cool and soothe inflammation, add 5 drops of camomile and 6 drops of lavender to cool bath water. Or, if the area is fairly small, apply a compress. Add 3 drops of camomile and 3 drops of lavender to a bowl of cool water. Use a soft cloth and lay the compress across the sunburned area. Afterwards apply the following blend to the sore skin: 10 drops of camomile and 15 drops of lavender in 50ml of base oil (consisting of 40ml of sweet almond oil, 5ml of wheatgerm oil and 5ml of jojoba). If the person cannot bear to be touched use the blend from a spray container.

> *Consult a doctor immediately if the burn is severe or large and if the person is in shock as there is a high risk of infection and fluid loss. Only ever apply* sterile *cloths or dressings to a burn.*

# CANDIDA ALBICANS AND LEUKORRHOEA

To relieve symptoms of vaginal thrush apply the following gel to the whole external genital area. Buy an unperfumed water-based gel from a chemist, add 2 drops of tea tree oil to 5ml (1 teaspoon) of the gel, mix very well then apply as above.

To help relieve discomfort and fight infection use a sitz bath twice a day. Add 2 drops of lavender and 2 of *tea tree (carry out a patch test first) to a large bowl of cool water. Disperse the oils evenly across the surface of the water and splash the genital area, then sit down in it and soak for at least 10 minutes.

Another alternative is *douching. A vaginal douche or enema pot can be bought at

most good chemists. Fill a sterile litre bottle with 500ml of warm, preboiled water and add 4 drops of tea tree oil, replace the lid and shake well. Then add another 500ml of water prepared in the same way, shake again to disperse the oil droplets even more and pour into the douche or enema pot. Douche morning and evening for up to *three days maximum.

Regular baths using the following combination are also helpful: add 4 drops of lavender and 4 drops of tea tree to a bath.

To help with feelings of depression, add 2 drops of bergamot *or* 2 drops of patchouli to the above bath recipe. These will not only uplift the spirits but will help combat the fungal infection too.

It is also advisable to treat your sexual partner using an appropriate method listed above even though he may not have any symptoms.

For leukorrhoea (a persistent and thick white discharge from the vagina) treat as above but receive a diagnosis from your doctor first.

These conditions can also benefit greatly from dietary changes, so consult an aromatherapist or other health professional for further advice.

---

*Check with your doctor if douching is appropriate for your particular case and do not over-use this method.*

*A vaginal douche should never be used during pregnancy.*

*Some of the above oils are not suitable for pregnant women, so refer to Chapter 6 for suggested recipes and treatment.*

*Consult your doctor for a diagnosis as the symptoms of candida albicans are similar to those of other serious infections.*

---

## CATARRH AND SINUSITIS

To relieve congestion use the *steam inhalation method: add 3 drops of eucalyptus *or* peppermint to a bowl of boiling water, drape a large towel over your head to create a mini steam room, close your eyes and inhale deeply.

While breathing fresh air at regular intervals, try not to let too much steam escape. Continue using this method for about five minutes.

Inhaling from a tissue sprinkled with a few drops of your chosen oil or blend (selected from any of the oils listed below) is also very useful, especially in cases of chronic sinusitis.

For catarrh caused by a cold use local massage to alleviate congestion. Massage from the nostrils, out along the underside of the cheekbones using firm pressing movements with your index fingers. Then using the same technique continue just above the eyebrows working from the outside in towards the top of the nose. Next, using gentle pressure, work down the sides of the nose and along the top of the cheekbones. Also massage the glands in the neck using circular then downward stroking movements. Do this with the following blend: mix 3 drops of eucalyptus, 4 drops of lavender and 3 drops of tea tree in 25ml of sweet almond oil. Regular massage treatments are also of benefit to promote efficient elimination of excess mucus and toxins.

For fighting infection and boosting the immune system take regular aromatic baths using 3 drops of eucalyptus, 4 drops of lavender and 3 drops of tea tree.

To help purify the atmosphere and clear the head use one or a selection of the following essential oils as a room fragrancer: sweet basil, bergamot, eucalyptus, juniper, lavender, lemon, pine needle, peppermint, *rosemary and tea tree. Add 5 to 10 drops to a vaporiser, bowl of warm water or a spray container.

As with other ailments, dietary changes and regular massage can benefit this condition, so consult an aromatherapist or other health professional for further advice.

*Steam inhalations should never be used for asthmatics as they aggravate the condition and can cause choking.*

*Rosemary oil should be avoided by people with high blood pressure, so if you suffer from this condition choose another oil from those listed above which appeals to you.*

*Some of the oils in this section should not be used by pregnant women, so refer to Chapter 6 for suitable essential oils for pregnancy.*

## CELLULITE (CELLULITIS)

For an anti-cellulite massage oil, mix 6 drops of grapefruit, 8 drops of juniper and 8 drops of *rosemary *or* 6 drops of cypress in 50ml of sweet almond oil. Alternatively, mix 6 drops of cypress, 8 drops of geranium and 4 drops of *fennel *or* lemon oil in 50ml of base oil. Apply the massage oil with firm, upward kneading and stroking movements to the affected areas.

Regular baths using one or a selection of the following oils is also helpful: cypress, sweet fennel, geranium, grapefruit, juniper, lemon, mandarin, orange and rosemary. Regular skin brushing and massage (see Chapters 5 and 9) are also indispensable tools when combating this condition.

To banish cellulite a balanced diet, regular exercise and ideally professional lymphatic drainage massage and/or regular skin brushing needs to be undertaken. Consult an aromatherapist or other health professional for further advice.

> *The above recipes are not suitable for pregnant women.*
>
> *Rosemary oil should be avoided by people with high blood pressure so use 6 drops of cypress instead.*
>
> *Fennel oil should be avoided by epileptics, so use 4 drops of lemon oil instead.*

## CHILBLAINS

Rub the following blend all over the feet and hands as well as into the affected fingers and toes. Mix 4 drops of black pepper, 4 drops of lavender and 4 drops of *rosemary in 25ml of sweet almond oil

> *Rosemary oil should be avoided by people with high blood pressure so use 4 drops of lemon instead.*
>
> *These oils should not be used by pregnant women, so refer to Chapter 6 for suitable essential oils for pregnancy.*

## COLD SORES *see* HERPES SIMPLEX

## COLDS

To help relieve the symptoms of cold viruses use the *steam inhalation method. Add 3 drops of eucalyptus *or* 3 drops of peppermint and 3 drops of lavender to a bowl of boiling water. Drape a large towel over your head to create a mini steam room, close your eyes and inhale deeply. Breathe in fresh air at regular intervals but try not to let too much of the steam escape. Continue with this method for about five minutes. Usually the steam inhalation method is enough to eliminate the sore throat which so often accompanies a cold. However, as an alternative treatment use a *gargle. Boil some water and leave to stand until warm, pour into a glass and add 2 drops of tea tree oil. Mix very well and use as a gargle. Inhaling from a tissue which has been sprinkled with a few drops of your chosen oil or blend of oils from the selection listed under room fragrancers is also very useful.

A local massage can help to alleviate congestion and stimulate the body's natural defences. Massage from the nostrils out along the underside of the cheekbones using firm pressing movements with your index fingers. Then using the same technique continue just above the eyebrows, working from the outside in towards the top of the nose. Next, using gentle pressure, work down the sides of the nose and along the top of the cheekbones. Also massage the glands in the neck, using circular, downward strokes and cover the chest and upper back areas too. Apply the following blend using the above techniques: mix 4 drops of lavender oil, 4 drops of lemon oil, and

*Steam inhalations should* never *be used for asthmatics as they aggravate the condition and can cause choking.*

*Do not swallow essential oils; they should not be used internally.*

*Rosemary oil should be avoided by people with high blood pressure, so choose another oil listed in this section which appeals to you.*

4 drops of tea tree essential oil in 25ml of sweet almond oil.

To help purify the environment and keep your head clear, choose an oil or selection of oils from the following list and use as room fragrancers: sweet basil, bergamot, eucalyptus, juniper, lavender, lemon, myrtle, peppermint, pine needle, *rosemary and tea tree. Simply add 5 to 10 drops to a vaporiser, bowl of warm water or a spray container. The humidity caused by using the room spray or bowl of water methods can be very beneficial to dry coughs, especially at night.

Persistent cold infections may indicate a low immune system, so consult an aromatherapist or other health professional for further appropriate advice. Also see section on asthma.

# CONSTIPATION

Massage the abdomen using small circular strokes while simultaneously working in a clockwise direction. Also work firmly over the lower back area with the following blend: mix 4 drops of black pepper, 10 drops of *sweet marjoram and 10 drops of *rosemary in 50ml of sweet almond oil and apply as above working in a clockwise direction. Massage these areas every day to help ease this condition.

If the cause is stress related, the oils listed for anxiety and nervous tension are helpful. Choose an appropriate oil or blend of oils to use in the following ways. For a bath, add between 3 drops of an oil and 10 drops *in total* if using a selection of oils. For a massage, mix a maximum of 25 drops in 50ml of base oil. For room fragrancers, add between 5 and 10 drops to a vaporiser, bowl of warm water or a spray container.

*Marjoram should be avoided by people with very low blood pressure, so use mandarin instead.*

*People with high blood pressure should avoid rosemary oil, so also use mandarin instead.*

*None of the above essences is suitable for pregnant women. For suggested recipes and treatment refer to Chapter 6.*

This condition often benefits from massage, changes to diet, lifestyle and examining possible skeletal problems. Consult an osteopath, chiropractor, aromatherapist or other health professional for further advice. If the constipation persists, consult your doctor.

## COUGHS

To help relieve coughs caused by viruses use the *steam inhalation method. Add 3 drops of eucalyptus and 3 drops of lavender to a bowl of boiling water, drape a large towel over your head to create a mini steam room, close your eyes and inhale deeply. Breathe in fresh air at regular intervals but try not to let too much steam escape. Continue using this method for about five minutes.

Alternatively use an antiseptic *gargle. Boil some water and leave to stand until warm, pour into a glass and add 2 drops of tea tree oil. Mix very well and use this as a gargle.

For a local massage oil, mix 4 drops of bergamot, 4 drops of frankincense and 4 drops of sandalwood in 25ml of sweet almond oil. Thoroughly massage the lymph nodes (glands) just under the jaw, the throat, neck, chest and upper back areas.

To help purify the atmosphere choose an oil or selection of oils from the following list and use as room fragrancers: bergamot, eucalyptus, juniper, lavender, lemon, peppermint, pine needle and tea tree. Just add between 5 and 10 drops of your chosen oil or selection of oils to a vaporiser, bowl of warm water or a spray container. The humidity generated by the room spray and bowl of hot water methods is very helpful for some dry coughs.

Aromatic baths using any of the oils mentioned in

*Steam inhalations should never be used for asthmatics as they aggravate the condition and can cause choking.*

*Do not swallow essential oils, they should not be taken internally.*

*Some of the above oils should not be used by pregnant women, so refer to Chapter 6 for suitable essential oils for pregnancy.*

this section are useful to keep the immune system strong, as are regular full-body massage treatments, preferably from an aromatherapist. For a bath, add between 3 drops of one essential oil and 10 drops *in total* if using a selection of oils. For a massage blend mix a maximum of 12 drops *in total* of essential oil in 25ml of a base oil such as sweet almond. Also see listings under asthma and bronchitis.

## CUTS AND GRAZES

Add 4 drops of lavender oil to a small bowl of cool water and clean the wound carefully, wiping outwards away from the cut. Then apply 2 drops of neat lavender oil. If the wound is bleeding apply firm pressure using a clean cloth or gauze to which 2 drops of lemon oil have been added. If the wound is deep or large cover it by adding 5 drops of lavender oil to a plaster or gauze which will then need to be taped at the outside edges.

*If the cut or wound is severe seek medical attention immediately.*

*Lemon oil is not suitable for children or people with sensitive skins, so refer to Chapter 7 for suggested treatments.*

## CYSTITIS AND URETHRITIS

To help relieve the pain of cystitis and urethritis (inflammation of the urethra), apply a compress to the bladder area. Add 2 drops of bergamot, 2 drops of camomile and 2 drops of lavender to a small bowl of warm water for the compress.

Alternatively, apply the following blend: mix 4 drops of bergamot, 4 drops of sandalwood and 4 drops of tea tree in 25ml of sweet almond oil. Stroke the oil onto the bladder area regularly.

Gentle body massage can also be very comforting. Use the above oils but make enough for a treat for the whole body by mixing double the doses of essential oils in a 50ml bottle of sweet almond oil. You could also use a blend of the following oils: add 2 drops of bergamot, 2 drops of camomile and 2 drops

of lavender to a bowl of warm water. Mix well and use this to wash the area carefully after each urination.

> *If the discomfort does not clear after home treatment consult a doctor as the infection may spread to the kidneys.*
>
> *Some of these oils are not suitable for pregnant women. For suggested recipes and treatment refer to Chapter 6.*

Regular use of any of the following cleansing oils in the bath are useful for combating this condition: bergamot, eucalyptus, juniper, lavender, lemon, pine needle, sandalwood and tea tree.

## DEPRESSION

Individuals with depression may experience many different symptoms.

Aromatic baths are very comforting and effective for this condition, as is regular massage. To help create equilibrium, add 4 drops of bergamot, 3 drops of geranium and 3 drops of ylang-ylang to a warm bath and soak for at least 15 minutes, inhaling the aromas. For lethargy, add 3 drops of an oil from the following list or a *total of 6 drops (if using a selection of oils) to a bath *or* use your chosen oil or blend for a stimulating room fragrance as described below: *sweet basil, geranium, *juniper, *peppermint and *rosemary.

The following essential oils are particularly good for uplifting the spirits: bergamot, clary sage, geranium, grapefruit, jasmine, neroli, patchouli, rose, sandalwood and ylang-ylang. For an uplifting massage oil, mix 3 drops clary sage, 5 drops of ylang-ylang and 3 drops of jasmine or 4 drops of sandalwood in 25ml of sweet almond oil.

Any of the above oils or those listed under anxiety and nervous tension can be used to create a general 'lifting' effect in your environment. Just add 5 to 10 drops to a vaporiser, bowl of warm water or a spray container. Alternatively, sprinkle a few drops of your chosen oil or blend on a tissue and inhale at regular intervals.

This condition can benefit greatly from counselling, regular massage, caring friends and positive changes in lifestyle and/or diet. Consult an aromatherapist or other appropriate health professional for further details. Also see listings for insomnia and stress.

> *Sweet basil, juniper and peppermint should be used in low dilution only, i.e. 3 drops in a bath and 1 per cent in a massage oil.*
>
> *Rosemary oil should be avoided by people suffering from high blood pressure, so choose another oil which appeals to you in this section.*
>
> *Sweet marjoram oil should be avoided by people suffering from severe depression as if it is over-used it has a 'dulling' effect upon the senses.*
>
> *Some of the above oils should not be used by pregnant women, so refer to Chapter 6 for suitable essential oils for pregnancy.*

## DERMATITIS *see* ECZEMA

## DIARRHOEA

For diarrhoea caused by food or a virus, gently massage the abdomen using small, circular strokes in a clockwise direction and also use the following blend across the lower back area: mix 5 drops of cypress, 3 drops of eucalyptus and 5 drops of tea tree in 25ml of sweet almond oil.

Take an aromatic bath by adding 2 drops of geranium, 2 drops of lavender and 1 drop of peppermint.

For diarrhoea caused by emotional or nervous problems, massage the abdomen and lower back as above using the following blend: mix 4 drops of geranium, 2 drops of neroli and 6 drops of sandalwood in 25ml of sweet almond oil.

Take regular aromatic baths by adding 3 drops of camomile, 3 drops of

lavender *and/or* 3 drops of clary sage *or* 3 drops of bergamot, 3 drops of lavender and 2 drops of neroli.

> *Some of the above oils should not be used by pregnant women, so refer to Chapter 6 for suitable essential oils for pregnancy.*
>
> *As always, if symptoms persist, seek medical advice.*

Any of the above essential oils may also be used as room fragrancers, either to help reduce the spread of viral infection or to relieve anxiety and nervous tension. Simply add 5 to 10 drops of an appropriate oil or blend to a vaporiser, bowl of warm water or spray container.

## DYSMENORRHOEA (PAINFUL PERIODS)

To help relieve dysmenorrhoea (painful periods) massage the lower abdomen and back using the following blend: mix 1 drop of camomile and 2 drops of clary sage in 5ml of sweet almond oil. Alternatively prepare and use a hot compress by adding 3 drops of clary sage to a bowl of warm water and then rest.

Try taking a warm, aromatic bath by adding 3 drops of clary sage and 3 drops of lavender and soaking for at least 15 minutes.

If the pain is accompanied by nausea the following suggestions may help: either put 1 drop of peppermint on a tissue and inhale from this occasionally *or* use 1 drop of peppermint as a room fragrancer.

## EARACHE

Massage the following blend around the whole ear, paying special attention to the area behind the earlobe, the cheekbone and neck. Mix 1 drop of camomile oil and 1 drop of lavender in 5ml of sweet almond oil. A warm compress using the same essential oils applied to the above areas can also help to ease discomfort.

> *Always seek medical advice concerning this sometimes misleadingly minor condition.*

# ECZEMA AND DERMATITIS

Buy calendula cream or an aqueous cream from a chemist, measure out 2 teaspoons and add 3 drops of camomile. Mix very well and apply to the affected patches of skin.

For weeping eczema add 1 drop of *myrrh to this cream recipe. Also take regular aromatic baths using 3 drops of camomile and 3 drops of lavender.

Eczema is often linked to stressful emotional states of mind so to combat this, gentle body massage would be helpful. Try the following blend: 4 drops of camomile *or* lavender and 3 drops of neroli in 25ml of base oil (20ml of sweet almond oil and 5ml of jojoba is ideal).

However, sometimes the eczema is so severe a massage would not be possible because of the discomfort it would cause. If this is the case, use one or a selection of the following oils as room fragrancers. Choose oils which have a calming and uplifting effect on the body and emotions: bergamot, camomile, Atlas cedarwood, clary sage, frankincense, geranium, grapefruit, jasmine, lavender, mandarin, sweet marjoram, myrtle, neroli, orange, patchouli, petitgrain, rose, sandalwood and ylang-ylang (see Chapter 3 for more details about the oils). Add 5 to 10 drops of your chosen oil or blend to a vaporiser, bowl of warm water or spray container.

For cases of allergic dermatitis where an external substance is the cause of the ailment, treat as above and avoid the allergen (the substance causing the allergy). The same applies to eczema arising from an allergy to dairy products or other foods and drinks.

Identifying allergies, and making dietary and lifestyle changes, can be of great help for this condition. Consult an aromatherapist or other health practitioner for further advice on these subjects.

*Some of the above oils should not be used by pregnant women, so refer to Chapter 6 for suitable essential oils for pregnancy.*

*Some of the above oils are unsuitable for young children, so refer to Chapter 7 for suggested recipes and treatment.*

# FATIGUE

Fatigue has many possible causes such as over-exertion, a
new baby, time changes, working or studying too hard,
'burning the candle at both ends', or anxiety and nervous
tension to name but a few. I have listed some helpful oils below, so
choose an oil or blend appropriate for your own needs.

From the following list add to a bath 3 drops of an oil or up to 6 drops
*in total* if using a selection of oils: *sweet basil, *black pepper, *eucalyptus,
*lemon and *peppermint. However, bergamot, grapefruit, juniper and
rosemary can be used in the usual quantities of between 3 drops if using one
oil and 10 drops *in total* if using a selection of oils to add to your bath. Soak
for at least 15 minutes and inhale these stimulating aromas.

To give you some guidelines, the following essential oils all tend to have a
balancing effect upon the body and mind: bergamot, geranium, petitgrain and
rosewood.

For a 'fruity' and re-energising bath combine 3 drops of geranium, 3 drops of
grapefruit and 3 of rosewood *or* 3 drops of grapefruit, 3 drops of lemon and 3 drops
of rosewood *or* 3 drops of bergamot, 3 drops of petitgrain and 3 drops of rosewood.

Regular massage can help with fatigue. Try a neck and shoulder or full-body
massage with the following relaxing yet harmonising blend: mix 5 drops of
myrtle, 4 drops of petitgrain and 3 drops of vetiver in 25ml of sweet almond oil.

Any of the oils mentioned above can be used as room fragrancers to create
similar effects in your environment. Simply add 5 to 10 drops of your chosen oil or
blend to a vaporiser, bowl of warm water or a spray container. Inhaling from a tissue
sprinkled with a few drops of your chosen essence or blend is also very useful.

For mental fatigue I would particularly recommend *sweet basil and
*rosemary.

Fatigue often benefits from receiving regular treatments from an
aromatherapist or other health professional. Consult a qualified therapist
for further advice on massage, relaxation, diet and lifestyle changes.

*Sweet basil, black pepper, eucalyptus, lemon and peppermint are all skin irritants
if used in excess so use them as directed, in low dilution only –
3 drops in a bath or 1 per cent in a massage oil. If you have very sensitive skin
use them as room fragrancers only or in very dilute form.*

*Rosemary oil should be avoided by people suffering from high blood pressure.
Select another oil which appeals to you from those listed in this section.*

*Some of these oils are not suitable for pregnant women. For suggested recipes and
treatments refer to Chapter 6.*

## FEVER

The following oils are helpful for reducing fever and combating
infection: bergamot, eucalyptus, lavender, peppermint and tea tree.

Use the following recipe as a
cool compress: add 3 drops of
eucalyptus and 3 drops of lavender
to a bowl of cool water. To cool the
sick person dab the body using a soft
cloth or sponge as often as necessary
until the *temperature falls or
medical help arrives.

*Always consult a doctor for a
diagnosis and when suffering from
or treating a person who has a
dangerously high temperature
(40°C or 104°F). For childhood
illnesses see Chapter 7.*

## FLU *see* INFLUENZA

## FRIGIDITY *see Chapter 8*

## GINGIVITIS

Gingivitis is an infection of the gums. To treat it, brush and floss teeth
regularly and massage the gums with clean fingers using gentle circular

*Do not swallow essential oils; they should not be taken internally.*

*Both peppermint and myrrh essential oils should be avoided by pregnant women. For suggested recipes and treatment refer to Chapter 6.*

movements. Also prepare the following *mouthwash: add 5 drops of lemon, 5 drops of *myrrh and 15 drops of *peppermint to a bottle containing 100ml of vodka. Shake before use and add 3 teaspoons of the mixture to a glass of warm water, then rinse the mouth well. Use regularly after brushing and flossing.

## GOUT *see* ARTHRITIS, GOUT AND RHEUMATISM

## GUM AND MOUTH INFECTIONS
*see* GINGIVITIS; HALITOSIS; AND MOUTH ULCERS

## HAEMORRHOIDS

To relieve discomfort and help to prevent haemorrhoids (piles) apply the following blend regularly to the cleansed anal area: mix 5 drops of cypress oil and 10 of geranium with 25ml of sweet almond oil or a homemade ointment. Or, commercial water-based gels (available from chemists)

*For recipes and treatment during pregnancy refer to Chapter 6.*

make an excellent base for essential oils. Mix 1 drop of cypress and 2 drops of geranium in 5ml (1 teaspoon) of gel and apply as above.

## HALITOSIS

Use the following *mouthwash regularly to combat bad breath: add 5 drops of *sweet fennel, 5 drops of myrrh and 15 drops of peppermint to a bottle containing 100ml of vodka. Shake well before using and add 3 teaspoons of the mouthwash to a glass of warm water then rinse the mouth thoroughly.

Besides being a sign of poor oral hygiene, bad breath may be linked to

digestive problems or a local infection. Consult an aromatherapist, your dentist or other health professional for further advice on these subjects.

> *Do not swallow essential oils; they should not be taken internally.*
>
> *None of the above essential oils should be used by pregnant women, so refer to Chapter 6 for suitable essential oils for pregnancy.*
>
> *Fennel oil should be avoided by people with epilepsy, so use 5 drops of lemon oil instead.*

# HANGOVERS

Although not exactly an ailment, I have been asked for my advice on this condition countless times over the years! For a total 'morning after' pick-me-up treatment use the following suggested techniques and recipes.

Take a stimulating bath using 4 drops of grapefruit, 4 drops of juniper and 4 drops of *rosemary. For headaches use a cold compress: add 3 drops of lavender and 3 drops of rosemary to a bowl of cold water, swirl the water so the oils disperse evenly. Place a clean cloth on the surface of the water so it picks up the oils, then apply the compress to the forehead and temples and rest if possible.

To clear the mind and keep you awake choose an oil or selection of oils from the following list: sweet basil, eucalyptus, juniper, lemon, peppermint and rosemary. Then sprinkle a few drops of your chosen oil or blend onto a tissue and inhale deeply. For feelings of nausea: sprinkle 2 drops of peppermint onto a tissue and inhale regularly.

Room fragrancers are a great idea for this condition. Use the oils listed above for a stimulating effect or camomile and lavender to help soothe and sedate.

> *Rosemary essential oil should be avoided by people suffering from high blood pressure, so choose another oil from the list above which appeals to you instead.*

Practical tips are to not drink on an empty stomach and to take 1,000mg of vitamin C and drink lots of water before going to bed.

# HEADACHES AND MIGRAINE

For a tension headache sprinkle a tissue with 1 or 2 drops of calming lavender oil and inhale deeply. (If this aroma is not liked, try camomile.) Also massage the forehead, neck and shoulder area to relieve muscle spasm with the following blend: 1 drop of camomile and 1 drop of lavender in 5ml of sweet almond oil. Sometimes a warm bath with 3 drops of lavender *or* 3 drops of camomile is helpful.

For a headache with feelings of nausea, sprinkle a tissue with 1 drop of refreshing peppermint oil and inhale deeply. Also gently massage the following blend around the temples and forehead (it may also be helpful to rub a little over the stomach area in a clockwise direction): 1 drop of *peppermint in 5ml of sweet almond oil. Alternatively make a cold compress using either 1 drop of lavender *or* 1 drop of peppermint in a small bowl of water. Apply to the forehead and rest.

> *Peppermint oil should not be used by pregnant women, so refer to Chapter 6 for suitable essential oils for pregnancy.*
>
> *It is best not to use essential oils during a migraine as aromas used at this time may aggravate the condition.*

### MIGRAINE

Treat a migraine at the *onset of an attack with lavender oil as for a tension headache.

Headaches and migraine are often helped by massage, dietary and lifestyle changes, so consult an aromatherapist or other health practitioner for further advice.

# HERPES (SIMPLEX AND ZOSTER)

Herpes simplex is responsible for cold sores (simplex I) and genital herpes (simplex II) while herpes zoster causes chickenpox and shingles.

### COLD SORES

As soon as an eruption is suspected, apply 1 drop of neat tea tree *or* geranium on a cotton bud to the area.

Massage the glands just under the jaw with the following blend: 5 drops of bergamot, 5 drops of lavender and 6 drops of tea tree in 25ml of sweet almond oil.

### GENITAL HERPES

Apply the following gel to external lesions *only* using cotton buds (but carry out a patch test first, see Chapter 2). Buy a water-based gel from a good chemist, add 2 drops of tea tree oil to 5ml (1 teaspoon) of the gel and mix well, then use as above.

To boost the immune system response, massage the whole body using the following blend: 6 drops of bergamot, 12 drops of lavender and 12 drops of tea tree diluted in 50ml of sweet almond oil. This blend can also be helpful when rubbed into the groin and other lymph nodes.

Take regular aromatic baths using 3 drops of bergamot, 4 drops of lavender and 3 drops of tea tree.

To help counteract stress, which often triggers an attack, use oils which have a relaxing and uplifting effect on the emotions, mind and body. Use either one or a selection of the following oils: bergamot, camomile, cedarwood, clary sage, frankincense, geranium, grapefruit, jasmine, lavender, mandarin, *sweet marjoram, myrtle, neroli, orange, patchouli, petitgrain, rose, sandalwood and ylang-ylang. Use between 3 drops of an oil and 10 drops *in total* if using a selection of oils in a bath.

### SHINGLES

Lightly dab the following blend over the sores and with gentle strokes apply it to either side of the spine as this is where the affected nerves are located: 6 drops of bergamot, 4 drops of camomile, 10 drops of lavender and 10 drops of tea tree diluted in 50ml of sweet almond oil.

Take regular aromatic baths using 3 drops of camomile, 4 drops of lavender and 4 drops of tea tree.

An aromatherapist or other health professional can offer useful holistic advice concerning lifestyle and dietary changes.

> *Consult a medical practitioner in cases of genital herpes and shingles.*
>
> *Some of the above oils should not be used by pregnant women, so refer to Chapter 6 for suitable essential oils for pregnancy.*
>
> *Marjoram oil should be avoided by people with very low blood pressure, so if you suffer from this condition choose another relaxing oil from those listed which appeals to you.*

## HIGH BLOOD PRESSURE *see* HYPERTENSION

## HIVES (URTICARIA OR NETTLE RASH)

If a large area of skin is affected take a warm aromatic bath using no more than 5 drops of camomile essential oil.

For more localised skin irritation apply the following soothing blend. Buy an aqueous cream from a good chemist, measure out 10ml (2 teaspoons), then add 2 drops of camomile oil. Mix well and lightly apply it to the affected areas.

This condition can suddenly flare up, for example, if someone has unwittingly eaten a food or in some way has come into contact with a substance they are allergic to, or if they are experiencing a great deal of stress. It is therefore useful to prepare a batch of the cream so that some is on hand when an eruption occurs.

To help prevent *stress-related hives, regularly use essential oils which have a relaxing and uplifting effect on the mind and body. Use one or a selection of the following oils: bergamot, Atlas cedarwood, clary sage, frankincense, geranium, grapefruit, jasmine, lavender, mandarin, marjoram, myrtle, neroli, orange, patchouli, petitgrain, rose, sandalwood and ylang-ylang. Add to a bath between 3 drops of an oil and 10 drops *in total* if using a selection of oils, and soak for at least

15 minutes inhaling the aroma. Alternatively your chosen blend of oils may be used for regular body massage. Use a maximum of 12 drops of essential oil *in total* diluted in 25ml of sweet almond oil.

Any of the above oils can also be used as room fragrancers to create a similar effect in your environment. Simply add 5 to 10 drops of your chosen oil or blend of oils to a vaporiser, bowl of warm water or spray container.

> **Never** *use oils from this list in the bath or on the skin* during *an outbreak of hives as they can aggravate the condition. However, they may be helpful emotionally at this time if used as room fragrancers.*
>
> *Some of the above oils should not be used by pregnant women, so refer to Chapter 6 for suitable essential oils for pregnancy.*

## HYPERTENSION

To help relieve persistent high blood pressure, massage the whole body using the following relaxing blend: 5 drops of clary sage, 4 drops of sweet marjoram and 2 drops of ylang-ylang *or* 2 drops of geranium oil.

Also take regular aromatic baths making use of the numerous relaxing essential oils, such as: camomile, clary sage, frankincense, lavender, mandarin, sweet marjoram, neroli, rose and sandalwood.

Adjustments to diet and lifestyle can improve or even help prevent this condition. Consult an aromatherapist or other health practitioner for further advice.

> *Note that rosemary oil should be avoided if suffering from this condition.*
>
> *Most of the above oils are not suitable for pregnant women. For suggested recipes and treatment refer to Chapter 6.*

# HYPOTENSION

To help relieve low blood pressure, massage the whole body using the following stimulating blend: mix 3 drops of black pepper with 3 drops of geranium oil and 6 drops of rosemary in 25ml of sweet almond oil.

Also take regular aromatic baths using 3 drops of a stimulating oil such as peppermint. For an invigorating combination try adding 4 drops of geranium and 5 drops of rosemary to a bath.

*Note that marjoram oil should be avoided if suffering from this condition.*

*Some of the above oils should not be used by pregnant women, so refer to Chapter 6 for suitable essential oils for pregnancy.*

Regular exercise and massage therapy from a professional is very useful for this condition. Consult an aromatherapist or other health practitioner for further advice on appropriate treatment.

# IMPOTENCE *see Chapter 8*

# INDIGESTION

To generally relieve discomfort caused by indigestion use the following massage oil: 5 drops of *peppermint in 25ml of sweet almond oil *or* 5 drops of *sweet fennel and 4 drops of lavender in 25ml of sweet almond oil. Gently massage the blend over the stomach and/or the abdomen using circular strokes always in a clockwise direction.

For indigestion with wind and griping pains use the following massage oil: mix 1 drop of black pepper, 3 drops of sweet fennel and 4 drops of *sweet marjoram oil in 25ml of sweet almond oil.

For feelings of nausea: mix 5 drops of peppermint oil in 25ml of sweet almond oil *or* mix 4 drops of lavender oil and 3 drops of fennel *or* camomile oil in 25ml of sweet almond oil. Gently stroke the blend over the stomach and abdomen. A tissue sprinkled with 2 drops of refreshing

peppermint oil can also be of help if inhaled at regular intervals.

For stress-related indigestion treat as above *or* to help prevent it, mix 4 drops of lavender, 5 drops of sandalwood and 3 drops of neroli *or* rose oil in 25ml of sweet almond oil. Massage over the stomach and/or abdomen as above and also apply to the pulse points on the wrist and neck areas. Using any of the oils listed under anxiety and nervous tension in the bath or as room fragrancers can also be helpful.

Dietary and lifestyle changes, regular exercise and, if the indigestion is stress related, massage and other techniques to promote relaxation can benefit this condition. Consult an aromatherapist or other health professional for further advice on these subjects.

*Essential oils should not be taken internally. A variety of herb teas like peppermint, ginger, fennel and camomile can help ease indigestion.*

*Fennel should be avoided by people with epilepsy so use lavender instead.*

*Marjoram should be avoided by people with very low blood pressure so use camomile instead.*

*Some of the above oils are not suitable for pregnant women. For suggested recipes and treatment see Chapter 6.*

## INFLUENZA

Generally, to help relieve symptoms of flu begin treatment as soon as the onset of the virus is apparent and get plenty of rest.

The *steam inhalation method is very useful to combat most symptoms. Add 3 drops of lavender and 3 drops of tea tree oil to a bowl of boiling water. Drape a large towel over your head to create a mini steam room, close your eyes and inhale deeply. Breathe in fresh air at regular intervals, but try not to let too much of the steam escape. Continue with this method for about five minutes. Ideally a steam inhalation should be used night and morning for a few days. It is also helpful to inhale regularly from a tissue sprinkled with a few drops of your

chosen oil or blend of oils selected from those listed in this section.

For a local massage to help relieve congestion and stimulate the immune system use the following techniques. Massage from the nostrils out along the underside of the cheekbones using fairly firm, circular movements with your index fingers. Then, using the same technique, continue just above the eyebrows working from the outside in towards the top of the nose. Next, using gentle pressure, work down the sides of the nose and along the top of the cheekbones. Using circular and downward strokes, massage the throat, neck, chest and upper back areas, paying special attention to the glands just under the jaw and those below the collarbone area. Use the above techniques when applying the following blend: mix 4 drops of lavender, 4 drops of orange and 4 drops of tea tree in 25 ml of sweet almond oil.

Generally, regular massage treatments can contribute to the prevention of illnesses of this type by encouraging and strengthening the body's own natural defences. However, remember never to massage a person who has a high *fever.

Warm aromatic baths are comforting when suffering from flu. Choose an oil or selection of oils from the following and add to a bath between 3 drops of an oil and 10 drops *in total* if using a selection of essences.

*Always consult a doctor when suffering from or tending a person with a dangerously high temperature (40° C or 104° F).*

*Steam inhalations should never be used for asthmatics, as the steam aggravates their condition and can cause choking.*

*Some of these oils should not be used by pregnant women, so refer to Chapter 6 for suitable essential oils for pregnancy.*

Useful oils are bergamot, black pepper, Atlas cedarwood, eucalyptus, geranium, juniper, lavender, lemon, sweet marjoram, myrtle, orange, peppermint, pine, rosemary and tea tree. Black pepper, sweet marjoram and rosemary are warming and useful for 'chill' type symptoms. On the other hand, bergamot, eucalyptus, lavender and peppermint all help to reduce fever.

For someone who feels too weak

to take a bath and has a *high temperature use a cool compress. Add 3 drops of eucalyptus and 3 drops of lavender to a bowl of cool water then use a soft cloth or sponge to dab the sick person's body carefully until the temperature falls or medical help arrives.

To help purify the sick room choose an oil or selection of oils from the following list (they are all suitable for use as room fragrancers): bergamot, eucalyptus, juniper, lavender, lemon, pine needle, peppermint and tea tree. Just add 5 to 10 drops of your chosen oil or blend of oils and add to a vaporiser, bowl of warm water or spray container. To reduce the risk of further infection it is advisable to use the room fragrancers until the sick person has regained his or her strength.

## INSECT BITES AND STINGS

For *bee stings, gently remove the sting with tweezers and apply 1 drop of lavender oil directly to the painful area. Apply hourly until there is improvement. Try not to scratch the area as this encourages infection. However, if this does occur apply the following blend to the infected site regularly: mix 2 drops of lavender and 2 drops of tea tree in 5ml (1 teaspoon) of sweet almond oil.

For the bites and stings of other common insects including *wasps and mosquitoes, treat in the same way as bee stings. To help relieve itching and inflammation, add 4 drops of camomile, 4 drops of lavender and 4 drops of tea tree to a bath *or* bathe the affected areas with 2 drops of camomile, 2 drops of lavender and 2 drops of tea tree.

As a preventative measure use an oil or blend of oils which repels insects. These oils are particularly useful when used as a room spray, in a vaporiser or in a bowl of warm water. Alternatively sprinkle a few drops on damp cotton wool or kitchen towel and wipe or fix these

*Seek medical help immediately if allergic symptoms like breathing difficulties or collapse occurs.*

*Avoid using the following insect repellent oils if pregnant: basil, citronella, lemon verbena, lemongrass and peppermint.*

around door jambs, steps and window frames. Choose from the following list: sweet basil, citronella, eucalyptus, lavender, lemon verbena, lemongrass, patchouli or peppermint.

## INSOMNIA

A relaxing aromatic bath just before going to bed can help reduce anxiety and induce calm. Add 4 drops of camomile and 5 drops of lavender to a warm bath and soak for at least 15 minutes, inhaling the soothing aroma.

Alternatively sprinkle 2 drops of neat lavender oil on a tissue or on your night wear and inhale deeply *or* 1 drop of lavender may be applied to pulse points on the wrists and neck.

An evening massage is also useful for relieving nervous tension. Pay special attention to neck, shoulders and facial areas when using the following blend: mix 3 drops of camomile, 5 drops of lavender and 4 drops of *sweet marjoram in 25ml of sweet almond oil *or* for a change use 4 drops of mandarin, 3 drops of rose and 5 drops of sandalwood in 25ml of sweet almond oil.

> *Marjoram oil should be avoided by people suffering from very low blood pressure, so use 6 drops of camomile and 6 drops of lavender in 25ml of base oil instead, or simply use the second recommended recipe.*
>
> *Some of these oils are not suitable for pregnant women. For suggested recipes and treatments refer Chapter 6.*

## ITCHING *see* PRURITUS

## LEUKORRHOEA *see* CANDIDA ALBICANS AND LEUKORRHOEA

## LOW BLOOD PRESSURE *see* HYPOTENSION

## MENOPAUSAL PROBLEMS

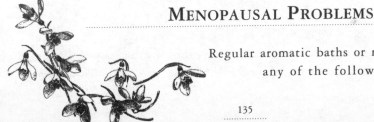

Regular aromatic baths or massages with any of the following oils will

promote hormonal harmony: clary sage, geranium and rose.

Baths and massage blends using the following essences will help to uplift the emotions and decrease anxiety: bergamot, clary sage, jasmine, neroli, rose and sandalwood. For essential oils to suit the changing needs of your skin see Chapter 9.

Regular treatments with an aromatherapist would be ideal. Gentle exercise like yoga and t'ai chi can do much to alleviate the symptoms of the menopause. Dietary changes should be also be considered.

## MENTAL FATIGUE *see* FATIGUE

## MIGRAINE *see* HEADACHES AND MIGRAINE

## MOUTH ULCERS

Apply 1 drop of neat tea tree to the centre of the mouth ulcer. Also prepare the following *mouthwash: mix 5 drops of lemon, 10 drops of peppermint and 10 drops of tea tree in a bottle containing 100ml of vodka. Shake well before use and add 2 to 3 teaspoons of the mixture to a glass of warm water, then rinse the mouth well. Brush the teeth after every meal and use the mouthwash regularly until the ulcers disappear.

Persistent bouts of mouth ulcers can sometimes indicate a low immune system, so consult an aromatherapist or other health professional for further advice.

> *Do not swallow essential oils; they are not to be taken internally.*
>
> *Peppermint oil should not be used by pregnant women, so refer to Chapter 6 for suitable essential oils for pregnancy.*

## MUSCULAR ACHES AND PAINS

To relieve aches and pains use the following *massage oil: 10 drops of lavender, 8 drops of *sweet marjoram and 6 drops of *rosemary in 50ml of sweet almond oil. For people who do a lot of sport, try using the following

blend: mix 4 drops of black pepper, 8 drops of juniper and 12 drops of rosemary in 50ml of sweet almond oil. For muscles lacking in tone the following oils are useful: black pepper, grapefruit, juniper and rosemary.

*Never massage injuries yourself – always seek medical advice and a health professional when dealing with injuries.*

*Marjoram oil should be avoided by people with very low blood pressure; use juniper oil instead.*

*Rosemary should be avoided by people with high blood pressure; use clary sage instead.*

*Some of the above oils are not suitable for pregnant women. For suggested treatment and recipes refer to Chapter 6.*

Warm aromatic baths will also help ease aching, overtired muscles. Choose an oil or selection of oils from the following: black pepper, camomile, clary sage, juniper, lavender, sweet marjoram, peppermint, pine needle, rosemary, sandalwood. Add to a bath between 3 drops of an oil and 10 drops *in total* if using a selection of oils.

Also see listings for arthritis, gout and rheumatism, and for sprains.

## NAUSEA

For nausea caused by indigestion, use the following blend: mix 5 drops of *peppermint in 25ml of sweet almond oil *or* 3 drops of *sweet fennel 4 drops of lavender *or* 3 drops of camomile in 25ml of sweet almond oil. Apply a little of the blend to the stomach and abdomen using gentle, clockwise strokes. Alternatively, if this is too uncomfortable, apply a warm compress to these areas. Mix 1 drop of fennel, 2 drops of lavender and 2 drops of peppermint in a bowl of warm water. Swirl the water so the oil disperses evenly. Place a clean cloth on the surface of the water so it picks up the oil, then apply.

For nausea caused by anxiety and nervous tension use the following blend: mix 4 drops of lavender, 5 drops of sandalwood and 3 drops of neroli or rose. Apply to the stomach area in a clockwise direction and to the pulse points on the wrist and neck.

Aromatic baths can be helpful for nausea. To refresh try adding 3 drops of orange and 3 drops of peppermint oil to a bath *or* for a relaxing effect add 3 drops of camomile and 3 drops of lavender to a warm bath.

For travel sickness sprinkle a tissue with 2 drops of peppermint oil and inhale deeply. If the cause is partly related to the stress of travelling, follow the treatment above for anxiety and nervous tension a few hours before your trip. For a more portable method sprinkle 2 drops of any of the above oils on a tissue and inhale deeply.

All essences listed in this section can also be used as room fragrancers, creating a refreshing yet calming effect in your environment. Add between 5 and 10 drops of your chosen oil or blend of oils to a vaporiser, bowl of warm water or spray container. Choose the oil or blend according to your individual needs and the underlying cause of nausea.

Also see listings for anxiety and nervous tension; hangovers; indigestion; and stress.

> *Fennel should be avoided by people suffering from epilepsy; use 3 drops of camomile oil instead.*
>
> *Some of the above oils are not suitable for pregnant women. For suggested recipes and treatment of morning sickness refer to Chapter 6.*

## NETTLE RASH *see* HIVES

## OTITIS *see* EARACHE

## PMS *see* PREMENSTRUAL SYNDROME

## PERIOD PAIN *see* DYSMENORRHOEA

## PILES *see* HAEMORRHOIDS

## PREGNANCY

*see Chapter 6 for suggested recipes and treatments of many common ailments*

# PREMENSTRUAL SYNDROME
## (PREMENSTRUAL TENSION)

To help relieve fluid retention: mix 5 drops of geranium, 4 drops of juniper and 3 drops of *rosemary in 25ml of sweet almond oil. Massage the blend over the areas which become affected, beginning this routine a couple of days before the fluid retention usually begins.

Regular massage treatments are very useful to reduce various premenstrual symptoms such as mood swings, fatigue and other symptoms of an emotional nature.

Aromatic baths using relaxing and uplifting oils are also very helpful at this time. Choose one oil or a selection from the following list: bergamot, camomile, Atlas cedarwood, clary sage, cypress, frankincense, geranium, grapefruit, jasmine, lavender, lemon, mandarin, *sweet marjoram, myrtle, neroli, orange, patchouli, petitgrain, rose, sandalwood and ylang-ylang. Clary sage, geranium and rose are especially useful as they exert a hormonal balancing effect. Use between 3 drops of an oil and 10 drops *in total* if using a selection of oils in a bath, then soak for at least 15 minutes inhaling the harmonising aromas.

Individuals experience different symptoms before menstruation, so here are some of the best oils to use for various emotional states of mind. For irritability and frustration: bergamot, jasmine, neroli and rose. For despondency: bergamot, clary sage, geranium, grapefruit, jasmine, lemon, mandarin, neroli, orange, patchouli, petitgrain, rose, sandalwood and ylang-ylang. For lack of confidence: jasmine, rose and ylang-ylang.

*Marjoram oil should be avoided by people with very low blood pressure so if you suffer from this condition choose another relaxing oil which appeals to you.*

*Rosemary oil should be avoided by people with high blood pressure, so in the recipe for fluid retention use 3 drops of cypress oil instead.*

A few drops of your chosen oil or blend can be sprinkled onto a tissue and inhaled

at regular intervals or even worn as a delightful perfume. One or a selection of the above oils can also be used in a massage oil or as room fragrancers, see Chapter 2.

For recipes and treatment of other symptoms of premenstrual syndrome refer to the following listings: anxiety and nervous tension; depression; fatigue; headaches and migraine; insomnia; spots; and stress.

This condition can benefit from regular massage, dietary and lifestyle changes, so consult an aromatherapist or other health professional for further advice.

## PRURITUS

For genital or anal pruritus (itching) take regular aromatic baths. To help relieve irritation add 4 drops of camomile and 4 drops of lavender to a warm bath.

Fungal infections like thrush (*Candida albicans*) can also be the cause of this condition. If this applies use the following recipe: 4 drops of lavender and 4 drops of tea tree in a warm bath. Alternatively use 2 drops of camomile and 2 drops of tea tree in a sitz bath or large bowl and use as a local wash. Clean and dry the area thoroughly. This method can be repeated up to three times a day.

## PSORIASIS

Psoriasis has often been linked to stressful states. To combat, use the essential oils which have a relaxing or uplifting effect on body and mind. Here are some examples: bergamot, camomile, cedarwood, clary sage, frankincense, geranium, grapefruit, jasmine, lavender, mandarin, marjoram, neroli, orange, patchouli, petitgrain, rose, sandalwood and ylang-ylang.

Treat with calendula cream or an aqueous cream as described for eczema. To help relieve itching and scaly patches on the scalp and around the hairline use the following blend: mix 12 drops of lavender oil in 20ml of jojoba and 5ml of avocado oil. Massage into the scalp, stroke around the hairline and use any excess to coat the hair. Next cover the hair with a warm

towel and leave on for at least two hours. Then work a mild pH balanced shampoo into the oiled hair, add water and shampoo out as usual. You may need to shampoo twice. This is not only therapeutic for the skin but makes for a luxurious hair treatment too.

Because of skin sensitivity it may not be appropriate to use massage, so room fragrancers are an ideal way to lift the spirits of the person suffering from this condition. Any one or a selection of the essences listed at the beginning of this section can be used as room fragrancers. This is a quick and effective method of creating a stress-free zone in your environment. Add 5 to 10 drops of your chosen oil or blend to a vaporiser, bowl of warm water or spray container.

*Some of the above relaxing and uplifting oils should not be used by pregnant women, so refer to Chapter 6 for suitable essential oils for pregnancy.*

This condition is ideally tackled by closely examining diet, lifestyle and hereditary factors. I would advise a consultation with a health professional for further support and advice.

## RHEUMATISM *see* ARTHRITIS, GOUT AND RHEUMATISM

## RINGWORM

To combat ringworm, mix 6 drops of lavender, 2 drops of *myrrh and 6 drops of tea tree in 25ml of sweet almond oil and apply to affected areas three times a day. As this condition causes itching and flaking skin (often on the scalp) you may prefer to use a cream base. Make a basic ointment or buy an aqueous cream from a chemist. Mix 10 drops of lavender, 5 drops of myrrh and 15 drops of tea tree in about 2 tablespoons of the ointment or cream and apply as above.

*Myrrh should not be used by pregnant women, so refer to Chapter 6 for suitable essential oils for pregnancy.*

To help eradicate the fungus, clothing and linen should be washed thoroughly in water to which several drops of tea tree have been added. If hand washing, always use protective gloves.

## SHINGLES *see* HERPES ZOSTER

## SINUSITIS *see* CATARRH AND SINUSITIS

## SORE THROAT

To help relieve hoarseness, thoroughly massage just under the jaw, the throat, neck and chest areas with the following blend: mix 6 drops of lavender and 6 drops of sandalwood in 25ml of sweet almond oil.

For sore throats caused by a virus use the following recipes and suggested treatments. Boil some water and leave to stand until warm, then pour into a glass and add 2 drops of tea tree oil. Mix very well and use this as a *gargle twice a day. For a local massage oil, mix 4 drops of eucalyptus, 4 drops of lavender and 4 drops of tea tree oil in 25ml of sweet almond oil. Massage using the same technique and areas as outlined above.

To help purify the atmosphere choose an oil or selection of oils from the following and use a room fragrancer: bergamot, eucalyptus, juniper, lavender, lemon, peppermint, pine needle and tea tree. To use, simply add between 5 and 10 drops of your chosen oil or selection of oils to a vaporiser, bowl of warm water or a spray container.

> *Do not swallow essential oils; they should not be taken internally.*
>
> *Some of the above oils should not be used by pregnant women, so refer to Chapter 6 for suitable essential oils for pregnancy.*

## SPOTS

For the occasional eruption, dab individual spots with 1 drop of neat lavender oil *or* 1 drop of neat tea tree oil. For further skin-care details see the entry on acne in Chapter 9.

# SPRAINS

To help relieve pain and inflammation, rest the joint, apply ice using a compress and elevate the injured limb – a method which is known as RICE. Apply the cold compress to the sprain as soon as possible. Add 3 drops of camomile and 3 drops of lavender to a bowl of ice-cold water. Swirl the water so the oils are evenly dispersed. Place a clean cloth on the surface of the water so it picks up the oil then apply to the affected area. Then wrap the compress and an ice pack around the affected joint. Repeat this treatment often and for gentle support use a crepe bandage.

> *A sprain should never be massaged. Always consult a doctor as a bone may have been fractured.*

# STRESS

These days this small word has an undoubtedly large impact on many lives. In ancient times when faced with an emergency situation several primitive responses took over in the body, preparing us to fight or flee from a dangerous situation. These responses are still with us and keep us safe, but problems can occur in modern-day life when a situation or someone stresses us and we hold onto that 'internal' tension. Common symptoms of stress are digestive upsets, headaches, loss of sex drive, exhaustion and a lowered immunity leaving us vulnerable to infectious illnesses. As well as causing physical problems stress affects our emotional and mental states too, giving rise to irritability, anxiety, depression and nervous tension.

Aromatherapy is a great way to tackle this condition with many appropriate anti-stress oils. Here are some of the best: bergamot, camomile, Atlas cedarwood, clary sage, cypress, frankincense, geranium, grapefruit, jasmine, lavender, mandarin, sweet marjoram, myrtle, neroli, orange, patchouli, petitgrain, rose, sandalwood and ylang-ylang. Select an oil or blend according to the effect you desire – for instance, stimulating, sedating, sensual – and also by which aroma appeals to you.

Look for the stress-related information listed under the ailment which applies to you or refer to the listing for anxiety and nervous tension.

Every individual reacts differently to the stresses and strains of life, therefore consult an aromatherapist or other health professional for further specific advice.

> *Some of the above oils should not be used by pregnant women, so refer to Chapter 6 for suitable essential oils for pregnancy.*

## SUNBURN *see* BURNS AND SCALDS

## THRUSH *see* CANDIDA ALBICANS AND LEUKORRHOEA

## TOOTHACHE

Dilute 1 drop of *clove oil in 5 ml (1 teaspoon) of sweet almond oil and rub directly onto the gum. Tincture of *myrrh is also helpful when applied to the gum surrounding the painful tooth.

> *Do not swallow; essential oils should not be taken internally.*
>
> *Clove oil and myrrh should not be used by pregnant women, so refer to Chapter 6 for suitable essential oils for pregnancy.*

## URINARY TRACT INFECTIONS
### *see* CYSTITIS AND URETHRITIS

## URTICARIA *see* HIVES

# VARICOSE VEINS

Gently stroke the legs in an upward direction, taking care to avoid the *varicose veins with the following daily aromatic blend. Mix 6 drops of cypress, 12 drops of geranium and 6 drops of juniper in 50ml of sweet almond oil.

Diet and lifestyle changes as well as gentle exercise often benefit this condition. Consult an aromatherapist or other health professional for further advice.

> *Use upward, gentle strokes on the legs in the direction of the heart. Never apply pressure directly to a varicose vein – massage should only ever be used above the problem area.*
>
> *Some of the above oils are not suitable for pregnant women. For suggested recipes and treatments refer to Chapter 6.*

# VERRUCAE AND WARTS

Verrucae or plantar warts are contagious and occur on the soles of the feet. Warts can occur anywhere on the body. Treatment for both ailments is the same. Apply 1 drop of neat tea tree oil daily and cover with a plaster.

| ESSENTIAL OILS / AILMENTS | Basil | Bergamot | Black pepper | Camomile | Carrot seed | Cedarwood | Clary sage | Cypress | Eucalyptus | Fennel | Frankincense | Geranium | |
|---|---|---|---|---|---|---|---|---|---|---|---|---|---|
| Anxiety and nervous tension | | ✔ | | ✔ | | ✔ | ✔ | | | | ✔ | ✔ | |
| Burns and scalds | | | | ✔ | | | | | | | | ✔ | |
| Catarrh | | | | | | ✔ | | | ✔ | | ✔ | | |
| Cellulite | | | ✔ | | | | | ✔ | | ✔ | | ✔ | |
| Colds and flu | ✔ | ✔ | ✔ | ✔ | | | | | ✔ | | ✔ | ✔ | |
| Constipation | | | ✔ | | | | | | | ✔ | | | |
| Cuts and grazes | | | | | | | | | | | | | |
| Depression | ✔ | ✔ | | | | | ✔ | | | | ✔ | ✔ | |
| Fatigue | ✔ | ✔ | | | | | | | | | | | |
| Haemorrhoids | | | | | | | | ✔ | | | | ✔ | |
| Headaches | | | | ✔ | | | | | ✔ | | | | |
| Indigestion | | | ✔ | ✔ | | | | | | ✔ | | | |
| Insomnia | | ✔ | | ✔ | | | | | | | | | |
| Mental fatigue | ✔ | | | | | | | | | | | | |
| Muscular aches and pains | | | ✔ | ✔ | | | ✔ | | | | | | |
| Premenstrual syndrome | | | ✔ | | ✔ | | ✔ | ✔ | | | ✔ | ✔ | |
| Sore throat | | | | | | | ✔ | | | | | ✔ | |
| Spots and blemishes | | ✔ | | | | | | | | | | | |
| Varicose veins | | | | | | | | ✔ | | | | ✔ | |
| Warts | | | | | | | | | | | | | |

| | Grapefruit | Jasmine | Juniper | Lavender | Lemon | Mandarin | Marjoram | Myrrh | Myrtle | Neroli | Orange | Patchouli | Peppermint | Petitgrain | Pine | Rose | Rosemary | Sandalwood | Tea tree | Ylang-ylang |
|---|---|---|---|---|---|---|---|---|---|---|---|---|---|---|---|---|---|---|---|---|
| | ✔ | ✔ | | ✔ | | ✔ | ✔ | | ✔ | ✔ | ✔ | ✔ | | ✔ | | ✔ | | ✔ | | ✔ |
| | | | | ✔ | | | | | | | | | | | | | | | | |
| | | | | | ✔ | | | ✔ | ✔ | | | ✔ | | ✔ | | ✔ | ✔ | | | |
| | ✔ | | ✔ | ✔ | ✔ | | | | | | ✔ | | | ✔ | | ✔ | | | | |
| | | | ✔ | ✔ | ✔ | | | ✔ | ✔ | ✔ | | ✔ | | ✔ | | ✔ | | | ✔ | |
| | | | | ✔ | | ✔ | ✔ | | | | ✔ | ✔ | ✔ | | | | | | | |
| | | | | ✔ | ✔ | | | ✔ | | | | | | | | | | | ✔ | |
| | | ✔ | | ✔ | ✔ | ✔ | | | | ✔ | | ✔ | | ✔ | | ✔ | ✔ | ✔ | | ✔ |
| | ✔ | | | | | | | | | | | | | | | | ✔ | | | |
| | | | ✔ | | | | | | ✔ | | | | | | | | | | | |
| | | | | ✔ | | | ✔ | | | | | ✔ | | | | ✔ | ✔ | | | |
| | | | | ✔ | ✔ | ✔ | ✔ | | | ✔ | ✔ | | ✔ | ✔ | | | | | | |
| | | | | ✔ | | ✔ | ✔ | | | ✔ | ✔ | | ✔ | | ✔ | | | | | ✔ |
| | ✔ | | | | | | | | | | | | ✔ | | ✔ | ✔ | | | | |
| | ✔ | | ✔ | ✔ | | | ✔ | | | | | | ✔ | | ✔ | | ✔ | ✔ | | |
| | | ✔ | ✔ | ✔ | | ✔ | | | | ✔ | | ✔ | | | ✔ | | | | | ✔ |
| | | | | ✔ | ✔ | | | | | | | | | ✔ | | | | ✔ | ✔ | |
| | | | | ✔ | ✔ | | | | | | | | | | | | | | ✔ | |
| | | | ✔ | ✔ | ✔ | | | | | | | | | | | | ✔ | | | |
| | | | | | ✔ | | | | | | | | | | | | | | ✔ | |

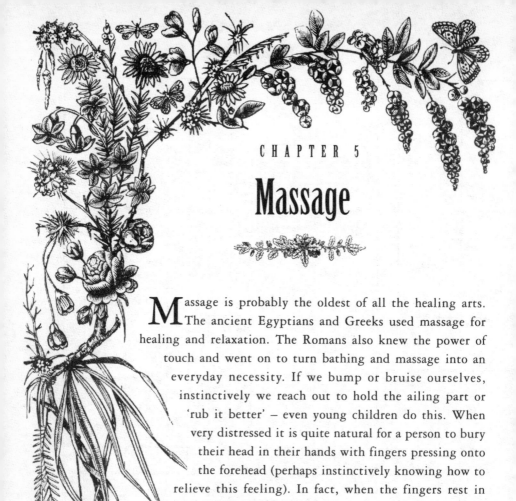

CHAPTER 5

# Massage

$M$assage is probably the oldest of all the healing arts. The ancient Egyptians and Greeks used massage for healing and relaxation. The Romans also knew the power of touch and went on to turn bathing and massage into an everyday necessity. If we bump or bruise ourselves, instinctively we reach out to hold the ailing part or 'rub it better' – even young children do this. When very distressed it is quite natural for a person to bury their head in their hands with fingers pressing onto the forehead (perhaps instinctively knowing how to relieve this feeling). In fact, when the fingers rest in this position they are touching two powerfully calming pressure points on the front of the forehead. Most people need touch in their lives: it is a way of communicating reassurance, love, friendship and, through the medium of massage, it is healing too.

Although aromatherapy can be used in many ways, it is perhaps best known through the medium of massage. The effects of this great healing art are enhanced by combining pure essential oils with the power of touch. If you aren't already the most popular person around, be prepared for things to change as you offer aromatherapy massages to friends and family. The more massage practice you gain on different bodies, the more skilful

your technique will become. Line up the whole family and prepare friends to be pampered. At its best an aromatherapy massage is a most pleasurable and sensual experience. Once you have discovered it you'll wonder how you survived without it!

Massage is an art, and just as we all draw differently, we approach touching and massage individually too. As long as some fundamental instructions are followed, after you become familiar with the basic techniques you can improvise and find what works best for your partner as well as yourself. Massage is a two-way experience with both recipient and 'giver' gaining much pleasure. It is like a conversation without words, as you 'listen' to what your partner's body is 'saying'. Creative massage, like art, takes imagination and intuition and can open the way for an amazing journey into the senses.

If by now you are feeling that massage is terribly complicated don't give up, it is a great asset to have at your fingertips. Aromatherapy massage is really quite straightforward once you've had some practice. Try doing a little at a time, starting with the back. Once you've mastered that, move on to another section of the body, perhaps the neck and shoulders. Get used to moving your hands in a flexible way sensing different skin textures and the varying tensions in or supple-ness of muscles. It can be difficult to learn a practical skill from a book: the 'hands on' approach is usually much easier. If you want to study further there are qualified therapists who run regular massage courses or workshops. There you'll get a chance to practise and fine-tune your technique on willing individuals as well as receiving a massage in return.

# DEVELOPING INTUITION

Massage can link all of the senses including the sixth, intuition. We all have this quality within us, however deeply it may have been buried, and all that is needed is a sincere desire to connect with it. Some fortunate people are able to attune themselves to this peaceful 'frequency' with ease. In others it may seem less accessible and like any tool which hasn't been used for a while it may be rusty and need a little attention before it may be relied on with certainty.

Meditation remains one of the most traditional ways to get 'in touch' with our intuition or 'inner voice'. No particular religion is needed nor specific clothing or equipment. It can be done anywhere at any time! Finding a way to still or 'centre' your mind, allowing negative thoughts to drift away and positive ones to replace them, can be very liberating. Through regular meditation it is possible to achieve much inner clarity, calm, happiness and even wisdom. Once you learn to connect with this peaceful, inner place you can reconnect with a deep and healing part of yourself.

However, some people say they find it hard to sit still or visualise mental images, and others just don't believe it is possible, or are not willing to try this technique. Meditation and deep relaxation mean different things to different people; for some it may be a quiet walk in the countryside or near the sea, others can reach this point through breathing techniques, music, prayer, chanting and even during a skilful massage. There are many paths to take to this enlightening state of mind and we will each be drawn to whichever one suits our individual personality and beliefs. These days there are a wide variety of cassette tapes or CDs offering guided visualisations or meditations, environ-mental sounds or New Age music, and these may help in getting you started with meditation. Some of the music tapes are also excellent to play during massage treatments. As you become more 'centred' and attuned to yourself it is likely that you will be able to concentrate and attune more easily to the needs of your partner.

# WHAT CAN
# AROMATHERAPY MASSAGE DO FOR YOU?

Massage stimulates the lymphatic system, the function of which is to nourish cells and help eliminate waste products and excess fluids from the body. This in turn boosts the efficiency of the immune response, strengthening the body's natural defences in combating infections. Another effect of massage is to improve the circulation, allowing oxygen and valuable nutrients to reach the organs and tissues of the body. As discussed earlier, massage can also relieve pain and psychologically it is very comforting. An American study in 1975 reported that the health of premature babies greatly improved when given regular massage and stroking. Massage generally encourages health and relaxation and provides an opportunity to reconnect with our emotions as well as the physical body.

There are several types of massage, but aromatherapy mainly draws upon a method which deals with the manipulation of the soft tissues of the body and is called Swedish massage. Some professional aromatherapists may also use fairly deep pressure-point techniques, lymphatic drainage massage and even reflexology as part of their treatments. When the art of aromatherapy is used with healing massage a winning combination is created. Not only do pure essential oils have an effect on the physical body but they also have an affinity with the mental and emotional levels. This powerful combination means that an aromatherapy massage can work on a physical ailment while influencing your mood too.

Many physical complaints can benefit from regular aromatherapy massage and some of these techniques are listed in Chapter 4. As essential oils have the ability to work on the mental and emotional planes as well as on a physical level, aromatherapy is ideal for treating symptoms of stress. However, you don't have to be feeling 'uptight' or 'under the weather' to reap the benefits of an aromatherapy massage – it is a treat to be enjoyed at any time.

## IMPORTANT POINTS TO NOTE
## BEFORE YOU BEGIN A MASSAGE

Before you begin there are some important safety points to remember and certain situations where massage should not be used. Before you give an aromatherapy massage check for the following information:

♦ Does your massage partner suffer from epilepsy, high or very low blood pressure, allergies or sensitivity of any kind (especially skin problems like eczema)?
♦ Is the person pregnant, a child or a baby?

If the answer is 'yes' to any of these questions avoid the essential oils which may be harmful for their condition. A list can be found in Chapter 2. Also, use low dilutions where appropriate and always check any safety notes listed under specific essential oils in Chapter 3.

## TIPS ON HOW TO AND HOW NOT TO MASSAGE

Before you begin a massage, check the following points:

♦ Ask your massage partner if he or she has a particular illness or are receiving medical or homeopathic treatment that may rule out massage or aromatherapy. If this is the case make sure you have their doctor's consent before proceeding with any massages. The following examples give you details of when you should NOT massage:
 • Never massage if someone has cardiovascular disease (disease of the heart, arteries or veins), cancer or any other swellings or bruises.
  • Do not massage if a person has a fever, an infectious or other skin dis-order which may spread (like ringworm or boils), broken skin (as can occur in eczema), a burn or sore sunburn.
  • Never massage directly over areas of

varicose veins or the eyeballs, and avoid working on all painful, inflamed and swollen areas (like joints or sciatic pain).

- Never massage recent scar tissue or fractured bones.
- Never massage a pregnant woman's abdomen. In fact if there is any complication in the pregnancy such as a risk (or history) of miscarriage or abnormally high blood pressure do not massage.
- Avoid using a massage blend on the genitals.
♦ Avoid massaging a person who has a full stomach.
♦ Check if your partner wears contact lenses and ask him or her to remove them before you begin.
♦ If massaging your baby take sensible precautions. NEVER apply oils to the face or hands as there is a risk of the baby rubbing his/her eye or sucking his/her own hand.
♦ Ensure that oils do not run into your partner's eyes or that you rub your eyes while you still have traces of massage oil on your hands.
♦ Consult an aromatherapist or other health professional if you have sciatica, sports injuries or other serious illness.
♦ Always use firmer pressure in an upward direction and towards the heart and very light pressure when moving the hands in a downward direction.
♦ Always massage the abdomen in a clockwise direction following the natural flow of the large intestine.
♦ Do not apply firm pressure over the backs of the knees, or drag the delicate skin around the eye area. Let your fingers float in a feather-light way over these places.
♦ Never work directly on the vertebrae of the spine. Instead use even pressured, long strokes on either side of the spine.
♦ Never massage a pregnant woman on her abdomen and don't apply too much pressure to her lower back. Simply use feather-light, circular strokes on her abdomen and gentle, long upward strokes on her back area.
♦ If massaging your baby or child never use heavy pressure. Only use very gentle stroking movements (effleurage) with some light circular movements with the thumbs or the flat of the hand.

Ensure your partner is as comfortable throughout the massage as possible. Let them move their neck and arms into new positions if necessary. While they are doing this stop massaging but keep a comforting hand on their body. If your partner feels uncomfortable after lying on their back for some time, ask them to bend their knees up or put a small, rolled towel under the back at waist level and this will help take pressure off the lower back. Once contact has been made, try not to lose touch with your partner. Ideally some kind of direct body contact should be kept throughout the massage. As you progress this will become easier.

Once you have your massage blend prepared put a little oil in the palm of one hand, then rub both palms together to warm the oil and apply to your partner's body. Never pour massage oil directly onto the body of the person you are working on as this gives them a shock and immediately prevents them from relaxing and trusting in your abilities. When giving a massage use enough of the blend to allow your hands to glide without resistance over your partner's body. Hairy people or those with dehydrated skin will need more oil than others. You should allow up to about 25ml of massage blend for a full body massage for a large adult. During the massage use more oil whenever you feel it necessary, although too much blend can cause you to slip and lose contact with your partner's body altogether!

## HOW TO MAKE YOUR OWN MASSAGE OIL OR BLEND

Before you apply essential oils to the skin they must always be diluted appropriately in a good-quality base oil. The only exceptions to this rule is applying 1 drop of neat lavender or tea tree oil, for example, to a cut or spot. Even then I recommend doing a patch test to check for any sensitivity before it is used. Base oils have a 'fatty' consistency and include vegetable, nut and seed oils, for example, apricot kernel, sweet almond, avocado, grapeseed and wheatgerm oil.

Details of which essences blend well with each other are listed under

individual essential oils in Chapter 3. These blending suggestions are guidelines only – each of us has personal preferences and you may discover an exotic blend of your own. When selecting an oil choose one which appeals to you and is also compatible with your physical, mental and emotional requirements. However, it is not advisable to blend a stimulating essential oil with a sedative one or to blend too many essences together. I would suggest using one or two in a blend to begin with, and when you know each essential oil very well a maximum of four may be used. But remember that the therapeutic effect of essential oils can be reduced by mixing too many essences together. When two or more compatible oils are blended together they can exert a synergistic effect, meaning that they enhance each other's actions, creating a powerful therapeutic effect.

Blending can take a few minutes or can be elevated to an art form, as shown by great perfumers who can take up to two years to create one fragrance! Making you own massage and facial oil, skin-care products and perfumes can be very satisfying and easy once you've had a little practice.

*It is important to realise that this is not accomplished by using large quantities of different oils. Instead a subtle blend of just two essences is likely to be superior.*

## TIPS FOR BLENDING ESSENTIAL OILS SUCCESSFULLY

Generally all flower oils work well together; woody oils enhance the resinous oils and other woody essences; the essential oils derived from herbs tend to blend harmoniously with each other; and the range of oils from fruits blend well with essences from their own botanical family. See Chapter 3 for details of where the essences come from and which botanical 'family' they belong to.

Smelling an oil straight from the bottle does not give your nose a true 'picture' of an essential oil. To receive a less concentrated impression you could try sniffing the lid of the bottle, but this is of no use if you want to prepare a

blend properly. Try imitating the following technique used by 'le Nez' literally 'the nose' (or noses) in the international perfume houses. These master perfumers often use 'smelling strips' to 'feel' the character of an aroma. When working they do not wear perfume themselves, do not attempt to 'sniff' when they have a cold and when blending they usually work in a fragrance-free or airy environment.

Smelling strips can be bought but a cheaper way is to make your own. Buy some blotting paper from a stationer and cut it into small strips. I draw around a 15cm (6 inch) ruler and then cut this small piece of paper lengthwise into four narrow strips. Then take your first chosen essential oil and put 1 drop of it onto the end of the smelling strip and mark it number 1. Note down each essential oil and corresponding smelling strip number on a separate piece of paper. If the slightest drop of oil gets onto your hand, rinse and dry your hands immediately (don't use scented soap) as this can blur your perception of your second choice of oil. Next try oil number 2 on the second smelling strip. Smell number 1 essence alone and number 2 alone, then without letting them actually touch move your nose between both of them, savouring their unique qualities and sensing if you like the overall 'theme' of these oils together. If you become confused about a certain aroma, take a break in fresh air and come back to it.

Another tip is carefully to write down your recipes to the drop, and keep them safe. It can be very frustrating to have created beautiful aromatic blends and then not recall quite how many drops of a certain oil you added. When you've decided on your selection of essential oils you then have to 'blend' them well.

Add a small amount of base oil (10ml if making a

> *Three very important points should be considered when blending:*
>
> - *Select an essential oil whose aroma is pleasing to you.*
> - *Choose an essential oil which not only suits your physical condition but is compatible with your mental and emotional needs too.*
> - *Always use the appropriate dilution for the person for whom the blend is intended. See Chapter 2 for details.*

25ml blend in total) to a clean bottle then add the drops of
essential oil (always following the recommended dosages).
Next gently swirl the bottle around in your hand to mix
the oils, then check that the aroma you've created still
pleases you. Then fill the bottle with the base oil, replace
the top and gently shake several times; this will blend the essential
and base oils fully.

Always label and date your blends so you know how fresh they are and
when to prepare more. Small adhesive labels and waterproof pens can be
bought in most stationery shops.

You may prefer to blend small amounts at first so that you can experiment and familiarise yourself with different essential oils. However, if you
have a particular favourite or need to use a blend regularly (for example, a
daily facial oil for acne) prepare larger amounts and always store your blends
in dark, glass bottles with screw tops in a dry, cool place. Keep them away
from sources of heat and out of direct sunlight. This way if blended with a
little wheatgerm oil they can stay 'fresh' for up to 16 weeks.

Of course, if preparing only a small amount of oil for massage, simply pour,
for example, 10ml of base oil into a small
bowl or saucer. Then add an appropriate
number of drops of your chosen essential oil
or blend of oils and mix very well, either with
your finger or a teaspoon. Again, it is a good
idea to keep a record of which essential and
base oils you used at the beginning of each
massage session for yourself and your partner.

> *Only ever use small amounts of*
> *essential oils in blends as they are*
> *all very powerful. A few drops is*
> *often all that is needed in a base*
> *oil so always keep to the suggested*
> *dilution in Chapter 2.*

## BASE OILS FOR DILUTING THE ESSENTIAL OILS

Before using pure essential oils for massage they must be diluted appropriately in a good-quality base oil (sometimes known as a 'carrier'
oil) as they are simply too concentrated for use directly on the
skin. Base oils have a 'fatty' consistency, for
example, extra virgin olive oil in small

amounts makes a good base oil to add to skin-care preparations but other less well-known base oils are more suitable for body massage. Sunflower, soybean and grapeseed are other suitable base oils. Most of these oils are vitamin rich so are ideal for use in skin-care preparations too. Base oils are derived from seeds, nuts and in the case of avocado oil, the fleshy part of the fruit.

Choose from the following examples according to your or your partner's individual needs and skin type.

> *Don't use a mineral oil as this is not readily absorbed like the base oils recommended here. Instead it forms a film on the surface of the skin and can clog the pores.*

### SWEET ALMOND OIL

Although there are many base oils, throughout this book I have mainly recommended the use of sweet almond oil. It is useful for all skin types, has no odour so does not detract from a blend of aromatic oils and is full of nutrients too. Ideal for skin care, this base oil can be used on its own, as an effective moisturiser for dry skin and even for very young babies.

### APRICOT KERNEL OIL

Apricot kernel oil has a light consistency and is odourless, so it does not detract from delicate aromatic blends. Apricot kernel is very versatile and its uses are similar to sweet almond oil. It is an ideal addition for skin-care preparations and a particularly good base for facial oils, especially where there is sensitivity or inflammation as in cases of acne.

### WHEATGERM OIL

Wheatgerm oil is an orange-yellow colour and is not odourless like the two oils mentioned above; in fact it is quite strong. For this reason use small amounts of wheatgerm – up to 10 per cent is ideal in a massage blend. For example, 50ml of blend would contain 45ml of sweet almond oil and 5ml of wheatgerm

> *Wheatgerm base oil should be avoided by people with an allergy to wheat.*

oil. Wheatgerm has a high vitamin E content which acts as a natural preservative and so if used in a blend it can help to lengthen its shelf life. This base oil is an excellent addition to a blend for stretch marks, scars and burns.

## AVOCADO OIL

Avocado oil comes from the fleshy part of the fruit of the avocado pear tree. In its unrefined state the oil is a dark green and has a quite strong, distinctive aroma. When blending only use small amounts – up to 10 per cent in a facial oil or massage blend. For example, 50ml of blend would contain 45ml of, say, sweet almond oil and 5ml of avocado oil. Avocado oil contains many vitamins and also has a high level of natural waxes and at times it may become semi-solid. If this happens simply place a little avocado oil in a bottle, put this into a cup of hot water for a few minutes and it will liquefy again. Avocado oil is ideal for more mature or very dry skin types.

## JOJOBA

Jojoba is actually a liquid wax which comes from the beans of a North American desert plant. It becomes semi-solid in cold conditions, so when this happens simply place a little jojoba into a bottle and put this into cup of hot water for five minutes or so and it will liquefy again. It is very enriching, so generally use only up to 10 per cent of jojoba in a massage blend – for example, 50ml of blend would contain 45ml of, say, apricot kernel oil and 5ml of jojoba. Unlike vegetable oils jojoba has a very long shelf life and so is an ideal addition to perfumes and other skin-care products. A little jojoba can be used on its own for babies with extremely dry skin, or for cases of eczema and psoriasis. It also suits most other skin types too and can also help in cases of acne. Great results can be achieved when used for both skin and hair care and today it is found in many commercial shampoos.

Base oils will keep for several months if refrigerated, but always remove your chosen amount of base oil well in advance of the scheduled massage time! If you decide to use a vegetable oil the best type to purchase are those that are cold-pressed.

## WHAT 'TOOLS' WILL YOU NEED?

♦ A good-quality base oil: select according to the appearance and
texture of your partner's skin type
♦ A small bowl or saucer
♦ A teaspoon (5ml) and a tablespoon (15ml) for larger fluid measurements
♦ A duvet or several thick blankets and a sheet
♦ Two large towels and two smaller towels
♦ A pillow
♦ And last but not least soft, warm hands

## PREPARING YOURSELF TO GIVE A MASSAGE

The first thing to do is to look at your hands. If they are not soft and
in good condition the massage will be uncomfortable for your
partner. Get your hands into shape by using an enriching hand
cream and by exercising them. One good stretch is performed by
interlacing your fingers so that your thumbs are touching and pointing upwards. Then draw your thumbs outwards, opening the palms
and then gently bending both thumbs and the palms of the hands
away from you. Next loosen your wrists by circling them and flexing
them first towards, then away from your body. Perform these exercises
daily and just before each massage to help gain flexibility in your
hands. As some techniques involve quite deep pressure, especially with
the thumb, it is important that your nails are short and without sharp
edges. Remove all rings, bracelets and your watch before starting.
Your comfort is important too, so for ease of movement wear soft,
loose-fitting clothes when you are giving a massage.

Some people have a natural gift of touch and give great
massages from the start; others need to train their hands. Learn to
let your hands be your 'eyes' and 'ears' and in time they will 'see' and
'listen' to your partner's body, their likes and dislikes. Always ask
your partner before you begin to let you know during the massage if they
feel uncomfortable, cold or if certain areas are too tender for you to work on.

From a practical point of view massage is much easier if your partner is naked. You can then work on the muscles freely without negotiating the lines of your partner's underwear. They in turn can enjoy the uninterrupted flow of your strokes and feel physically more comfortable. However, psychological comfort is equally as important and some people may not want to undress completely. This individual choice should always be respected. If your partner is very shy or for some other reason cannot be approached in the usual way, a foot or hand massage can be very soothing and also encourage a feeling of well-being.

Ask your massage partner to remove any jewellery and their glasses or contact lenses if they wear them. A towel should always be used to cover your partner's body from neck to toe. The only undraped area should be the one you are massaging. When working on the abdomen cover the breast or chest area with a smaller towel so your partner stays warm.

As an interchange of energies occurs between both people during massage, you may sense what mood your partner is in and they in turn may be able to sense yours. So never give a massage when you are in a hurry or feeling strong, negative emotions. Wait until a time when you are feeling calm, patient and in a positive frame of mind. You will also give a much better massage if you can meditate or 'still' yourself for a few minutes before your partner arrives and the massage begins. Massage is about caring and empathy for your partner's needs, so if you are feeling relaxed this will transmit to your partner and they will often relax too.

By following these simple suggestions you can begin to provide a truly comfortable and healing environment.

## PREPARING YOURSELF TO RECEIVE A MASSAGE

This is your time, so try (but not too hard) to concentrate on relaxing, on your breathing and on how you are feeling as the giver uses various strokes on your body. Tell the person giving the massage if you would rather not

undress completely, although your body should be covered with a towel at all times anyway. If your eyes are closed you become even more connected to the sensations. Resist the temptation to 'help' and stay relaxed as the giver gently moves your limbs – this will make it easier for the giver to work deeply and thoroughly on your muscles. *Do* tell the giver if certain points are too tender to be worked on or equally if you really enjoy a specific massage technique, but besides this there should be no conversation. Silence is not a common state for most of us, but it can be very healing and adds much to the whole experience of the massage. After the massage don't jump up and get dressed immediately, allow yourself some time to come back down to earth and savour your new-found state of body and mind.

## GENERAL PREPARATION

### WHEN AND WHERE TO GIVE A MASSAGE

Before you even begin to assemble your tools make sure that you choose a time when you will not be interrupted and unplug the telephone. The place where you give the massage should be as attractive as possible and the lighting should be subdued to induce maximum relaxation. Candles create a beautiful and sacred atmosphere but make sure they are standing in a safe place. Also choose a place which is quiet and not draughty. Heat it very well, as it is better that the room be too hot rather than too cold.

The best place to receive or give a massage is on a massage couch. However, as most homes don't come equipped with these, the floor is the next best place! Fold a double duvet in half or use layers of blankets to provide a thick, comfortable base for your partner to lie on. Also leave yourself some 'padding' at the outer edges as you will be spending a good deal of time kneeling or sitting, and in order to give a good massage you need to be comfortable too. Next cover this with your sheet and one of the large towels; use smaller towels to cover the pillow and the place where your partner's feet will be.

Although a bed may seem like an easier place to massage, unfortunately it isn't. The mattress instead of the muscles will absorb the pressure of your strokes giving little benefit to your partner. It can also be quite difficult for you, because the base is not firm enough, making kneeling difficult and ultimately forcing your muscles into awkward positions.

## OTHER PRACTICAL TIPS

The bowl for the oil should be put in a safe place where your partner cannot accidentally knock it over and cause stains. However, it must be easy for you to reach too – a low table is ideal when working on the floor.

A massage can be given in silence or low-volume music can be used. If you do decide to use music it should have an even tempo, not changing from quick to slow (many New Age music cassettes are appropriate). There may be a danger that the giver begins to massage in time with the musical rhythm, or becomes distracted by the music thereby forgetting to focus or 'listen' to their partner's body and needs. You could try massaging with and without music, note any differences and see which you and your partner prefer.

Once you begin to touch your partner it is best to stay silent except to reassure them or softly ask them to turn over in their own time. Conversation can detract from the touching experience and much can be gained through silence in this situation. You are able to focus totally on your partner and the recipient can sense your touch much more acutely and in doing so can deeply relax.

An aromatherapy massage should be a pleasurable experience for the recipient. If you are using a calming massage blend, your partner may be so relaxed that they fall asleep during or after the massage. Alternatively, if you use a stimulating massage blend, it is likely they will feel re-energised and invigorated. A treatment given by a skilled aromatherapist using pure essential oils can dispel many negative states restoring harmony to body, mind and emotions.

# SOME BASIC MASSAGE STROKES

### EFFLEURAGE

Don't be put off by this word! Effleurage is simply a technique which basically involves stroking either gently or more firmly with a constant rhythm. It consists of long, flowing, uninterrupted strokes which should be performed firmly in an upward direction (towards the heart) and much more lightly as your hands move in a downward direction. This technique is generally very relaxing and ideal for use on all parts of the body. Use it when you begin work on your partner, when you move from one part of the body to a new area and finally when you complete a massage. Under the title of effleurage I also include the feather-light stroking, and the cross-wise 'pulling' movements I describe in the massage sequence on page 168.

### KNEADING

Kneading is generally performed on the more fleshy areas of the body like the buttocks, thighs, back muscles and shoulders. It is particularly good for promoting the elimination of waste products from the muscles and for easing tension. Kneading does not use the knuckles as you do when kneading dough! However, the other necessary movements are very similar to the kneading most of us are familiar with. First, pick up the flesh in the palm of your hand and then gently squeeze it, while allowing your thumb to slide easily over this section of flesh. Immediately place your other hand ready to perform the same movement just slightly further along the muscle from where your first hand left off, allowing the flesh to pass from one palm into the next and so

> *Fairly firm pressure is suitable for areas of very knotted muscle on the back but care should be taken to apply only very light pressure on the face and other sensitive areas.*
>
> *Only use the lightest effleurage strokes when massaging babies and children. Any massage stroke should always be performed with even pressure and rhythm for the comfort of both the giver and receiver of the massage.*

on. Both hands should work rhythmically together and stay in contact with the skin at all times. I have also described a range of 'circling' movements involving thumb and fingertip pressure (see page 166).

For ease of home use I have outlined a full body massage sequence for you and also given advice on self-massage as well as tips on touching for babies and children. A step-by-step sequence designed specifically for lovers can be found in Chapter 8. If you don't want to give a full body massage, select the appropriate advice from the sequence below and work on any of the following areas: the back; *or* the face, neck and shoulders; *or* both feet; *or* both hands. I hope you have fun and enjoy the experience of both giving and receiving aromatherapy massage.

> *If pregnant, refer to Chapter 6 for details appropriate for you at this special time.*

## MASSAGE FOR FRIENDS

An aromatherapy massage is particularly enjoyable when shared with a friend (I have assumed the person receiving the massage in this case is a woman). Always check for any reasons why you shouldn't massage or use particular oils as well as noting other safety advice given on essential oils by referring to the section 'Important points to note before you begin a massage' on page 152 and Chapter 3 on the essential oils. For other tips on preparation and blending essential oils and base oils see the information given earlier in this chapter. When you are ready the following massage sequence can be used to give you guidelines and later inspiration for your own massage strokes.

*1. Ask your partner to lie on her front. Check that she is comfortable; she may prefer a pillow under her ankles. Now fold down the towel far enough to expose her lower back. Next, before applying any oil, gently rest your hands for a minute near the base of her spine and then begin to use quite quick effleurage strokes covering the*

whole of the back, maintaining fairly firm pressure going upwards and very light strokes when returning to the lower back area.

2. Then pour a little of your chosen massage blend onto your palm and rub your hands together to warm the oil (use more massage blend whenever you feel necessary throughout the duration of the massage). With your hands at either side of the base of her spine and your fingers facing towards your partner's head, use upward, gliding strokes to apply the oil. These strokes should be fairly firm when your hands are travelling upwards to the shoulder area, then gently sweep both hands out towards the outer edges of each shoulder, pointing your fingers outwards away from the spine. Your hands should then apply only the lightest pressure on their downward journey as you gently stroke the back and sides of her body. When you reach the top of her buttocks bring your hands up toward the base of the spine again. This should be one continuous, rhythmic movement without losing touch with your partner's skin. Continue with this method, each time starting the upward stroke slightly further out from the spinal area than the last, until you have covered the entire back and sides of her body.

3. If you feel any tension in the back gently knead these areas using the same rhythm and speed as in step 2. Trace small thumb circles from the base of the spine to the base of the skull, being careful not to apply too much pressure on her neck. Do this by circling the balls of your thumbs or fingers continuously in lengthwise strips (from base of spine to base of skull), gradually moving outwards from the centre of the back over any tense areas.

4. You may find that there is tension in the buttocks, if so gently knead them too. Keeping the fingers together and your thumb moving towards them in a squeezing movement, work across her hips from the spinal area out and then move back towards the centre of the back again. You can also try using the heel of your hand or your thumb carefully to apply circular pressure to very knotted areas. Then, with the flat of the hands, make light and even-pressured circular movements all over the buttocks, but especially the sides, and with even lighter circular strokes move up to the lower back area again. Cover the buttocks with the towel again while still leaving the back area exposed.

5. Next, *using long uninterrupted strokes, slide your hands up to the tops of her shoulders and knead these muscles lightly. The muscles here can often be very tight but also tender so work with care. Start at the base of the neck and knead outwards by gently picking up the flesh then squeezing and rolling the muscles between your fingers and thumb. (Do this by bringing your fingers towards you and letting the thumb slide over the top of the 'roll' of flesh. Do not pinch or hurt your partner.) Use first one hand then the other until you reach the upper arm. Repeat twice and then do the same along the top of the other shoulder.*

6. When *you feel the tense muscles soften, return to the base of the spine and briefly effleurage the whole of her neck, shoulder, back and buttock areas once more. Always work from the base of the spine upwards, using firmer movements towards the heart and with much lighter strokes when moving your hands in a downward direction. By now any tension she was experiencing should be melting away.*

7. Next *kneel to one side of your partner and in one long movement, using feather-light pressure, stroke downwards from the shoulders to the base of her spine. This can be done by splaying the fingers slightly and using the backs of your hands or fingertips, or you can alternate them for a more interesting sensation. Start with the area of the back farthest away from where you are kneeling and with flowing, lengthwise strokes cover the whole back and buttock areas until you reach the side closest to you.*

8. Now *position yourself at your partner's feet and with several long, fairly light and flowing strokes (effleurage) cover her whole leg. These movements should flow continuously from ankle to knee and knee to the top of the thighs. The massage technique as always should be fairly firm on the upward stroke and light when bringing the hands back down the body. Be sure not to apply heavy pressure to the backs of her knees, instead lightly glide over this area. Return to the lower leg and lightly knead these muscles with the squeezing and rolling action (as described for the tops of the shoulders). Next, using the palms of both hands at the same time, glide up to just above the knee, then knead the thigh area. After this flex the knee so it is at a right angle to the thigh. Using one hand*

to support the leg, grasp the calf and with the other hand and firmly slide it downwards to the back of the knee. Repeat this until the whole of the lower leg has been covered. Next effleurage the leg again in an upward direction. These strokes should become lighter and lighter each time you stroke up and float down the length and sides of her leg. Repeat this three times. To finish off, use feather-light touches by trailing your fingertips from the top of the thigh to her toes.

9. Next bring your hands down to the ankle again and keeping your fingers together place them (pointing to the floor) on the inside of the ankle. From here firmly yet very slowly draw your hands across her lower leg toward you. As one hand begins to lift off the leg use your other hand to take its place, stroking exactly the same strip of skin. As this second hand begins to lift slowly from the leg, replace the first hand slightly above it covering a new area of skin. Use this rhythmic, pulling technique all the way up the inside of the leg to her buttocks without pausing. Repeat this process starting from the top, this time covering the outside of the leg. Perform this pulling technique twice up each side of her leg. Next with one hand under the foot and one on top, slide the hands downwards at the same time and slowly off the foot and toes. Then move on to the other leg and repeat the whole sequence.

10. Ask your partner to turn over. As she does so lift the towel a few inches above her and this time cover her from the upper chest to her toes. If she had a pillow supporting her ankles before take it out now. Kneeling at her feet, circle the ankle bone with the fingertips of both hands. Then slide your hands gently up a little until you are holding either side of her leg just above the ankle with your fingers resting on top of her shin bone. Your fingers should now be held together and pointing towards her knee. From this position stroke the oil up the front of her lower leg to the top of the thigh in one flowing movement – your hands should part briefly as you glide around the kneecap, then sweep upwards together again. When you reach the top of the thigh let your hands separate and again in one flowing movement lightly stroke down either side of the leg until you reach the top of her foot. Perform this stroke twice more. Then bend her knee up and place one hand on either side of the bent knee. From here stroke down firmly to the groin area (this helps promote lymphatic flow) then gently lower the leg again. Next, repeat the pulling

*technique that you used on the back of the leg at step 9. Start with your hands resting on the inner ankle and slowly perform the stroke until you reach the top of the inner thigh, and then starting at the top cover the outside of her leg. Next, with one hand steadying the top of the foot, use the other thumb to massage the sole of her foot. Very gently pull each toe and then with one hand between her foot and the floor and one hand on top of the ankle lightly stroke downwards and off at the toes. Then position yourself on the other side and repeat the whole sequence along the front, inner and outer areas of her other leg and foot.*

*11. Now position yourself above her head. With the backs of both hands stroke out from the centre of her upper chest to the upper arms, then turn your hands over and continue the stroke by gliding the palms down to the elbows. Bring your hands up again and this time slide your fingers between the floor and her shoulders, sweeping slowly inwards and upwards to the base of the skull. Repeat this four times beginning and ending with your hands at the centre of the upper chest each time. This is an excellent stroke for relaxation.*

*12. From this position with your hands side by side and fingers pointing toward her feet, use light pressure to glide them down the centre of her body. When you reach the area just below her navel bring your hands outwards over each hip and glide them back up, covering the sides of her body, ribcage and finally her upper chest. When you reach her armpits draw both hands together to meet in the centre of the upper chest again. This long, flowing stroke is very relaxing and helps to connect many areas of the body. Do this four times. When you reach the upper chest position for the last time, stroke lightly down the breast bone and glide both hands out and up towards the armpits, encircling the breasts. Or carefully place your palms on both breasts and together gently move them in circles toward each other.*

*13. Next move to sit near one of her hands. Effleurage from the wrist up to her shoulder covering the front and back of the arms, then glide both your hands lightly down to her fingertips again. Repeat this three times. Next move onto her hand; with your fingers touching her palm (under her hand) and your thumbs on top,*

use gentle, upward and outward strokes with the thumbs. At the same time use your fingers to press and stroke her palm. Then rotate each finger; holding it just above the joint nearest to the hand, very gently pull each one towards you. We often take our hands for granted as we use them everyday. However, a surprising amount of tension can be released through a hand massage. To complete this section of the massage use several slow, feather-light strokes in a downward direction from the shoulder to her fingertips. Then move to the other side and repeat on her other hand and arm.

14. Next sit to one side of your partner's torso and gently rest one hand on her abdomen. Keep it still for a few seconds allowing you both to connect with this very sensitive area. Then using your flattened palm and fingers perform small circular strokes while simultaneously moving in a clockwise direction. Continue with these and gradually move outward smoothing one large 'circle' around the edges of her abdomen. Use two hands for this slow movement and always keep one hand on her body (this stroke is very good if constipation is a problem). When massaging this area strokes should always be performed carefully, not for too long and in a clock-wise direction to follow the natural flow of the large intestine. After circling the whole of the abdomen, glide your hand upwards from the soft area between the ribcage and slowly over the breast bone and onto the centre of the upper chest.

15. Kneel above her head and place your hands on the centre of her upper chest with fingers pointing inwards. Next draw your hands slowly outwards, across the chest to the tips of her shoulders. Then with palms facing up slide your fingers between the floor and her shoulders with your thumbs resting on top near the collarbone. From this position slowly sweep inwards toward the base of her neck and then stroke gently upwards to the base of the skull. This is a very sensitive area but it often holds much tension so work very carefully here. From the base of the skull, with your fingers still facing inwards, continue the slow, careful stroke up the back of her head, through her hair and eventually gently separate your hands as they leave her head altogether. Repeat this sooth-ing stroke three times.

16. Now we come to perhaps the most relaxing area for massage –
the face. Interlace your fingers so they are pointing inwards and
place them gently in the centre of her forehead. From this position
slowly draw your fingers apart and smooth them outwards
across her forehead and down to the temples. Then, keeping your
fingers still and together, use slight pressure to circle the temples twice.
While maintaining the lightest touch with the face glide your hands back
up to the interlaced position on the forehead again. Repeat this several times being
careful to avoid the eye area. Next, using your fingertips, gently pinch along her
eyebrows (being careful to avoid the eyeballs), then stroke down the nose and make
tiny circular movements with the balls of your middle fingers on the outside of her
nostrils. Continue with these small, circular strokes across the cheekbones and then
glide the fingers smoothly up toward her ears. Repeat this stroke four times. Then
with the tips of your forefingers touching, place them between her nostrils and upper
lip. Slightly splay your other fingers and rest them lightly on her chin and neck, but
not over her mouth. From this position stroke smoothly outwards and up to the
earlobes. Then using the tips of your fingers continue this light, flowing stroke
straight down over the jaw, sides of the throat, collarbone and then out towards the
armpits. Perform a few circles using quite firm pressure with the flat of your hand
where the armpit and upper chest meet, then place both hands at the starting position
above her upper lip again. Repeat this as a flowing stroke four times. Massage of the
face, neck and shoulders can help alleviate headaches and melt away nervous
tension.

17. For the next stroke keep your fingers together and your palms flat. Place one
hand so the palm is next to her ear with your fingers pointing to her chin. Then
slowly and very lightly stroke up across her cheek toward the temple area. As soon as
your first hand reaches the top of her cheekbone begin to trail it off very gently into
her hair and then lift off completely. As soon as this hand reaches her hairline
begin to move your other hand upwards retracing the exact movements of the
first stroke. Then as the second hand starts to lift off replace it with the
first, covering the same area yet again. This is an
incredibly soothing stroke and should be repeated
three times with both hands. Next run your

*fingers through your partner's hair starting at one ear crossing the crown and ending at her other ear. Use slow, rhythmic, 'raking' movements with your fingers very gently pulling sections of her hair toward you. Repeat this action until every part of the hair has been 'finger combed'.*

*18. Finally, complete the aromatherapy massage in style. Cover her with the towel from throat level to her toes. Move to the position you used for massaging the abdomen and place your hands lightly on each of her shoulders. Starting here, use one feather-light stroke down her arms and off the tips of her fingers. Return to shoulder level and this time run the fingertips of both hands down the outside of the front of her body. Then return again to the upper chest and this time run your fingertips down the centre of her torso and continue in one long stroke down her legs and off the tips of her toes. Replace your hands lightly on the top of her thighs and with splayed fingers run the length of her leg twice more covering any areas missed last time. Then repeat the whole technique once more. Lightly hold your partner's feet for about 15 seconds to help them come back down to earth then slowly release your hold. Although lengthy to describe, these finishing strokes should take about a minute.*

An aromatherapy massage can have a potent effect on many levels so allow your partner time to rest for a while after such a wonderful treat.

# BABY MASSAGE USING VERY LIGHT EFFLEURAGE

Before you begin refer to the safety information earlier in this chapter and check that you are using one of the very few essential oils suitable for babies and that it is used in very low dilution. Refer to Chapters 2 and 7 for lists of suggested essential oils and dilutions. For useful preparation tips for a massage see information given earlier in this chapter on pages 160-161. Make sure your hands are warm and the baby doesn't get cold or uncomfortable at any time.

In my experience all babies loved to be massaged; some wriggle and kick excitedly, some get bored after a short time and others are happy to be stroked all day! You know your own baby best so tailor your home massage routine according to his needs. Choose a time when your baby is not too hungry or too full and a time when you are feeling calm. Lay him on his back so you can initially maintain eye contact, and talk to him during the massage. Use only *very light* effleurage movements in an upward direction on his body, and your strokes should be feather-light when you bring your hands down to begin again.

Start by holding his feet in both of your hands and gently stroking up his legs. From here, using the balls of your fingers, carefully stroke across his abdomen in a clockwise direction (this can help with constipation and colicky pains) and up to his chest. Starting in the centre very gently stroke outwards to his upper arms using both sets of fingers at the same time and then lightly down his arms. Then use a few very light strokes down the length of his body before turning him over. Massage his back *very lightly* using the method given below in 'Children's massage'.

> *Use sensible precautions when massaging your baby.* Never *apply an aromatherapy massage oil to your baby's face or hands as there is a risk of him rubbing it in his eyes or sucking on his own hands.*

# Children's Massage
# Using Light Effleurage

Children love being cuddled and a massage is usually very well received, especially if it doesn't last too long. I tend to find that a foot, hand, leg *or* back rub is enough to give your child a treat as well as soothe any minor physical ailments. As usual before you begin refer to the safety information earlier in this chapter and check that any essential oil and dilution you use is suitable for your child. Refer to Chapters 2 and 7 for suggested essential oils and dilutions.

## A Basic Back Massage

*1. Use very light effleurage strokes up either side of the back (from base of spine to base of skull) with the palms and relaxed fingers of your hands. When you reach the shoulder area spread your fingers wide and in one continuous stroke bring your hands lightly down the back to the base of the spine again. Without losing contact with your child's skin repeat this action until the whole of the back has been stroked. When you want to complete the massage or move to a different area of the body, gradually make your strokes lighter until they are feather-light and slow, then gently lift your fingers off altogether.*

*2. Next position your hands on either side of your child's lower back, with your fingers pointing upward and both thumbs almost touching. Slowly trace circles up either side of your child's spine (never on the vertebrae) to the base of the neck and out across the shoulders using very light thumb pressure. Although the thumb is actually performing the circles, keep the flat of both of your hands in light contact with your child's back and allow them to slide gently upwards too. Repeat this twice. Finally complete the massage as you started it by using some flowing effleurage.*

The long effleurage movements I described first can be used on their own if you and your child prefer. This stroke has a constant rhythm which is calming, comforting and often sends children soundly to sleep.

## A BASIC LEG MASSAGE

With your hands together and fingers pointing upward use light effleurage in an upward direction. These long even-pressured strokes should flow from ankle to knee then knee to groin with even lighter pressure when your hands return downward to the ankle again. Repeat this several times on the front and back of your child's legs. Always work on both legs otherwise your child may feel lopsided! Also be careful to stroke very lightly over the backs of the knees and to glide around the kneecaps.

### HAND FOOT OR TUMMY MASSAGE

Follow the techniques using *very light* pressure as described in the 'Massage for friends' sequence.

## SELF-MASSAGE

If you don't have anyone available to share a massage with, you can do it yourself. Self-massage is great because you know exactly how much pressure to apply to areas and it is also an ideal way to practise your massage techniques! Some of the strokes you need are very similar to those described in 'Massage for friends', so to clarify certain techniques fully please refer to these numbered sections where appropriate.

*1. Start by taking a few deep breaths and gently stretching your body. Then when you are ready begin to massage your scalp – as if you were shampooing your hair. When you've covered the whole head run your fingers through your hair. Then, this time using your chosen massage oil, move onto your face. Using the balls of your fingers repeat the strokes listed in step 16 of the 'Massage for friends' sequence on your own face, neck and upper chest.*

*2. Next with one hand, grasp the back of your neck and squeeze and release the muscles between your palm and fingers. With the head held upright work firmly*

*from the base of the skull down to the base of the neck. Then reach across to your left shoulder and using the same technique work from the base of the neck along the top of your left shoulder to the upper arm. When you've done this three times repeat on your right side. These techniques are very useful for relieving tension and headaches.*

*3. Still using the squeeze and release movements, work down both arms, then stroke up to each shoulder area again. Next massage your left hand, mainly using firm, circling movements with your right thumb. When every part of the hand has been covered repeat on the right hand with your left thumb.*

*4. Now move on to your upper chest and effleurage this area well. Kneel or stand up and reach around so that you can massage just below your waist level on your back. Work in a circular motion all over the lower back and buttocks from the centre to the outside of the hips. Now glide your hands around to your solar plexus area and repeat the methods listed in step 14 of the 'Massage for friends' sequence on your own abdomen. Keep your hands still on the centre of your chest for one minute to 'connect' quietly with your heart. Then sit down again, relax and begin to knead your thigh slowly, working from the knee to the groin. When you have covered this whole area bend your knee up and reaching down to your ankle stroke firmly up the back your lower leg to the knee and then up to the groin. Repeat the strokes in number 9 of the 'Massage for friends' sequence along the length of your own leg and foot. Then repeat all the movements on your other leg.*

*5. Position your leg so you can massage your foot. Using both hands, but especially firm thumb pressure, cover every inch of your foot, especially the sole. Important pressure points are located here which relate to various organs and systems within the body. Repeat on the other foot. Now take some deep, slow breaths and allow yourself to rest fully.*

CHAPTER 6

# Pregnancy and Aromatics

Aromatherapy can be very beneficial in pregnancy not only to relieve common complaints like backache, but also to help bring harmony to your changing emotions. Some essential oils refresh and uplift your mind and body, while others help you relax. Some people sail through pregnancy and feel nothing but a sense of well-being. However, if you do experience any of the minor ailments common to pregnancy there is usually an essential oil or blend to help alleviate them.

Although aromatherapy can be used in many ways aromatic baths, massages and room fragrancers will probably be the most useful at this special time. Essential oils can also be of use in labour in the form of a massage blend, compress or a mood-enhancing room fragrancer. Regular, warm aromatic baths can help melt away muscular and emotional tension giving you an opportunity to really relax. Massage with essential oils can relieve aching muscles and help to ease the pain of varicose veins as well as relieve other minor ailments. I can also recommend yoga and gentle swimming as great ways to help improve your stamina, breathing techniques and keep you active throughout your pregnancy. These days there are local classes and many excellent books geared to the needs of expectant mothers.

In this chapter I have tried to cover most common complaints occurring in pregnancy. For more information once your baby has arrived see Chapter 7. If you can, consult a qualified aromatherapist who will give you valuable advice and support throughout your pregnancy as

well as providing luxurious body treatments. (Chapter 14 gives details of how to find an aromatherapist.) It is also important to discuss using aromatherapy with your midwife and doctor early on in your pregnancy. Some medically trained people now recognise the benefits of essential oils and positively encourage their use.

This is a special time when you must take extra care of yourself and your unborn baby. For this reason I have listed some oils which are not suitable for use at this time. Again an *asterisk refers you to safety and other important notes in the box below, so please read them carefully.

Avoid the following essential oils throughout pregnancy: angelica, basil, carrot seed, cedarwood, clary sage, clove bud, cinnamon leaf, citronella, fennel, hyssop, juniper, lovage, marjoram, melissa, myrrh, origanum, parsley, peppermint, rosemary, sage, tarragon, thyme and any other essential oils listed as toxic in Chapter 2 such as pennyroyal, etc.

Both lavender and camomile are extremely useful 'pregnancy' oils, but they are also very mild emmenagogues (which means they promote menstruation). Both of these essences should also be avoided in the first three months of pregnancy if there is a history or serious risk of miscarriage. Otherwise they may be used in pregnancy at the recommended dosages.

Cypress, jasmine and rose should be avoided for the first 20 weeks of pregnancy after which they may be used moderately and with care.

Although clary sage oil is listed under those to be avoided during pregnancy, it is useful once labour has started. Clary sage (salvia sclarea) essential oil should not be confused with sage oil (salvia officinalis) which should only ever be used by a qualified aromatherapist.

Finally, if you cannot find information about an essential oil or are unsure if it is suitable for you or those you care for, do not use it. Always consult a qualified aromatherapist for professional advice. And before you use an essential oil read the safety information and suggested methods of use outlined in Chapter 2 as well as any safety notes listed for specific oils in Chapter 3.

## RECOMMENDED ESSENTIAL OILS

Some of the above essential oils, like lemon and tea tree oil, are better used mainly as room fragrancers or for applying only to an affected area (for example, on the legs if varicose veins become a problem). Others make luxurious additions to massage oils like neroli, petitgrain and ylang-ylang oil. Essences like frankincense and lavender can make deeply relaxing bath oils, much needed in the latter stages of your pregnancy.

> *In my experience the following essential oils are suitable for use during pregnancy: *camomile, *cypress, frankincense, geranium, grapefruit, *lavender, lemon, mandarin, neroli, orange, patchouli, petitgrain, *rose, sandalwood, tea tree, ylang-ylang.*
>
> *\*Check if and when you should use the \*asterisked essences by reading the information on page 178 of this chapter.*

## RECOMMENDED BASE OILS

Base oils which are especially useful in pregnancy are sweet almond, *wheatgerm and jojoba. Wheatgerm oil is especially good for scarring and is therefore ideal for preventing stretch marks. If you create your own massage blend and aren't going to use it right away, add 10 per cent wheatgerm oil to help prolong its shelf life. This means that a 50ml bottle of massage blend should contain 5ml (1 teaspoon) of wheatgerm oil and 45ml of another base oil like sweet almond.

More details of various base oils and tips for successfully blending essential oils can be found in Chapter 5.

> *If you suffer from a wheat allergy you should avoid wheatgerm oil and use jojoba instead.*

## RECOMMENDED DOSAGES IN PREGNANCY

Because of the sensitive and changing state of you and your unborn baby you should use half (or less) of the usual dosage for adults. This applies when trying out any of the suggested applications outlined in Chapter 2. This means using a 1.25 per cent dilution or less.

> Do not take essential oils internally *and always keep to the recommended dosages appropriate for pregnancy.*

## HOW TO CHOOSE AN ESSENTIAL OIL

It is always important that you select an essential oil whose aroma pleases you. This is even more so when pregnant as your sense of smell is heightened (as well as every other emotion!). An essence which doesn't appeal to you is unlikely to have a positive effect upon your mood and sense of well-being. Choose an essence which suits your physical, mental and emotional needs. For detailed information on specific essential oils and tips on blending essential oils refer to Chapters 3 and 5, but here are a few of my favourite blends for pregnancy.

### Relaxing bath blends
Mix 2 drops of mandarin and 3 of sandalwood in 10ml (2 teaspoons) of sweet almond oil and add this blend to a warm bath *or* mix 2 drops of camomile (Roman) and 3 drops of lavender in 10ml (2 teaspoons) of sweet almond oil and add the blend to a warm bath.

### Relaxing massage blends
Mix 3 drops of lavender and 3 drops of neroli essential oils into 25ml of sweet almond oil *or* mix 2 drops of frankincense, 2 drops of lavender and 2 drops of neroli essential oils into 25ml of sweet almond oil.

### Uplifting massage blend

Mix 2 drops of petitgrain, 3 drops of sandalwood and 1 drop of ylang-ylang essential oils.

> *After 20 weeks of pregnancy you may choose to add 2 drops of rose or jasmine instead of petitgrain to the last recipe.*

## HOW TO USE ESSENTIAL OILS IN PREGNANCY

### AROMATIC BATHS

Simply add between 2 drops of an essential oil *or* 5 drops in total, (if using a selection of oils) to 2 teaspoons of a good-quality base oil like sweet almond. Mix very well and then just before you step into the warm bath add the blend and swirl the water around to disperse the oil evenly on the surface. Then soak for at least 15 minutes inhaling the wonderful aromas. I would advise that no more than three essences be blended at one time, in fact an essence used alone can still create a unique and delightful effect.

### COMPRESSES

These can be helpful during labour and for breast engorgement or inflammation. Fill a medium-sized bowl with water and add 4 drops of a suitable essential oil, then swirl the surface of the water so the oil disperses evenly. Next place a clean, folded cloth on the surface of the water so it picks up the essential oil and then apply it to the sore breast (or other area) or in the case of labour to just above the pubic hair. As soon as the compress loses its required temperature, place it on the surface of the water and apply again.

> *A hot compress should be comfortably warm and not so hot it scalds the skin. To ease breast discomfort a cold compress can bring more relief for some conditions (such as mastitis), so use cold water instead of warm.*

### MASSAGE BLENDS

Always dilute essential oils in a good-quality base oil before applying them the skin. Add up to 6 drops in total to 25ml of base oil in a small bowl or saucer, mix well using your finger or a teaspoon. This provides plenty of oil for a full-body massage for a large adult. Use 3 drops in 10 to 15ml (2 or 3 teaspoons) for a back or leg massage. If you wanted to prepare a larger amount of massage blend add 12 drops of essential oil in total to a bottle containing 50ml of base oil. Then replace the cap and tilt the bottle from side to side several times until the essential and base oils are well blended.

### ROOM FRAGRANCERS

Any of the following methods will diffuse wonderful aromas through-out the atmosphere. Depending on the size of the room you would like to fragrance, add between 5 and 10 drops of essential oil to a vaporiser. Alternatively add the same amount of drops to a bowl of hot water or a spray container (I use a plant spray). For this last method fill the spray with about 100ml of water, add the essential oil and shake well before spraying. However, if the essential oil is kept in plastic for any length of time, it causes the plastic to deteriorate, so a ceramic sprayer would be a wiser investment.

> *When using any of the above methods ensure that the vaporiser or other container of the essential oils is put in a safe place out of the reach of children and pets.*

In the following pages you will find many ailments which are often experienced in pregnancy and aromatherapy recipes to help relieve them. The ailments are arranged in alphabetical order so you will find both antenatal and post-natal complaints in the same section.

*It can be fun to create your own relaxing bath and massage blends and satisfying to treat yourself or those you care for. However, if you are in the slightest doubt as to what you are treating or if symptoms persist seek the advice of your midwife or doctor immediately. Because of your increased sensitivity at this time inform your midwife and doctor of any ailments, pains or excess fluid which develops.*

*Always keep to the recommended dosage and don't be tempted to add more drops. In the case of essential oils more does not mean a better therapeutic effect; they are powerful natural substances and should be treated with care. Also check if an essential oil is suitable for you by reading the information at the beginning of this chapter and referring to Chapters 2 and 3.*

## ACHES *see* MUSCULAR ACHES AND PAINS

## ANXIETY AND NERVOUS TENSION

It is perfectly natural to feel apprehensive, especially as your due date approaches. Every woman reacts individually (but sometimes very emotionally) to everyday stresses at this time. The very rapid changes that your body and mind undergo can be compared to no other period of your life, and this may lead to feelings of excitement and joy but also may involve heightened emotional sensitivity with feelings of vulnerability or even depression. Regular aromatic baths and aromatherapy treatments can help transform 'blue' moods and work towards restoring harmony.

Take regular aromatic baths. Add between 2 and 5 drops of essential oil (in total) to 2 teaspoons (10ml) of a base oil like sweet almond oil. By prediluting the essential oils you create a moisturising treat for your skin. Add the blend to a warm bath, just prior to stepping in and swirl the water around to ensure that the droplets are evenly distributed. Then soak for at least 15 minutes inhaling the wonderful aromas.

### An uplifting bath

Add one or a selection of the following essences: bergamot, grapefruit, jasmine, mandarin, neroli, orange, patchouli, petitgrain, rose, sandalwood, ylang-ylang.

### A relaxing bath

These oils also help soothe upset emotions. Try one or a selection of: camomile, frankincense, geranium, lavender, mandarin, neroli, rose, sandalwood.

### A harmonising bath

Use one or a selection of the following essential oils: geranium, grapefruit, lavender, patchouli, petitgrain, rose, sandalwood, ylang-ylang.

If possible have regular aromatherapy treatments or arrange for your partner or a friend to massage you lightly using any of the following blends.

### An uplifting massage blend

Mix 2 drops of petitgrain, 1 drop of ylang-ylang and 2 drops of sandalwood *or* patchouli *or* jasmine into 25ml of sweet almond oil.

### A relaxing massage blend

Mix 2 drops of frankincense, 2 drops of lavender and 1 drop of neroli into 25ml of sweet almond oil. *Or* mix 3 drops of camomile (Roman) and 3 drops of lavender essential oil into 25ml of sweet almond oil.

### A harmonising massage blend

Mix 1 drop of geranium, 2 drops of rose and 2 drops of lavender *or* bergamot into 25ml of sweet almond oil.

For practical tips refer to the massage section later in this chapter on pages 193-194.

# BREASTS

For *sore* breasts use the following blend: mix 2 drops of camomile (Roman) and 2 drops of lavender in 15ml (3 teaspoons) of sweet almond oil. With fingers together yet relaxed, use the balls of the fingers to apply this blend lightly to the breasts. Work around the whole area but always toward the nipple and with fairly firm circular strokes where the breast and underarm meet.

For *engorged* breasts massage using the above technique and the following blend: mix 2 drops of geranium oil and 2 drops of lavender in 15ml (3 teaspoons) of sweet almond oil. Also prepare a hot compress (as described at the beginning of this chapter) by adding 2 drops of geranium and 2 of lavender to a medium-sized bowl of water, then use a clean cloth as a compress.

> *If symptoms do not improve in 12 to 24 hours seek the advice of your midwife or doctor.*

See also the listing under nipples.

# CANDIDA ALBICANS

Apply the following gel to the external genital area. Buy a tube of unperfumed, water-based gel from a chemist, then add 1 drop of lavender and 1 drop of tea tree to 5ml (1 level teaspoon) of gel. Mix together very well and apply.

To help relieve discomfort and fight infection use a sitz bath twice a day. Add 2 drops of lavender and 2 drops of tea tree to a large bowl of cool water or to a shallow bath (not too hot). Swirl the water to disperse the droplets evenly across the surface of the water and splash the genital area thoroughly. Then sit down in it and soak for at least 10 minutes, or as long as is comfortable.

Alternatively, you could take regular aromatic baths. Add 2 drops of lavender and 3 drops of tea tree to the bath water. To soothe any feelings of frustration or depression which may occur because of

> *Do not use the gel internally.*

this complaint add 1 drop of bergamot *or* camomile *or* patchouli to this bath blend.

It is advisable for your sexual partner to use the above treatments as well, (especially the gel), even though he may not have any symptoms.

> Never *use the douche method during pregnancy and always carry out a patch test before you use a new oil – see Chapter 2 for instructions. Also inform your midwife or doctor to ascertain a medical diagnosis as the symptoms of candida albicans are similar to those of other serious infections.*

# CONSTIPATION

To help relieve discomfort caused by constipation, regularly and gently massage the areas described below with this aromatic blend: mix 2 drops of mandarin and 1 drop of patchouli essential oils in 12ml (2.5 teaspoons) of sweet almond oil. Then, using small circular strokes, massage your lower back, buttocks and, if you feel comfortable, around the sides of your abdomen. If you decide to stroke this area use the balls of your fingers and work around the edges of the abdomen with small circular movements while simultaneously moving in a clockwise direction. To complete the back and abdominal massages trace very light large circles with the palms of your hands.

> *Always use light strokes in a clockwise direction on the abdomen to follow the natural flow of the large intestine. Don't stroke here for too long; literally one minute should be enough once you are used to the massage technique.*

# CRAMPS

To help relieve cramps, which often occur in the late stages of pregnancy, try the following blend. Mix 1 drop of cypress, 3 drops of lavender and 2 drops of geranium in 25ml of sweet almond oil. Massage this into

the feet and legs using fairly firm strokes in an upward direction. Work from toes to ankles, ankles to knees and knees to groin, then let your hands glide very lightly back down to your toes. Repeat several times, better still ask your partner or a friend to do it for you!

## CYSTITIS AND URETHRITIS

Urinary tract infections are unfortunately quite common during pregnancy. To help relieve discomfort use the following methods. Add 3 drops of lavender *or* bergamot *or* sandalwood to a large bowl of warm water or a shallow bath. Swirl the surface of the water around to disperse the droplets evenly on the surface of the water before sitting down. Then soak for about 10 minutes or as long as is comfortable. Alternatively this aromatic water may be used to carefully wash locally after urinating.

> *Inform your midwife or doctor straight away if you suspect you have a urinary tract infection.*

## FATIGUE

Regular aromatic baths are excellent 'pick me ups' although if you feel tired, do rest. It is not a good idea to be in conflict with your body at this time so try to relax and 'go with the flow'. As pregnancy progresses most women learn to catnap when they can, especially if they have other young children to care for.

However, try fragrancing your environment (as outlined at the beginning of this chapter) with the following refreshing essential oils: geranium, grapefruit, lemon, orange, petitgrain. Also try the following aromatic bath: 2 drops of grapefruit and 3 drops of petitgrain *or* sandalwood.

## FLUID RETENTION *see* OEDEMA

# GINGIVITIS

Gingivitis or inflammation of the gums is quite common during pregnancy. Hygiene is the key here, so brush and floss your teeth regularly, and with circular movements massage your gums with clean fingers. Also use the following *mouthwash: add 3 drops of bergamot and 12 drops of mandarin oil to a bottle containing 100ml of vodka. Shake very well before use and then add 3 teaspoons of the mouthwash to a glass of warm water and rinse your mouth.

> *Do not swallow mouthwash containing essential oils. They should not be taken internally.*

# HAEMORRHOIDS

To relieve discomfort and help prevent haemorrhoids (piles) use the following gel regularly on the cleansed anal area. Buy a water-based gel from a chemist and measure out 5ml (1 teaspoon) into a small jar. Add 1 drop of cypress and 1 drop of geranium oils. Mix very well and apply.

# HEARTBURN *see* INDIGESTION

# HIGH BLOOD PRESSURE *see* HYPERTENSION

# HYPERTENSION

Hypertension (high blood pressure) can occur during pregnancy and regular massage treatments will help with this condition. So try using the following blend: mix 3 drops of ylang-ylang and 3 of geranium *or* neroli in 25ml of sweet almond oil.

For a relaxing aromatic bath: add 2 drops of frankincense and 2 drops of sandalwood *or* lavender to a warm bath.

> *Diet and lifestyle changes can also benefit hypertension. Consult an aromatherapist or other health professional, i.e. your midwife, for further advice. Your blood pressure will be checked throughout your pregnancy by your midwife, however, if you notice any signs of sudden or excessive amounts of fluid retention inform your midwife or doctor immediately.*

# INDIGESTION

To help relieve discomfort and heartburn in the later stages of pregnancy, use the following blend: mix 3 drops of mandarin oil *or* 3 drops of sandalwood in 12ml (1.5 teaspoons) of sweet almond oil. Rub it onto your breast bone and on the soft area just below, between your ribs.

> *When working on the stomach or abdomen always stroke in a clockwise direction.*

See also listings in this section under nausea and constipation.

# INSOMNIA

An evening bath using one or a selection of the following oils will help: camomile, lavender, mandarin. Use up to 5 drops in total in 2 teaspoons of sweet almond oil, then add the blend to the bath and soak for at least 15 minutes. Alternatively, sprinkle 2 drops of neat lavender on a tissue or on your night wear and inhale deeply.

An evening face, neck and shoulder massage is also very helpful to melt away nervous tension. Mix up to 4 drops of the above essential oil or oils in total in 15ml of sweet almond oil.

# MASTITIS

Mastitis is an inflammation of the breasts which can occur while breastfeeding. Initially you may prefer a hot compress but later, to relieve the heat

and discomfort of mastitis, choose a cool one. Add 2 drops of geranium and 2 drops of lavender and use a compress as outlined.on page 181. Repeat every two hours.

To help reduce the risk of mastitis recurring massage the breasts regularly with the following blend or at the first sign of symptoms. Buy an unperfumed aqueous cream from a chemist, measure out 25ml (5 level teaspoons) and put this into a clean, dry jar. Add 5 drops of camomile, 5 drops of tea tree then mix well and apply the cream to the breast area using the following massage routine. If you prefer mix 3 drops of camomile and 3 drops of tea tree into 25ml of sweet almond oil. With fingers together and relaxed, work around the whole area using the fingertips, but always towards the nipple. With firm circular movements massage especially where the breast meets the underarm.

*If symptoms do not clear within 12 hours or you develop a high temperature before that time, contact your midwife or doctor immediately. It is also very important to wash off all traces of essential oils before you next feed your baby.*

## MORNING SICKNESS *see* NAUSEA

## MUSCULAR ACHES AND PAINS

For aching muscles gently massage the affected areas with the following massage blend. Mix 4 drops of camomile, 4 drops of geranium and 5 drops of lavender into 50ml of sweet almond oil. Always massage in an upward direction towards the heart. See the massage section at the end of this chapter for hints.

## NAUSEA

Unfortunately one of the best essential oil remedies for nausea should not be used during pregnancy. Try sipping herb teas like camomile with a little honey to settle your stomach.

Alternatively try using one or a combination of the following essences as room fragrancers: grapefruit, lemon, mandarin or orange. Simply add 5 to 10 drops to a vaporiser, bowl of hot water or a spray container to create an instantly refreshing atmosphere.

## NIPPLES (SORE OR CRACKED)

Buy an unperfumed, water-based gel from a chemist and measure out 5ml (1 teaspoon) into a small jar. Add 1 drop of camomile (Roman), mix very well and apply to painful nipples straight after your baby's feed so you can leave it on for the maximum time before the next breastfeed. See also the listing under breasts.

> *Wash off the gel with a* mild *soap and water and let your breasts 'air dry' before next feeding your baby.*
>
> *Calendula cream is also an excellent remedy for cracked nipples and can be bought at most healthfood shops.*

## OEDEMA

Oedema (fluid retention) is a common problem especially in the latter stages of pregnancy. To help relieve swollen feet and legs apply the following blend as described below. Mix 3 drops of cypress oil and 3 drops of geranium in 25ml of sweet almond oil. Using long, fairly firm strokes, work in an upward direction towards the heart. If you don't have someone to do this for you sit on the floor and work around your toes and feet using thumb circles then sweep upward toward the ankle. Then stroke from ankle to knee, then knee to groin. Glide your hands very lightly back down to your toes and repeat several times on each leg.

> *Inform your midwife or doctor immediately if you notice any sudden or excessive fluid retention as this can be a sign of more serious illness.*

# PERINEUM

The perineum is the area between the vagina and anus. In the days following the birth take regular sitz baths to help prevent infection and promote healing. Add 2 drops of lavender and 2 drops of tea tree to a large bowl of warm water (or a shallow bath). Swirl the surface of the water so the droplets are dispersed across the surface of the water before sitting down. Then soak for at least 10 minutes or as long as you are comfortable. If you are advised not to take baths then use the aromatic water in the bowl as a local wash for the genital area.

# PILES *see* HAEMORRHOIDS

# SKIN CARE

During pregnancy some women 'bloom'; others find the changes that occur in the body upset their normally clear skins. For the odd eruption, dab single spots with 1 drop (*only*) of tea tree *or* lavender oil. For a 'balancing' facial oil suitable for all skin types, mix 2 drops of ylang-ylang *or* lavender oil and 4 drops of sandalwood in 23ml of sweet almond or apricot kernel oil and 2ml of jojoba (just under half a teaspoon). Apply to the face, avoiding the eye area, after cleansing. Leave on the skin for about 10 minutes then remove any excess with a tissue. Chapter 9 has recipes for specific skin types .

# STRETCH MARKS

To help prevent stretch marks try the following blend. Mix 6 drops of neroli and 6 drops of lavender in 45ml of sweet almond oil and 5ml (1 teaspoon) of wheatgerm oil. This creates a beautiful aroma which you can use daily to combat stretch marks and it is emotionally uplifting as well. Massage the blend over your buttocks, breasts and any other 'tight' areas but just *stroke it lightly* over the abdomen (always in a clockwise direction).

## TEETH AND GUMS *see* GINGIVITIS

## URINARY TRACT INFECTIONS
### *see* CYSTITIS AND URETHRITIS

## VAGINAL THRUSH *see* CANDIDA ALBICANS

## VARICOSE VEINS

Like fluid retention, this complaint is common to late pregnancy. To relieve discomfort apply the following blend as described below: mix 2 drops of cypress, 3 drops of geranium and 1 drop of lemon into 25ml of base oil. Gently stroke the legs in an upward direction taking care to *avoid* any *varicose veins. Cover the whole of the legs using long, even and upward strokes with the palm of each hand.

> *Use upward, gentle strokes in the direction of the heart. Never apply pressure directly to a varicose vein, massage should only ever be used above the problem area.*

## PRACTICAL MASSAGE HINTS FOR PREGNANCY

Before massaging, see Chapter 5 for the basic strokes, hints on how to and how not to massage and sequences and tips on blending oils. Massage during pregnancy should be light and relaxing, so use mainly effleurage (stroking) and light kneading around the shoulders and thighs. Sometimes receiving a skilled face, hand or foot massage can be as soothing as a full-body treatment. Chapter 7 contains a section on self-massage but only use light strokes and heed the contra-indications (circumstances where you should not massage) on page 194.

As the pregnancy progresses different positions must be used for massage. One comfortable position is to sit astride a chair padded with pillows with the person who is giving the massage kneeling behind you. Another is for you to lie on your side with a pillow between your knees.

*Also listed in Chapter 5 is important safety information and contra-indications (that is, when massage is not suitable). There are a few more contra-indications to add when massaging yourself (or your partner) during pregnancy:*

- *Avoid working on the lower back or abdomen for the first three months of pregnancy.*

- *Do not massage the abdomen during pregnancy. Simply stroke lightly over it, always moving in a clockwise direction.*

- *Do not apply deep pressure to the lower back (unless your partner is in labour and is comfortable with this).*

- *If there is any complication in the pregnancy, such as a risk (or history) of miscarriage or abnormally high blood pressure, do not massage at all.*

- *Read the safety information in Chapter 2. Check in Chapter 3 and the beginning of this chapter for the suitability and uses of certain essential oils for you at this special time.*

Choose whichever you are most comfortable with – this can be a good way to practise how you may feel during labour. It is important for your birthing partner to know which strokes you enjoy before you get to the labour room!

## RECOMMENDED ESSENTIAL OILS FOR LABOUR

Essential oils that are especially useful for labour massage are: bergamot, clary sage, frankincense, jasmine, lavender, neroli, rose and ylang-ylang. Choose the essences for your own labour blend according to your preferences and intuition. I have found combining clary sage, neroli and rose essential oils to be very helpful and a clary sage compress invaluable. I hope you find them as much use as I have.

# THE BIRTHING PARTNER'S ROLE IN LABOUR

Every woman reacts differently to labour and childbirth, but if she has chosen you as her birthing partner, be patient and flexible to her needs. Have the prepared labour blend of oils to hand along with other favourite essential oils. Essences like bergamot, lavender or lemon can be used to purify the atmosphere in the labour room as well as refresh and uplift all of the occupants!

A hot compress using clary sage can help ease the contractions. Prepare as described at the beginning of this chapter and apply it just above the pubic hair as required. During labour listen to what your partner wants – she knows how, where and when massage should be given, and what level of pressure is bringing her relief. Most women need firm pressure applied to the sacrum (the triangle of bone in the lower back) at the onset of strong contractions. Work using the required pressure here and out across her buttocks, then glide your hands back to the base of the spine and repeat. Make sure your partner is comfortable before you begin.

This is a very emotional time and as labour progresses to the transition stage she may just want to be held or sometimes not touched at all. This is when a tissue sprinkled with, for example, frankincense or neroli oil is invaluable. These oils will help her relax, concentrate and encourage her to find that extra energy needed to deliver her baby.

## AFTER THE BIRTH

Once you have rested after the birth and your baby is content (and if your midwife agrees) take a warm bath. An aromatic soak at this time is a boon. Besides soothing any sore areas it will help to 'balance' you after the hard work and excitement. Add 3 drops of lavender and 2 drops of mandarin *or* neroli to a bath. This is most definitely the time to pamper yourself so have a relaxing soak for as long as is comfortable.

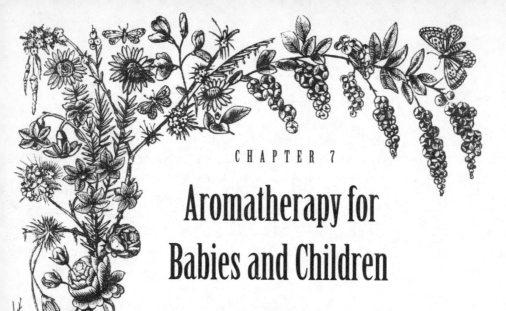

## CHAPTER 7

# Aromatherapy for Babies and Children

Although most of this book relates to adults and teenagers and their needs, this chapter is dedicated to childhood ailments. Essential oils should always be treated with care but especially so when treating babies and children. Very few oils are 'mild' enough for babies and young children and even these should be used very sparingly. Only use 'mild' essential oils for older children too, that is none described as having high toxicity or skin irritation.

> *Before you begin, read the safety and other important information in Chapter 2. Always keep to recommended dosages according to age and other considerations. Also read any safety notes listed for specific essential oils in Chapter 3.*

In my experience I would recommend only the following essential oils be used for babies and young children (that is, from two weeks to five years old): camomile, lavender, mandarin and rose.

I have found the following essential oils most useful for older children (six years to 12 years old): bergamot, camomile, Atlas cedarwood, clary sage, eucalyptus, geranium, lavender, mandarin, neroli, orange, rose, rosemary, sandalwood, tea tree, ylang-ylang.

## HOW TO USE AROMATHERAPY FOR BABIES AND CHILDREN

Baths, massages and room fragrancers are the most useful methods of using aromatherapy for babies and children. Older children also enjoy being massaged but tend to 'graduate' on to fragrant foot baths and girls especially love aromatic perfumes. Using room fragrancers in the home can be of benefit to the whole family. Depending upon the essential oils used they can create a mentally stimulating atmosphere, ideal for older children's homework time. Other essences can soothe upset emotions while others can help with mood swings of more 'hormonal' members of the family! They are also extremely effective when used for their purifying and uplifting properties if your child is unwell. Whether sprayed or vaporised in the home, essential oils like bergamot, eucalyptus and tea tree will help to speed healing and reduce the risk of an infection spreading.

*It is very satisfying to treat those you care for using essential oils but if you have the slightest doubt about what you are treating or if symptoms persist, seek medical advice immediately. Use the dosage information below as a guide when preparing your own aromatic blends, according to the age and condition of your child. Always keep to the recommended dosage and read the safety information in Chapters 2 and 3 before using essential oils.*

## RECOMMENDED DOSAGES

**From two weeks to one year old**
For a massage blend, use 1 or 2 drops of a suitable essential oil in a 50ml

bottle of base oil like sweet almond. For a bath mix just 1 drop of suitable essential oil with 15ml (3 teaspoons) of base oil. Add to the bath water and swirl the water around well to disperse the oil. (See Chapter 5 for details of baby massage.)

### From one year to five years old

For a massage blend, mix 2 or 3 drops of essential oil in 50ml of base oil like sweet almond. For a bath, mix 2 or 3 drops maximum of essential oil with 15ml (3 teaspoons) of base oil. Add to the bath water and swirl the water around well to disperse the oil evenly. (See Chapter 5 for details of children's massage.)

### From six years to 12 years old

For a massage oil use a 1.25 per cent dilution or less. For example, add 12 drops of a suitable essential oil in total in a 50ml bottle of base oil like sweet almond. For a bath, mix between 2 drops of a suitable essential oil or 5 drops *in total* (if using a selection of oils) with 10ml (2 teaspoons) of base oil. Add this prediluted blend to the bath then swirl the water around well to disperse the oil evenly.

## PRACTICAL SAFETY HINTS

♦ If you want to fragrance your baby's room, put the vaporiser in the room about 10 minutes before he goes to sleep. Then remove it, as some essential oils can be overpowering for a young baby.If a faint fragrance is left in the atmosphere the essences are still effective and your baby will be more comfortable.

♦ Essential oils always need to be diluted in a fatty base oil like sweet almond oil before being applied to the skin. The only exception to this rule is when 1 drop of lavender oil may be applied, for example, to a cut or insect sting.

♦ For appropriate dosages when using other methods refer to the listings in Chapter 2.

> *Never leave young children unsupervised in the bath as they love to splash and may harm themselves by accidentally swallowing essential oil or getting some in their eyes. If they do, seek medical help immediately. Be careful of this when bathing your baby too.*
>
> *Essential oils should never be taken internally as they can damage the lining of the digestive tract and some oils are toxic if swallowed. Eucalyptus oil can be very healing if used externally but is toxic if taken internally. It has proved fatal even when small amounts have been swallowed, so* always *keep bottles out of children's reach.*

## ACHES AND PAINS

These usually occur in the leg muscles of growing children. To ease uncomfortable aches use the following blend: for six to 12 year olds, mix 4 drops of lavender oil and 4 drops of rosemary oil in a 50ml bottle of base oil like sweet almond. Shake well and again each time you use the blend. Massage the legs from ankle to knee and knee to thigh, then very lightly stroke down to the ankle again and repeat. If the aches come near bedtime use 4 drops of clary sage instead of the rosemary oil to induce relaxation. For details of children's massage see Chapter 5.

## CHICKENPOX

Use a room fragrancer in the home to purify the atmosphere – bergamot, eucalyptus, lavender or tea tree are all good choices. If you have a baby or young child, put him in a tepid bath, three or four times a day to which the following has been added: 1 drop of camomile and 1 drop of lavender (prediluted together in 2 teaspoons of base oil) and 3 tablespoons of baking soda. For older children use this blend to dab onto the spots: pour 50ml of witch hazel into 100ml bottle, add 4 drops of camomile, 3 drops of lavender and 3 drops of tea tree, then top up the bottle with 50ml of lavender flower water. Shake well and again each time you use the blend. These measures will help to soothe irritation and promote healing.

# COLDS

To help reduce infection and speed healing use a room fragrancer in the home. Use oils like tea tree and eucalyptus as they also have a clearing effect upon the respiratory system. Lavender and tea tree baths will help to boost your child's immune system and help him relax at bedtime. Mix the appropriate amount of essential oil for your child's age in 2 or 3 teaspoons of base oil and add to a warm bath. For older children (six to 12 years old) 1 drop of tea tree oil *or* lavender can also be sprinkled onto a tissue and inhaled regularly.

# COLIC

To help relieve discomfort mix 1 drop of camomile very well in a 50ml bottle of sweet almond oil. Shake well and again each time you use the blend. Apply to your baby's abdomen using gentle, clockwise strokes, also rub across his lower back. Massage him regularly in this way to help prevent colic. For details of baby massage see Chapter 5.

# COUGHS AND CROUP

For coughs, choose from any of the following essential oils to use as a room fragrancer in your child's room: eucalyptus, lavender, myrtle, sandalwood or tea tree. Use the hot water in a bowl method (repeatedly) to provide humidity in the sick room as this is of great help for dry coughs. Prepare a massage blend using equal parts of lavender and myrtle oil, mixing the appropriate amount of essential oil for your child's age in a 50ml bottle of base oil like sweet almond. Shake well and again each time you use it. Gently rub a small amount of this blend around his chest, throat and upper back area. For croup, treat as above and when coughing is severe fill the bathroom with steam and hold him until the worst is over. Regular chest 'rubs' will help to calm your child's and your emotions.

# CRADLE CAP AND DRY SKIN

For cradle cap, mix 1 drop of geranium and 1 drop of tea tree in a 50ml (3.5 tablespoons) bottle of sweet almond oil. Apply this blend over the crusty areas, being careful to avoid the fontanelle (the 'soft spots' between the baby's skull bones). Use daily until improvement is shown. Sweet almond oil can be used alone on new-born babies with dry skin. If it hasn't disappeared within a few days use some nourishing jojoba.

> *Be careful that the oil doesn't trickle into your baby's eyes at any time. If it does, seek medical help immediately*

# CUTS AND GRAZES

Add 2 drops of lavender oil to a bowl of cool water and clean the wound carefully, wiping outwards away from the cut. Then apply 1 drop of neat lavender oil. If possible leave open to the air but put a plaster on if needed.

> *If the cut or wound is severe seek medical attention immediately.*

# ECZEMA

Regular aromatic baths using equal parts of camomile and lavender oil will calm frustration and help to reduce inflammation. Also combine equal parts of camomile and lavender oil – 1 drop of each (if a baby) or up to 6 drops of each (if six to 12 years old) – with 2 tablespoons of calendula cream, mix well and apply to the affected areas. Calming room fragrances can help relieve upset emotions, so try: camomile, Atlas cedarwood, lavender, mandarin, neroli or rose. To uplift emotions try bergamot, clary sage, geranium, orange or ylang-ylang. Dietary changes can be of great help for this condition. Consult an aromatherapist or other health professional for advice. Also see page 255 for details of the National Eczema Society.

# EARACHE

Use the appropriate amount of the following essential oils according to your child's age. Mix camomile and lavender in equal parts in a 50ml bottle of base oil like sweet almond. Shake well and again each time you use the blend. Gently massage a small amount around the whole ear, and work behind the earlobe, on the neck and across the cheekbone area. A warm compress applied to these areas can also help to ease discomfort.

*Always seek medical advice concerning this condition.*

*In the case of babies and young children be especially aware that essential oils must be kept out of the eyes and must not be swallowed.*

# FEVERS

Use a room fragrancer with purifying essences such as eucalyptus and tea tree or bergamot and lavender. A lukewarm lavender bath will also help to induce sleep and soothe distress.

*Always consult a doctor when a child has a high temperature (over 40°C or 104°F).*

# HEAD LICE

Section your child's hair and massage the following blend into the scalp, covering the hair shafts from root to tip. Mix 15 drops of eucalyptus, 15 drops of geranium, 20 drops of lavender and 25 of rosemary in 100ml of base oil. Shake very well and again each time you use the blend. Cover the hair and leave for at least three hours. Then work some shampoo into your child's oiled hair, add water and wash thoroughly. This will make it much easier to remove the oil from the hair. Next, use a fine-toothed comb to remove the lice and eggs. For the treatment to be successful, repeat it every two days for about a week. It is best for the whole family to undergo this

> *Be careful that the blend doesn't trickle into your child's eyes at any time. If it does seek medical help immediately*

process but it's not such a hardship. The essences smell sweeter than the proprietary lotion and act as a conditioning treatment for the hair.

## INDIGESTION

To soothe tummy ache and intestinal discomfort, prepare a massage oil using neroli *or* mandarin *or* camomile. Use the recommended dosages for your child's age and mix them in a 50ml bottle of base oil. Shake well, then again each time you use it. Then, using circular strokes, apply the blend to your child's abdomen in a clockwise direction. This blend will also soothe your child's emotions and help to induce relaxation.

## INSOMNIA

To help soothe your baby to sleep try using 5 drops of lavender as a room fragrancer. Alternatively an evening massage using 1 drop of camomile and 1 drop of lavender oil in 50ml often works wonders. You could also try 1 drop of lavender *or* camomile in 3 teaspoons of base oil added to a bath. For an older child use as above but with appropriate dosages for their age group.

## NAPPY RASH

Regular baths with 1 drop of lavender oil in 3 teaspoons of base oil will help to prevent nappy rash. However, once it has erupted, mix 1 drop of lavender oil and 1 drop of tea tree (if you are treating a young baby) in 4 teaspoons of calendula cream and apply every time you change his nappy. Also keep him as dry as possible and to ensure it clears quickly have some nappy-free time each day.

# RASHES

To relieve inflammation and itching caused by heat rash, for example, use a massage blend made from equal parts of camomile and lavender oil and apply regularly to the affected area.

> *If symptoms persist seek medical advice.*

# SORE THROAT

Make a massage oil with equal parts of lavender and tea tree and rub under the jaw, over the throat, neck, chest and upper back area. Do this twice a day. Also use purifying room fragrancers throughout the house to reduce risk of infection and to speed healing. In addition, use the bowl of hot water method in your child's room at night with purifying essential oils like bergamot, eucalyptus and myrtle.

# TEETHING

Mix 1 drop of camomile and 1 drop of lavender oil in 50ml of sweet almond oil. Shake well and stroke a small amount along your baby's jaw and around his ear area. This will soothe the pain, calm him and induce sleep.

> *Be aware at all times that essential oils must be kept out of the eyes and must not be swallowed. If they are, seek medical help immediately.*

# WARTS AND VERRUCAE

Apply 1 drop of neat tea tree to your child's wart or verruca daily and cover with a plaster.

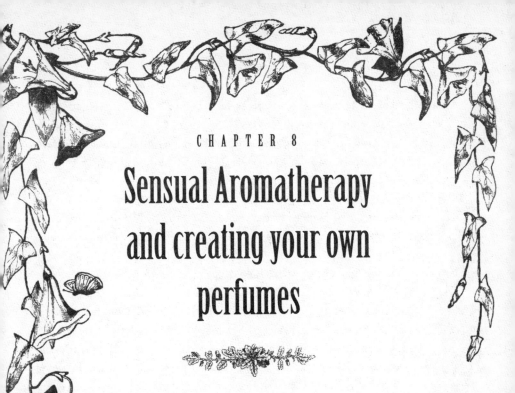

CHAPTER 8

# Sensual Aromatherapy and creating your own perfumes

For centuries people have nibbled beetroots, consumed large amounts of oysters and even powdered rhino horn in pursuit of the ultimate aphrodisiac. But there has always been a more pleasurable way to saturate your senses – aromatherapy. Essential oils are much more than sweet-smelling scents, they have many healing properties and can also be mood enhancing. Some essences have a relaxing, refreshing or uplifting effect on both mind and body while others are credited with aphrodisiac properties. Pure essential oils can be used sensually to create fragrant baths, massage blends, natural perfumes and environmental fragrancers. Turn to Chapter 2 to learn how to prepare all of these aromatic products and more.

## AROMATIC ATTRACTION

For centuries both sexes have used perfume to beautify and express themselves. Pleasing fragrances attract attention and of course the opposite sex. We each have our own unique, chemical aromas called pheromones which work as sexual attractants. They are released onto the skin by tiny glands in the

body. Sexual arousal causes more of this scent to be produced. Through our sense of smell we respond instinctively to others' pheromones which can provoke a like or dislike and even a memory response from the brain within seconds. In fact, the way we perceive aromas can cause us to feel quite differently towards different people; these emotions may range from repulsion or ambivalence to being passionately attracted. If a particularly positive feeling is perceived from a member of the opposite sex the body reacts accordingly with increased breathing rate, heart rate and other signs associated with falling in love or lust!

Throughout history there is evidence of most cultures using aromatic oils for health and for pleasure. Oils of cedarwood, rose, neroli, frankincense, myrrh and juniper are all frequently mentioned in ancient texts. The Queen of Sheba entranced Solomon with her scents of myrrh and frankincense and in Eastern harems essences were used to beautify and for sexual pleasure. Although women are often associated with the use of seductive perfumes, men also loved to use scents. Men of ancient Greece and Rome anointed themselves using aromatic oils or fragrant floral waters both before and after bathing. In fact rosewater was prized by the Romans as a refreshing aphrodisiac and was used liberally at their orgies together with other sensual essences.

## THE ART OF BLENDING

It was not until the twentieth century that chemicals were used to copy many natural essences. These synthetic aromas make up the bulk or whole of many of the perfumes we know today, although some of the world's finest fragrances continue to use essential oils like rose and jasmine. Perfumery is an art and in some cases it can take two years or more to create one fragrance. Top perfumery houses take hundreds of basic ingredients and blend them in varying proportions until they harmonise perfectly.

In the nineteenth century a French perfumer named Piesse devised a way of describing different aromas. He compared them to the notes on a musical scale, so that they were interpreted as having top, middle and base

'notes'. The top notes are the first impression you receive when you smell a fragrance, the middle notes form the main body, the 'theme' around which the perfume is often built and the base notes 'fix' the other essences, holding the whole blend together. Although this system is still widely used today there is sometimes disagreement as to where certain aromas belong on the 'scale'. However, top notes evaporate quickly, middle notes tend to last longer and the base notes of the perfume are the longest lasting. Throughout Chapter 3 you will find a 'Perfumery note' for each of the 32 essential oils described. This may be useful for you to refer to if you want to imitate great perfumers when creating your own aromatherapy blends. However, ultimately let your own aroma preferences and intuition be your guide when blending.

## CREATING YOUR OWN PERFUMES

Most people have at least one perfume which they use daily or perhaps just for certain occasions. Your choice of perfume can express a little of who you are or who you'd like to be. In response others may have their own ideas of what you are like or even your mood from the fragrance you wear!

The advantage of a skin perfume made from essential oils is that it can induce an uplifting, relaxing or sensual effect as well as being sweet-smelling. Create your own unique fragrance by diluting pure essential oils in jojoba, a liquid wax. Unlike vegetable oils, jojoba has a very long shelf life. In cold temperatures it will become semi-solid, so when this happens simply warm it in the palm of your hand or place it in a cup of hot water for five minutes and it will liquefy again.

Preparing your own perfume is quite easy once you've selected your essential oil or blend of oils. Tips for successful blending are given in Chapter 5 or you may want to balance your perfume by using essences which correspond to the top, middle and base note idea, as described above. You don't necessarily have to use a blend of essential oils to create a beautiful skin perfume. Essences like rose, neroli or jasmine are all exquisite aromas if used on their own.

When you've decided what kind of perfume and effect you'd like to create,

blend it as follows. Depending upon how strong you'd like the aroma to be, add up to 6 drops of essential oil to a bottle containing 10ml (2 teaspoons) of jojoba. Add just one drop, gently swirl the bottle around to mix the oils and check that the aroma still pleases you. Continue until the required strength is reached – this is also a good way to learn how just one drop too many can change the overall aroma or effect of a blend. Replace the cap and gently shake the bottle several times to ensure the oils are well mixed. Blended skin perfumes are better if left for at least two weeks and shaken a little each day. Always store your perfumes and aromatic waters in a cool, dry place out of direct sunlight.

Alternatively prepare an aromatic water using your favourite essential oils – see Chapter 9 for directions. Make a refreshing and uplifting Cologne water by adding the following essences to 400ml of pure spring water: 15 drops of bergamot, 5 drops of lavender, 10 drops of lemon, 10 drops of petitgrain and 5 drops of rosemary.

> *For children use 1 to 2 drops of essential oil only in 10ml of jojoba. Before you begin always check the suitability of an oil and the safety information in Chapters 2 and 3.*

Here are some ideas when creating fragrances for men and children, which in my experience are popular.

**Aromas for children:**
Geranium, lavender, mandarin, orange, ylang-ylang.

**Aromas for men:**
Sweet basil, bergamot, cedarwood, cypress, jasmine, juniper, lemon, mandarin, myrrh, myrtle, patchouli, petitgrain, pine, rose, sandalwood, vetiver, ylang-ylang.

Here are some essential oils and their 'characters' to give you some guidelines when blending:

### Floral
Geranium, jasmine, lavender, neroli, rose.

### Woody
Cedarwood, cypress, juniper, sandalwood.

### Herbal
Camomile, clary sage, sweet marjoram, rosemary.

### Citrus
Bergamot, grapefruit, lemon, mandarin, orange.

### Resinous
Frankincense, myrrh.

### Sensual
Jasmine, patchouli, rose, sandalwood, ylang-ylang.

## WHERE TO USE PERFUME

Apply perfume behind the ears, at the base of neck, nape of neck and even on the hair. For truly sensual moments put perfume between the breasts, back of the knees, waist and tops of thighs.

## A LOVING TOUCH

Frigidity and impotence often have a psychological cause, but stress, side-effects of drugs, blood pressure problems and other illnesses can impair a person's sexual desire or ability to make love. Regular aromatherapy treatments can be of benefit as can yoga, shiatsu and acupuncture. For home treatment, take aromatic baths and exchange massages with your partner. Massage can encourage communication, under-standing and can even help to heal rifts. A loving touch used in combination with a sensual, aromatic massage blend can also ease anxieties and have a calming effect

on mind, body and emotions. However, even if you already have a satisfying sex life, using aromatherapy can enhance your pleasure. Some essential oils are credited with aphrodisiac properties and if essences like jasmine or clary sage are blended they can often induce euphoria! A few ways to enjoy the pleasurable art of massage and the sensual qualities of pure essential oils are to:

♦ Set the scene by using appropriate room fragrancers to enhance your and your lover's mood.

♦ Fragrance pillows, bed linen and underwear using your favourite essential oils.

♦ Apply a sensual massage oil to your body before you bathe, then soak for at least 15 minutes inhaling the vapours. This luxurious treatment leaves your skin smooth and silky to the touch.

♦ Share an aromatic bath with your lover. For an even more sensuous experience apply a massage blend before you step into the bath. As the warm water envelops your bodies a thin film of oil will remain, making it easy to massage each other.

♦ Mist your body with a small amount of floral or homemade aromatic water after a warm bath. Small atomisers can be bought at most good chemists.

♦ Exchange aromatherapy massages with your partner using oils of your choice or any of the following 'aphrodisiac' essences: clary sage, jasmine, myrtle, neroli, patchouli, rose, sandalwood, vetiver, ylang-ylang. Jasmine, myrtle, rose and sandalwood have been used for sexual pleasure since ancient times.

> *Do not use sweet marjoram if you are trying to induce sensuality – it is an anaphrodisiac, that is it decreases sexual desire. Avoid using essential oils on the delicate tissues of the body as they can cause irritation.*

## MASSAGE FOR LOVERS

An aromatherapy massage can be very sensual when shared with a lover. Before you begin always check for any contra-indications (any reasons why you shouldn't use a particular oil) and other safety information given on essential oils by referring to Chapters 2 and 3. Chapter 5 gives tips on preparation and blending of oils

and outlines various basic strokes like effleurage (stroking), kneading and fairly firm thumb circles. When you are ready the following massage sequence can be used, initially as a guide and later as an inspiration for your own way of touching. I have assumed the person receiving the massage in this case is a man.

If you don't want to give a full body massage select the appropriate advice from the following sequence and work on any of the following areas: the back; or the face, neck and shoulders of your partner or both feet; or both hands or the solar plexus area. Have fun and enjoy the luxurious experience of both giving and receiving an aromatherapy massage.

*1. When your partner is lying on his front, check that he is comfortable – he may prefer a pillow under his ankles. Next, before applying any oil, gently rest your hands near the base of his spine, then very gently sit across his thighs or buttocks. It is important that you and he are comfortable in this position, if not sit to one side of him.*

*2. Pour a little of your chosen massage blend onto your palm and rub your hands together to warm the oil. Don't use too much oil at once, but keep replenishing as necessary during the massage. Place your hands either side of the base of his spine with your fingers facing towards your partner's head, then use upward, gliding strokes to apply the oil. Use fairly firm strokes when your hands are travelling upwards to the shoulder area, then, pointing your fingers outwards away from the spine gently sweep both hands out towards the outer edges of each shoulder. Then, applying only the lightest pressure, gently stroke down the back and sides of his body. When you reach the top of his buttocks bring your hands up towards the base of his spine again in one continuous, rhythmic movement. You should always avoid losing touch with your partner's skin. Continue with this method, each time starting the upward stroke slightly further out from the spinal area than the last, until you have covered the entire back and sides of his body.*

*3. Gently knead any areas of tension using the same rhythm and speed as the last technique. It may be easier to change your position and sit at the side of your partner as you work on each section of his back. Alternatively hold your original position, and using your body weight apply fairly firm pressure through your thumbs. Trace small thumb circles*

*from the base of his spine to the base of his skull, but be careful not to apply too much pressure on his neck. Do this by rotating the balls of your thumbs or fingers continuously in vertical strips (from base of spine to base of skull) and move outwards gradually either side of the spine releasing any tense areas as you go.*

*4. If you find that there is tension in the buttocks gently knead them as well. Use a squeezing movement, keeping the fingers together and moving the thumb towards them. Work across his hips from the spinal area out and then back towards the centre of the back again. You can also carefully apply circular pressure to very knotted areas by using the heel of your hand or your thumb. Finally, make light and even pressured circular movements with the flat of the hands, all over the buttocks but especially the sides. Then, with even lighter circular strokes, move up to the lower back area again.*

*5. Slide your hands up to the tops of his shoulders using long uninterrupted strokes, and then knead these muscles lightly. The shoulder muscles are often very tight but also tender, so work with care. From the base of his neck, knead outwards by gently picking up the flesh then squeezing and 'rolling' the muscles between your fingers and thumb. You can do this by bringing your fingers towards you and letting the thumb slide over the top of the 'roll' of flesh. Be careful not to pinch or hurt your partner. Use first one hand then the other until you have worked your way along to the upper arm. Do this twice more and repeat along the top of the other shoulder.*

*6. Once the tense muscles have softened, move back to the base of the spine and use gentle effleurage over the whole of the neck, shoulder, back and buttock areas again. By now any stress your partner may have been feeling should have melted away. Stroke upwards very lightly to the outer tips of each shoulder. Then slowly lift your hands off of his body and place them on the floor either side of him. Then lean forward, turn your head to one side and gently lie on his back in silence. From there move your hands to the tips of his shoulders and using the backs of your hands (and/or nails), lightly stroke along the full length of his arms, hands and fingertips. This is very sensual for both the giver and receiver of the massage as your torso connects with his back.*

7. *Slowly bring your arms back to his elbows and off onto the floor again and raise yourself up. Next kneel to one side of your partner and in one long movement using feather-light pressure, stroke downwards from the shoulders, to the base of his spine. You can do this either by splaying your fingers slightly and using the backs of your hands or your fingertips, or you can try both for a more interesting sensation. Cover the whole of the back and buttocks starting with the area of the back farthest away from where you are kneeling with flowing, lengthwise strokes, and finishing with the side closest to you.*

8. *Next position yourself at your partner's feet and cover his whole leg with several long, fairly light and flowing strokes (effleurage). These movements should flow continuously from ankle to knee and from the knee to the top of the thighs. Don't apply heavy pressure to the backs of his knees, but glide over this area lightly. Go back to the lower leg and lightly knead these muscles with the squeezing and rolling action described above for the tops of the shoulders (step 5). Then, using the palms of both hands, glide up at the same time to just above the knee, and knead the thigh area, working lightly all over and paying special attention to the inner thigh which is a sensitive area for both sexes. After this place the thumbs together and stroke along the very centre of the leg muscles, moving from his lower leg to the top of his thigh. These strokes should become lighter and lighter each time you push up and float down the length and sides of his leg. Repeat this three times. To finish, trail your fingertips using a feather-light touch from the top of his thigh to his toes.*

9. *Bring your hands down to the ankle again. Keep your fingers together and place them (pointing to the floor) on the inside of the ankle. Firmly and very slowly draw your hands one by one across his lower leg towards you. As one hand lifts off the leg immediately use your other hand to take its place, stroking the same strip of skin, then as this second hand begins to lift slowly from the leg, replace the first hand slightly above it covering a new area of skin. Without pausing, use this rhythmic, pulling technique right up the inside of his leg to his buttocks. Repeat this process starting from the top and this time covering the outside of his leg. Perform this pulling technique twice up each side of his leg. Now with one hand on top of the foot and one underneath, slide both hands downwards and slowly*

off his foot and toes. Spending extra time caressing the feet and toes can heighten the experience for your partner, as long as he is not ticklish! Repeat the whole sequence again on his other leg.

10. Ask your partner to turn over. If he had a pillow supporting his ankles before you may want to take it away now. Kneel at his feet, and circle the ankle bone with the fingertips of both hands. Gently slide your hands up a little until you are holding either side of his leg just above the ankle with your fingers resting on top of his shin bone. Hold your fingers together and point them towards his knee. Using the palms of your hands, stroke the oil up the front of his lower leg to the top of the thigh in one flowing movement — part your hands briefly as you glide around the kneecap, then sweep upwards together again. At the top of the thigh let your hands separate and lightly stroke down either side of the leg again in one flowing movement until you reach the top of his foot. Perform this stroke twice more. Repeat the pulling technique that you used on the back of the leg earlier, starting with your hands resting on the inner ankle. Perform the stroke slowly until you reach the top of the inner thigh, and then starting at the top cover the outside of his leg. Then, steady the top of the foot with one hand and use the thumb to massage the sole of his foot. Toes can be a very sensual and sensitive. Massage each toe and holding the tip try gently rotating each one in turn. Very gently pull each toe and then with one hand between his foot and the floor and one hand on top of the ankle lightly stroke downwards and off at the toes. Move to the other side and repeat the whole sequence along the front, inner and outer areas of his other leg and foot.

11. Move to kneel above his head and stroke out from the centre of his upper chest to the upper arms with the backs of both hands. Then with the palm of your hands, continue the stroke by gliding the palms to down to the elbows. Return to the tip of his shoulder and slide your fingers between the floor and his shoulders, sweeping slowly inwards and upwards to the base of the skull. Glide your hands down his neck and on to the collarbone area. Repeat this four times beginning and ending with your hands at the centre of the upper chest each time. This is an excellent stroke for relaxation.

12. *Still kneeling above his head, with your hands side by side on his upper chest and fingers pointing toward his feet, use light pressure to glide down the centre of his body. When you reach the area just below his navel bring your hands outwards over each hip then glide them back up covering the sides of his body, ribcage and finally his upper chest. At his armpits bring both hands together to meet in the centre of the upper chest again. This long, flowing stroke helps to connect many areas of the body and is very relaxing. When you reach the upper chest position for the last time, stroke down the breast bone lightly then glide both hands up and out towards the armpits. (If your massage partner is a woman, lightly stroke down the breast bone and, gliding both hands out toward the armpits, encircle the breasts. Or carefully place your palms on both breasts and together gently move them in circles towards each other.)*

13. *Next position yourself near one of his hands. Using a gentle, stroking action (effleurage), move from the wrist up to his shoulder covering the front and back of the arms, then lightly glide both hands down to his fingertips again. Repeat this three times. Then move on to his hand. With your fingers touching his palm and your thumbs on top, use gentle upward and outward strokes with your thumbs. Use your fingers to press and stroke his palm rhythmically at the same time. Rotate each finger holding it just above the joint nearest to the hand and very gently pull each one towards you. The hands are often taken for granted yet they are very receptive to sensual touch. Finally, use several slow, feather-light strokes in a downward direction from the shoulder to his fingertips, then move to the other side and repeat on his other hand and arm.*

14. *Now move to one side of your partner's torso and gently rest one hand on his abdomen. Keep it still for a few seconds to enable you both to 'connect' with this very sensitive area. Then perform small circular strokes using your flattened palm and fingers while simultaneously moving in a clockwise direction. Continue with these strokes and gradually move outward smoothing one large 'circle' around the edges of his abdomen. Use two hands for this very slow movement and always keep one hand on his body (therapeutic touch in this area can help rid the body of emotional tension). When massaging here the strokes should always be performed carefully, not for too long and in a clockwise direction to follow the natural flow of the large intestine. When you have circled the whole of the abdomen, glide your hand*

*upwards from the soft area between the ribcage and slowly over his breast bone and onto
the centre of the upper chest.*

*15. Position yourself above his head again and place your hands on the centre of his
upper chest with your fingers pointing inwards. Draw your hands slowly outwards,
across his chest to the tips of his shoulders. With palms facing up, slide your fingers
between the floor and his shoulders with your thumbs resting on top near his collarbone. Slowly sweep inwards towards the base of his neck and then stroke gently
upwards to the base of the skull. Work very carefully here as this is a very sensitive
area and often holds a lot of tension. With your fingers still facing inwards,
continue the slow, careful stroke from the base of the skull, and up the back of his
head, through his hair and eventually separate your hands gently as they leave his
head altogether. Repeat this soothing stroke three times.*

*16. Now we come to one of the most sensual and relaxing area for massage – the
face. With your palms resting lightly on his forehead stroke them back towards his
hairline. Repeat this three times. Then using your middle fingers gently trace circles
around the eye area (being careful to avoid the eyes themselves). Using upward and
outward strokes cover his cheek and chin area, then move out to his temples and
gently circle here three times. Then try tracing shapes with your fingertips around
the edges of your lover's ears. Now run your fingers through his hair starting at one
ear crossing the crown and ending at his other ear. Use slow, rhythmic, 'raking'
movements with your fingers very gently pulling sections of his hair towards you.
Carry on until every part of his hair has been 'finger combed'.*

*17. To complete the aromatherapy massage, move to the position you used for massaging
his abdomen and place your hands lightly on each of his shoulders. Use one feather-
light stroke down his arms ending off the tips of his fingers. Return to shoulder level
and this time run the fingertips of both hands down the outside of the front of his body.
Now return to his upper chest and this time run your fingertips down the centre of his torso
and continue in one long stroke down his inner thighs and off the tips of his toes. Continue
until you have covered his entire body. These finishing strokes can be as brief or lengthy as you
choose. Then cover him with a warm towel or duvet. Lightly touch your partner's feet for a few
seconds to allow him to come back down to earth then slowly release your hold.*

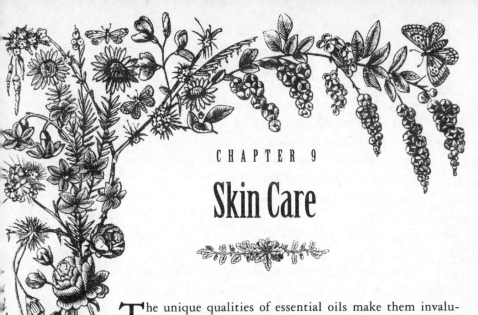

# CHAPTER 9

# Skin Care

The unique qualities of essential oils make them invaluable when used for skin care. Besides being of benefit to the skin they also work to improve your health and sense of well-being. Aromatherapy skin-care preparations provide an effective and natural alternative to commercial products which often contain harsh chemical preservatives and colourants. In addition they are fairly easy and satisfying to make as well as a joy to use. By making your own products you have the knowledge that the ingredients are fresh and natural and that you have created a unique combination of your favourite fragrances. You can also have fun experimenting and vary the essential oils periodically according to the changing needs of your skin.

To a greater or lesser degree all essential oils are antiseptic and stimulate new cell growth. The latter effect is particularly notable in the cases of neroli, lavender and frankincense (it is interesting that these are also credited with rejuvenating properties). Essential oils also have a pH value which is compatible with the skin's protective acid mantle, unlike alkaline soaps which upset this important balance. Some essences normalise the production of sebum, the skin's natural oil, bringing balance to both oily and dry skins. Others

promote the elimination of impurities and waste products from the skin, or have hormonal balancing or anti-inflammatory properties. These qualities are especially helpful for congested, inflamed skin or in cases of acne. When blended in a good-quality base oil and used for facial massage, the effect of the essences can be very beneficial for many skin disorders. These qualities plus the way essential oils are readily absorbed through the skin makes aromatherapy a vital addition to your skin-care routine.

> *Most skin types can benefit from the creams, facial oils, floral waters and face masks described in this chapter. However, if you have highly sensitive skin or a tendency to skin allergies, even very low dilutions may cause a reaction.*
>
> *When using a new essential oil it is always wise to carry out a skin patch test to check for allergic reaction. For further details see Chapter 2 for safety and other important information.*

## THE SKIN

The skin is the largest organ of the body and has a sensitive and intricate structure. Besides providing an outer protective casing, it eliminates waste products through the pores in sweat, which is acidic. It also contains a multitude of nerves which sense variations of temperature, pain and other external stimuli so that the body can react appropriately to them. Vitamin D is also formed by the action of sunlight upon the skin. But, although beneficial in small doses, the sun's rays can be very damaging to the skin. Too much sun can cause inflammation, burning and premature ageing. In an attempt to protect the body from over exposure to the sun's rays, melanin (a natural pigment) is produced which leads to a darkening of the skin. Incredibly while all these processes are taking place the skin is also tirelessly working to renew itself.

The skin's outer layer is called the epidermis and consists of dead, keratinised cells. These cells usually flake off imperceptibly when the skin

is rubbed or washed. Below the surface, however, is an abundance of activity. Put simply this deeper layer is like a cell-making factory. Essential nutrients and oxygen are supplied to this layer by tiny blood vessels which help to correct temperature changes as well as to ensure the growth of healthy, new cells. These cells make their way up to the surface of the skin and then in time they flake off. The next major layer of the skin is called the dermis. It consists of fibrous tissue, nerves, lymphatic and blood vessels and sweat glands. The sebaceous glands are also located here. They produce sebum (the skin's natural oil) which helps keep the skin protected and lubricated so that it doesn't dehydrate. Both the sweat and sebaceous glands play an essential role in forming an acid mantle which helps to protect the surface of the skin from harmful substances and germs. The dermis also contains the fibres which help to give the skin its elasticity and 'youthfulness'. It is the changes which take place here that contribute mainly to the visible signs of the ageing process such as the formation of wrinkles.

## HOW ESSENTIAL OILS WORK ON THE SKIN

Essential oils need to be *diluted in a good-quality vegetable oil or other suitable base (for example, a cream or ointment) before they can be applied to the skin. In this state their small molecules are safely and readily absorbed by the skin. They penetrate deeply through the layers of the skin to capillaries (tiny blood vessels) through which they pass into the main bloodstream. From here they are transported via tissue fluids around the body, influencing various organs or systems according to their individual properties.

The oils can take as little as 30 minutes to be very well absorbed, but this depends upon the condition of the skin; it takes longer for essences to travel through fatty or congested tissue. Heat improves absorption, so apply your facial or body oil after a bath. If you're massaging a friend remember to cover them with a large, warm towel and ensure the temperature in the room is comfortably warm too. The heat and friction

coming from your hands also helps the blend to have the required effect. Eventually the oils pass out of the body through the skin or via the lungs or kidneys. However, the wonderful effects of an aromatherapy massage or facial can last for several hours or more. Essential oils can enter the body very quickly through inhalation and we also receive benefit via our sense of smell. In this way aromas can also affect our hormonal and nervous systems, moods, emotions and even trigger memories.

*Essential oils are very powerful so always dilute them as described in Chapter 2.*

## SKIN IMBALANCES

Skin imbalances can be caused by many different factors, but the skin is a direct reflection of our inner health. If the other organs responsible for eliminating waste from the body are not functioning efficiently, the skin will respond by 'throwing out' impurities which can in turn overload the skin. This mainly occurs because of illness, allergy or following an unhealthy diet. Hormonal fluctuations are another cause of skin imbalances. These occur during puberty, pregnancy and the menopause. However, taking medication like the contraceptive Pill can also induce the same effects.

The weather is another enemy of the skin – extremes of heat or cold and too much exposure to the sun should be avoided. It is now widely accepted by dermatologists (skin specialists) that the sun's rays are very damaging to the skin because of the danger of skin cancer and as a cause of premature ageing.

Spending lots of time in centrally heated or air-conditioned environments encourages dehydration and conversely some medication can cause oily skin and hair. Smoking, too much alcohol, stress and lack of exercise also create problems for the skin, but these are all things which we can change in our lives. Unfortunately we have little control over growing levels of pollution in our everyday environment. This is why it is imperative to nourish and protect our skins as much as we can by carrying out a regular skin-care routine.

# YOUR EIGHT-POINT PLAN
## TO A HEALTHY SKIN

*1. Nourish your skin from the inside by eating a healthy, well-balanced diet with lots of fresh, vitamin-rich foods.*

*2. Drink plenty of pure spring water (six to eight glasses per day).*

*3. Have regular body or facial massage treatments or do it yourself (see Chapter 5 for a detailed massage sequence). Massage is of great benefit to the skin as the circulation and lymphatic system are stimulated. These in turn improve the supply of oxygen-rich blood and help to improve the elimination of waste products from the skin. Skin brushing is also an excellent technique to use for this purpose (see Chapter 10) and even used in the bath, essences like cypress and juniper can also have a general detoxifying effect.*

*4. Take regular aerobic exercise, preferably in the fresh air. This will ensure that a good amount of life-giving oxygen reaches the cells throughout the body.*

*5. Get plenty of 'beauty' sleep.*

*6. Use essential oils in your bath or as environmental fragrancers to enhance relaxation and lower emotional stress. Practices like meditation, yoga and t'ai chi can also bring peace to both mind and body.*

*7. Take precautions to protect your skin from pollution, harsh sunlight and other extreme weather conditions.*

*8. Use aromatherapy in your daily skin-care routine. Cleansing, toning, exfoliating (removing dead cells) and moisturising your skin is very important and the appearance and texture of skin can be further enhanced through the use of pure essential oils.*

## ESSENTIAL OILS FOR DIFFERENT SKIN TYPES

The skin undergoes many changes in your lifetime because of the factors listed earlier in this chapter. In order to meet the changing needs of your skin you will need to vary the essential and base oils you use when appropriate. For details of base oils for different skin types see Chapter 5. From the following essential oils select an oil whose aroma appeals to you and also suits your skin type. Then choose one of the several ways I've listed to experiment in making your own, unique skin-care preparations. Have fun!

> *Always refer to Chapter 2 for safety and other important information and Chapter 5 for tips on how to blend essential oils successfully.*

**Normal skin**
Camomile (Roman), frankincense, geranium, jasmine, lavender, myrtle, neroli, rose, sandalwood, ylang-ylang.

**Dry skin**
Camomile (Roman), frankincense, geranium, lavender, myrrh, neroli, rose, sandalwood, ylang-ylang.

**Oily skin**
Bergamot (bergaptene free only – marked FCF – see Chapter 3), cedarwood, cypress, geranium, grapefruit, juniper, lavender, lemon, patchouli, petitgrain, rosewood, sandalwood, tea tree, ylang-ylang.

**Combination skin**
Geranium, lavender, rose, rosewood, sandalwood, ylang-ylang.

**Sensitive skin**
Camomile (Roman), lavender, rose, rosewood.

**Congested skin**
Carrot seed, geranium, grapefruit, lavender, mandarin, myrtle, orange, rosemary.

**Mature skin**
Clary sage, fennel, frankincense, geranium, jasmine, lavender, myrtle, neroli, rose, rosewood, sandalwood.

## HOW TO MAKE AND USE FACIAL OILS

Use a dilution of up to 1.25 per cent when making a facial oil, for example, add 12 drops of essential oil to a 50ml bottle of good-quality base oil (see Chapter 5 for details of base oils). Replace the cap and tilt vigorously from side to side until well blended.

Body oils can be made in the same way but using a dilution of up to 2.5 per cent, that is 25 drops of essential oil in 50ml of base oil (see Chapter 2).

The shelf life of your facial oil can be lengthened by adding 10 per cent wheatgerm oil to the base oil (5ml in 50ml of base oil). This nourishing base oil is also excellent for scars, stretch marks and burns. Apply the moisturising facial oil night and morning after cleansing, using upward and outward strokes on the face and neck (downward on the nose) and light circles around the eye area. This should be done gently and with scrupulously clean fingers. Leave on for a minimum of 10 minutes then if necessary tissue off any excess. For details of skin ointments and creams see Chapter 2.

*If you have very sensitive skin halve the recommended amount of essential oil.*

## HOW TO MAKE AND USE
## FLORAL AND AROMATIC WATERS

Floral waters are often sold as a by-product of distilling essential oils – for example rose, neroli and the classic lavender water. They are gentle and ideal for cleansing and toning all skin types. They are also great for travelling in hot climates when the fragrance of neroli or geranium not only freshens you but also uplifts your spirits. Another favourite of mine is to pour some floral or homemade aromatic water into a spray container and mist my body with it after a bath. Cleanse or tone the face and neck using a little floral or aromatic water on damp cotton wool and wiping gently over the skin. To make an astringent for oily skin or acne, blend 25ml of witch hazel with 75ml of orange flower water

(neroli) and shake well before use. If the skin is very congested add up to 10 drops of lavender essential oil if desired.

You can prepare your own aromatic waters. Depending upon the strength required, add up to 15 drops of your chosen essential oil or oils to 100ml pure spring water, shake very well before use and apply as above. Store your floral and aromatic waters in airtight containers and keep them in a dark, cool place which will encourage them to keep longer. The following are especially fragrant and useful as waters: camomile (Roman), clary sage, geranium, lavender, neroli, petitgrain, rose and rosewood. The possibilities are endless . . .

## HOW TO MAKE AND USE FACE MASKS

A face mask improves the local circulation and helps to eliminate impurities from the skin. Use a facial steam (see below) to prepare your skin for this mask or treat yourself to a weekly mask while soaking in a warm bath.

Mix 3 level teaspoons of green clay with 1 or 2 teaspoons of spring water in a small bowl. Then add between 1 and 3 drops of essential oil to suit your skin type. Mix very well and, avoiding the eye area, apply to the *face, neck and upper chest. Leave for 15 minutes (or until dry) and then gently wash off using cool water. Orange flower (neroli), lavender or any other floral water may be used instead of plain water depending upon your skin type. A quarter of a teaspoon of cornflower (*centaurea cyanus*) is optional and may be added to the recipe to help soothe the complexion. If you cannot obtain green clay use 'light' kaolin. All these ingredients are available from good chemists, healthfood shops or reputable suppliers of pure essential oils.

> *This method should never be used by asthmatics as it aggravates their condition and can cause choking.*
>
> *It is also not suitable for people with broken 'thread' veins.*

# How to Make and Use a Facial Steam

Fill a large bowl or basin with water which has been boiled, then add between 2 and 5 drops of your chosen essential oil depending on your skin type. Pin back hair from your face and drape a large towel over your head to create a mini steam room. Breathe fresh air at regular intervals while trying not to let too much aromatic steam escape. Stay under the towel for up to four minutes if you have dry or sensitive skin and up to eight minutes if your skin is oily or congested. Then splash your face thoroughly with cold water, pat dry and apply a light cream or aromatic facial oil. This method is ideal for oily or congested complexions as it opens the pores and encourages the elimination of waste products. Yet it is also of benefit to dry skin as the steamy atmosphere has a 'plumping' effect upon the skin cells.

# How to Make and Use an Exfoliating Scrub

This is a quick and inexpensive way of creating your own face and body scrub. Finely grind some almonds and store in a jar. Wash your face with warm water and then measure out a teaspoonful of the ground almonds in your palm. Mix in a little warm water using your finger and then with gentle, circular strokes wash your face with the scrub. Rinse off using tepid water and pat the skin dry. This method sloughs off dead skin cells very effectively, improves circulation and leaves the skin glowing with vitality. This is especially useful for giving your skin a treat in the winter months.

For recipes and suggested treatments of the following and other skin conditions refer to the appropriate chapters: for acne, boils, eczema, psoriasis, spots and sunburn see Chapter 4, for stretch marks see Chapter 6.

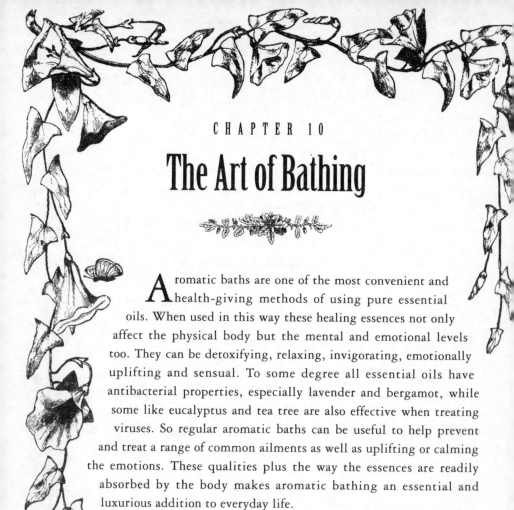

CHAPTER 10

# The Art of Bathing

A romatic baths are one of the most convenient and health-giving methods of using pure essential oils. When used in this way these healing essences not only affect the physical body but the mental and emotional levels too. They can be detoxifying, relaxing, invigorating, emotionally uplifting and sensual. To some degree all essential oils have antibacterial properties, especially lavender and bergamot, while some like eucalyptus and tea tree are also effective when treating viruses. So regular aromatic baths can be useful to help prevent and treat a range of common ailments as well as uplifting or calming the emotions. These qualities plus the way the essences are readily absorbed by the body makes aromatic bathing an essential and luxurious addition to everyday life.

## CHOOSING ESSENTIAL OILS AND PREPARING YOUR BATH

First ask yourself what effect you'd like from your aromatic bath, then select an essential oil whose aroma pleases you and also suits your physical and emotional needs. For example, if you have a cold, lavender oil will help to combat infection and has a very relaxing effect, on the other hand bergamot oil combines the ability to fight infection and induces an emotionally uplifting effect. Use only two or three essences in the bath. When you know each one very well you may choose to use a maximum of four, although just two

can often have a more powerful effect than four – less generally means more with essential oils. See Chapter 5 for successful blending tips.

The bath water should be warm and never too hot as this is damaging to your skin and causes the essences to evaporate off very quickly. For best results wash your underarms, hands, feet and genital area with a pH balanced soap while the bath is running. The pH balance soap is important because the skin protects itself by forming an acidic film over its surface which is known as the 'acid mantle' (see Chapter 9). Most commercial soaps are alkaline which disrupts this fine balance, stripping the skin of oil and even causing irritation. Washing yourself before you take your bath removes any obvious grime and some dead skin cells allowing the skin to benefit more from the essential oils.

Always add the drops of essential oil just before stepping into the bath; if you add them before this most of the essences will evaporate so you won't receive their full benefit through your skin. Make sure that doors and windows are closed so the aromatic vapours are not wasted. Next add to your bath between 3 drops of your chosen essential oil and 10 drops if using a selection of oils. Essential oils cannot be diluted in water just dispersed, so always *swirl the water around well to ensure the essences are evenly distributed across the surface of the water. Then soak in the bath from 15 to 30 minutes, inhaling the wonderful aromas. Warm water is relaxing whereas cool water is invigorating. For a skin toning or instant wake-up treatment you may choose to finish your bath with a cool shower or simply splash your body briefly with cold water.

## MORE BATHING 'ESSENTIALS'

To improve local circulation, eliminate impurities and slough off dead skin cells (exfoliate), gently use a skin scrub made from finely ground almonds or treat yourself to an aromatic face mask while you soak. After your bath apply your favourite massage oil or mist your body with some fragrant floral water or homemade aromatic water (see Chapter 9 for details of preperation). For a different but equally luxurious effect, wash, then use a massage oil all over your body before stepping into the bath. As the warm water envelops your skin you still

remain covered with a thin film of oil; this is ideal if you want to massage yourself in the bath and is a great treat for your skin too. Details of how to make and use all of the above preparations can be found in Chapter 9. Have fun experimenting!

---

*Never leave young children unsupervised in a bath. Not only is it dangerous to leave them in water, they also love to splash and may harm themselves by accidentally swallowing essential oil or getting some in their eyes. If they do, seek medical help immediately.*

*Before you create your own bath blends always read the safety notes in Chapters 2 and 3, keep to the recommended dosages and check that an essential oil is suitable for you or the person for whom the bath is intended. For babies, children and adults with sensitive or dry skin always dilute essential oils in 2 or 3 teaspoons of a 'fatty' base oil like sweet almond.*

*Always swirl the bath water before getting in because 'globules' of essential oils may irritate the genital area if you sit on them. Swirling the water breaks up the essential oils into tiny droplets.*

---

## SKIN BRUSHING

Another valuable addition to your bathing ritual is skin brushing. This involves regularly using a natural bristle brush over the surface of the skin *before* you bathe or shower. This has the effect of stimulating the circulation and lymphatic flow which helps to eliminate waste products from the body. Besides removing dead skin cells, regular brushing can also be of help in banishing cellulite. For further details see Chapter 4. Skin brushing is an invigorating self-treatment which restores energy, leaving your skin glowing with vitality.

Once you've brushed your skin a few times the following sequence should take you between three to five minutes.

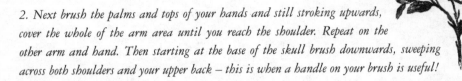

1. *Begin by brushing the sole of your foot, then the top of it, then move on to the ankle and leg. Briskly work up the sides, front and back of the leg and continue over the buttocks to the mid-back area. Repeat on the other foot, leg and hip.*

2. *Next brush the palms and tops of your hands and still stroking upwards, cover the whole of the arm area until you reach the shoulder. Repeat on the other arm and hand. Then starting at the base of the skull brush downwards, sweeping across both shoulders and your upper back – this is when a handle on your brush is useful!*

3. *Come back to the front of your body and brush the upper chest using downward strokes toward the heart, paying special attention to the area just below each collarbone.*
4. *Next carefully begin to brush your abdomen. Start at the lower right side and use clockwise sweeping strokes to follow the natural flow of the large intestine.*

5. *When you've completed this sequence, using long strokes, wipe a warm flannel all over the body. Using clean water wash the hands, feet, underarms and genital area using a pH balanced soap and then take a warm aromatic bath.*

---

*Brushing should always be carried out on dry skin using brisk, short strokes in the direction of the heart. Be firm and thorough but don't brush so hard you cause yourself discomfort. This treatment is too strong for delicate tissues so avoid the breasts, genital area and face and work carefully over the abdomen and along the inside of the arms. If possible buy a skin brush which has a detachable handle as this is invaluable for reaching your back.*

*Never skin brush if you have a skin infection and avoid varicose veins altogether.*

---

## RECIPES FOR AROMATIC BATHS

### Invigorating bath

For an enlivening start to the day use the following blend of essential oils in a warm bath. To enhance the effect finish with a cool shower or splash your body briefly with cold water. For a more fruity aroma add 3 drops of lemon oil instead of geranium.

| | |
|---|---|
| Sweet basil oil | 2 drops |
| Geranium oil | 3 drops |
| Rosemary oil | 4 drops |

### Relaxing bath

For a deeply relaxing bath at the end of the day add the following essential oils to a full, warm bath. For a more floral quality add 3 drops of neroli oil instead of sweet marjoram.

| | |
|---|---|
| Clary sage oil | 3 drops |
| Lavender oil | 4 drops |
| Sweet marjoram oil | 3 drops |

### Revitalising bath

This combination of essences in a warm bath is ideal to use when you've had a long day and need re-energising.

For a less fruity aroma but equally reviving effect add 3 drops of rosewood instead of grapefruit oil.

| | |
|---|---|
| Geranium oil | 3 drops |
| Grapefruit oil | 3 drops |
| Myrtle oil | 4 drops |

### Emotionally uplifting bath

To melt away stressful or negative thoughts and uplift your spirits use the following combination of essential oils in a warm bath. Soak for at least 15 minutes inhaling the aromatic vapours. If you feel like treating yourself add 2 drops of rose *or* jasmine essential oil instead of petitgrain.

| | |
|---|---|
| Bergamot oil | 4 drops |
| Clary sage oil | 3 drops |
| Petitgrain oil | 3 drops |

### Sensual bath

For a sensual bath for one or two add the following essential oils to a warm bath. Do make sure the blend is pleasing to both of you. For a more 'earthy' aroma use 3 drops of patchouli instead of myrtle oil, *or* leave out rose and myrtle altogether and substitute them

with 3 drops of jasmine.

| | |
|---|---|
| Sandalwood oil | 4 drops |
| Myrtle oil | 3 drops |
| Rose oil | 1 drop |
| Ylang-ylang oil | 2 drops |

## Purifying bath

Use this bath to help strengthen the body and combat infections like colds and flu. If desired use 2 drops of penetrating eucalyptus instead of bergamot oil.

| | |
|---|---|
| Bergamot oil | 3 drops |
| Lavender oil | 4 drops |
| Tea tree oil | 3 drops |

## Children's bath

If children see you relaxing in a fragrant bath it won't be long before they want one too! Mix the following essential oils into 2 to 3 teaspoons of base oil, then add to warm water to create a delightful bath. The dosages are suitable for children over six years old. This combination is ideal for bedtime as it soothes the emotions.

| | |
|---|---|
| Mandarin oil | 2 drops |
| Lavender oil | 2 drops |

## CHAPTER 11

# Aromacare for Men

Of course the benefits of aromatherapy are for everyone but most of the following recipes relate specifically to men. Essential oils can be effective for treating a wide range of common ailments (see Chapter 4), but they also work on the mental and emotional levels.

Each essence has different properties, some induce a relaxing, uplifting or sensual effect, while others stimulate mental clarity. Aromatherapy is versatile, and mood-enhancing atmospheres can be created very easily. Within minutes a mentally refreshing or de-stressing effect can quite literally transform moods at home or in the work place. Aromatic baths, massage oils, skin-care preparations and perfumes can also be made quite simply and used for healing or purely for pleasure. Descriptions of how to prepare all of these and more can be found in Chapter 2.

## STRESS-RELATED CONDITIONS

Because essential oils work on many levels, aromatherapy is an ideal choice for combating stress. The high-pressured, fast-moving world in which we live often means that individuals lose touch with their basic physical and emotional needs. A hectic lifestyle and poor

nutrition compound the strain on an already stressed person's mind, body and emotions. This can lead to irritability, anxiety, confusion and depression. If this internal tension is held in, or worse ignored, problems can occur and physical symptoms of dis-ease may be experienced. Common complaints include headaches, digestive upsets, exhaustion and lowered immunity which leaves us vulnerable to infectious illnesses. Men can experience impotence, hair loss, and hypertension (persistent high blood pressure) which puts strain upon the heart. Aromatherapy combined with massage, diet and lifestyle changes can significantly improve many of these conditions.

A course of treatments from an holistic aromatherapist would be ideal if you think you are suffering from any of these problems. These consultations would also provide an opportunity for you to discuss any stressful situations in a safe and confidential environment. However, if this is not possible try using any of the following relaxing and balancing essential oils in the bath or diluted in a base oil for massage: bergamot, camomile, Atlas cedarwood, clary sage, frankincense, geranium, grapefruit, lavender, mandarin, sweet marjoram, neroli, patchouli, petitgrain, rose, sandalwood and ylang-ylang.

*For other 'men's problems', like prostatitis (inflammation of the prostate gland), heart problems, etc., always seek the advice of a medical practitioner and a professional aromatherapist.*

## MASCULINE AROMAS

I am often asked the same question by men who need to go back to work or on to a social occasion straight after an aromatherapy treatment. They want my assurance that they won't leave the clinic smelling too feminine. At this point I explain how essential oils blend together and describe how many wonderful masculine aromas are available. Here are some examples, a description of each oils' unique fragrance can be found in Chapter 3: sweet basil, bergamot, cedarwood, clary sage, cypress, frankincense, jasmine, sweet marjoram, myrrh, myrtle,

neroli, patchouli, petitgrain, pine, rosemary, sandalwood, ylang-ylang.

I have suggested some aromatic bath recipes at the end of this chapter, but why not try creating your own bath blends using between one and three of the above essences. When selecting an essential oil choose one which appeals to you and is compatible with your physical, mental and emotional needs.

---

*Before you use essential oils refer to the safety and other important information, in Chapters 2 and 3. These also give advice on and details of 32 essential oils; which oils blend well with each other and techniques for using aromatherapy. Tips for successful blending and several step-by-step massage routines for all the family are given in Chapter 5. A sensual massage sequence is also outlined in Chapter 8. Have fun experimenting!*

---

## HAIR LOSS AND HAIR CARE

Hair loss can be caused by illness, shock, stress, glandular imbalance and the side-effects of medication. Aromatherapy can be very beneficial for this condition when combined with regular massage and appropriate dietary changes. However, hair loss can also be hereditary and cannot be successfully halted or reversed to my knowledge through using essential oils.

To stimulate circulation and in turn supply essential nutrients to the scalp, add 18 drops of rosemary, 18 drops of lavender and 9 drops of cedarwood to a bottle containing 300ml of pure spring water. Shake very well before use and apply 2 teaspoons of the aromatic water daily as follows: using small, circular strokes work thoroughly and firmly (but not vigorously) all over the scalp and around the hairline. Leave this on the scalp and comb hair through as normal.

For a nourishing hair conditioner, apply the following once a week to *dry* hair. Gently warm 20ml of jojoba then add 4 drops of cedarwood, 4 of rosemary and 4 drops of ylang-ylang. Mix the essential oils

well and massage the scalp as above. Also 'oil' the hair from root to tip. Next wrap the hair in a warm towel and leave for at least two hours. Next, work a pH balanced shampoo into the oiled hair, then apply water and shampoo out and rinse as usual.

### GENERAL TIPS FOR THIS DISORDER

First massage the head, then use a pH balanced shampoo and end by briefly rinsing the scalp with cold water. Also beneficial are daily aromatic baths and regular massage treatments (see Chapter 5 for self-massage) using any of the relaxing or balancing essential oils. These all help to reduce muscle tension and stress levels while uplifting the spirits.

## AROMATIC BEARD CONDITIONER

This luxurious treatment leaves the beard subtly fragrant as well as feeling silky smooth. At the same time the blend will nourish and heal the skin while its sensual aroma induces relaxation. Gently warm 10ml of jojoba and then add 5 drops of sandalwood. Mix very well and gently massage the blend into *dry* facial hair. Leave on for at least one hour then carefully rinse the beard with warm water and pat dry with a clean towel.

## AROMATIC AFTERSHAVE SPLASH

Shaving can sometimes leave the delicate facial skin sore and inflamed. An alternative to alcohol-based aftershave is the following soothing, antiseptic splash. Add 10 drops of bergamot and 10 of lavender oil to a bottle containing 150ml of rosewater and 50ml of witch hazel. Shake the bottle vigorously before use. Close your eyes and carefully splash a little of the aromatic water over the face and neck area.

*Keep your eyes closed when using this splash. Always avoid any of the oils getting into your eyes.*

The splash blend is also useful for cuts. Simply add a little to a damp cotton wool bud and apply directly to the skin.

For details of facial moisturisers and other useful skin-care information see Chapter 9. Suggested treatments for many common ailments can also be found in Chapter 4.

## AROMATIC BATH RECIPES

### Revitalising bath
To re-energise both mind and body add the following essential oils to a warm bath: 4 drops of bergamot, 3 drops of cypress and 2 drops of juniper. Swirl the surface of the water around to disperse the oil. Then step into the bath immediately and soak for at least 15 minutes inhaling the refreshing aromas.

### Relaxing bath
This relaxing bath also has an uplifting effect on the emotions. Add the following combination of essential oils to a warm bath: 3 drops of clary sage, 3 drops of frankincense and 4 drops of sandal-wood. Swirl the surface of the water around to disperse the oil. Then step into the bath immediately and soak for at least 15 minutes inhaling the soothing aromas.

### Anti-stress bath
For a deeply relaxing, anti-stress bath add the following essential oils to a warm bath: 4 drops of clary sage, 4 drops of sweet marjoram and 2 drops of ylang-ylang. Swirl the surface of the water around to disperse the oil. Then soak in the bath and unwind for 15 to 30 minutes. For a different aroma use 3 drops of bergamot oil *or* mandarin instead of the ylang-ylang.

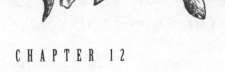

CHAPTER 12

# Travel First Aid Kit

Aromatherapy provides a fragrant and effective way to treat minor injuries, freshen up, repel unwanted insects and much more when you are travelling. The ability of essential oils to affect the physical, emotional and mental spheres makes them useful for both long hauls and shorter trips, alleviating jet lag and travel sickness. Essential oils can bring relief to stings, sunburn and prickly heat and help to refresh you in hot climates. Conversely, après ski aromatherapy eases the pain of aching muscles and cold sores as well as nourishing dry skin. The versatile properties of essential oils make them useful for cuts, minor wounds, stomach upsets and many more common ailments. These potent essences also have the practical advantage of being sold in small bottles – ideal for travelling. Don't leave home without them!

For first aid I would also strongly recommend Bach Flower Remedies. These are not essential oils, rather they are aqueous infusions of flowers in a brandy base which work in a similar way to homeopathy. Bach's Rescue Remedy is invaluable in an emergency for helping to rebalance feelings of shock and fear. A whole range of Dr Bach's Flower Remedies are available with leaflets from good health-food shops and chemists.

*Always check Chapter 2 to see if an essential oil is suitable for use by you or the person for whom it is intended.*

# OILS 'ESSENTIAL' FOR YOUR TRIP

Whenever you go away you should always take: camomile, eucalyptus, geranium, grapefruit, lavender, peppermint, rosemary, tea tree, plus a selection of base oils and a 5ml teaspoon for measuring these and creams.

## BRUISES

Add 2 drops of camomile and 2 drops of lavender to a bowl of ice water and apply a cold compress to the affected area. To help with inflammation use 2 drops of camomile and 1 drop of lavender in 5ml (1 teaspoon) of base oil.

> *Arnica homeopathic remedy or ointment (not essential oil) is excellent when treating shock and bruising.*

## BURNS AND SCALDS

Immediately run cold water onto the site of the burn for at least 10 minutes. If this is difficult then immerse the affected area in ice-cold water *or* apply a sterile, ice-cold compress using 4 drops of lavender for the same amount of time. For very minor burns, apply 2 drops of lavender oil directly to the burn and repeat up to four times a day. It may be necessary to cover the burn, if this is the case add 5 drops of lavender oil to a sterile dressing and gently cover it. Re-apply lavender oil up to four times a day.

> *Seek medical attention immediately if the burn is severe.*

## COLD SORES

As soon as an eruption is suspected put 1 drop of neat tea tree *or* geranium oil on a cotton bud and apply to the area. Also massage the glands just under the jaw line with the following blend: 5 drops of bergamot (bergapten free only – labelled FCF – see 'Caution' under bergamot in Chapter 3), 5 drops of lavender and 6 drops of tea tree.

## CUTS AND GRAZES

Add 4 drops of lavender oil to a small bowl of cool water and clean the wound carefully, wiping outwards away from the cut. Then apply 2 drops of neat lavender oil. If the wound is bleeding, apply firm pressure using a clean, dry cloth or gauze to which 2 drops of lemon oil have been added.

*If the cut or wound is severe seek medical attention immediately.* If the wound is deep or large, cover it by adding 5 drops of lavender oil to gauze which will then need to be taped at the outside edges.

## DIGESTIVE UPSETS

These can come in many forms. If diarrhoea or constipation are the problem see the listings in Chapter 4. For food poisoning, rest and regularly drink water to which a little salt, honey and Bach's Rescue Remedy has been added. This will help prevent dehydration and alleviate much distress. Use 1 or 2 drops of peppermint to fragrance the room *or* lavender which will help calm the sick person. Adding 1 to 3 drops to 5ml (1 teaspoon) of base oil lightly applied to the abdominal area can also be useful.

*Seek medical advice if symptoms persist.*

# FAINTING

If feeling faint sprinkle 3 drops of peppermint *or* rosemary oil onto a tissue and inhale deeply. If someone has actually fainted do the same and hold the tissue under their nose, also loosen any tight clothing and raise their legs slightly. In both cases Bach's Rescue Remedy is very effective.

> *Seek medical assistance immediately if the person does not revive within a few minutes.*
>
> *Make sure the person is still breathing and that their airway is clear.*

# INSECT BITES AND STINGS

For bee stings, gently remove the sting with tweezers and apply 1 drop of lavender oil directly to the painful area. Apply hourly until there is improvement. For the bites and stings of wasps, mosquitoes and other common insects again treat with 1 drop of lavender oil. To help relieve itching and inflammation, bathe the site with warm water to which 2 drops of camomile, 2 drops of lavender, and 2 drops of tea tree have been added *or* take regular aromatic baths using these oils. Try not to scratch the affected area as this encourages infection. However, if this does occur, apply the following blend regularly: mix 2 drops of lavender and 2 drops of tea tree in 5ml (1 teaspoon) of base oil.

Some effective *insect repellents* are: sweet basil, citronella, eucalyptus, lavender, lemon, lemon verbena, lemongrass, patchouli or peppermint. Sprinkle a few drops of essential oil onto damp cotton wool or kitchen towel and fix or wipe these around door jambs, steps, window frames the edges of your sheets and legs of the bed. Alternatively use the spray container method throughout your living space.

# JET LAG

Use the following essential oils in your bath to revive you: 2 drops of geranium, 4 drops of grapefruit and 4 drops of rosemary. Use 2 drops of peppermint *or* rosemary oil on a tissue and inhale at regular intervals for an emergency 'wake-up' treatment. To help you relax and sleep try: 5 drops of lavender and 5 drops of camomile (Roman) *or* sandalwood in a warm bath. Alternatively any of these oils may be used as room fragrancers in a spray container or bowl of hot water.

## MUSCULAR ACHES AND PAINS

Mix 10 drops of lavender oil, 8 drops of sweet marjoram and 6 drops of rosemary in 50ml of base oil. Massage into the muscles always stroking towards the heart. Warm aromatic baths also help to ease overtired, aching muscles. Choose from the following: black pepper, camomile, clary sage, juniper, lavender, sweet marjoram, peppermint, pine needle, rosemary, sandalwood.

> *Black pepper, peppermint and pine needle can irritate the skin so should be used in a 1 per cent dilution or 3 drops maximum in a bath.*

## PRICKLY HEAT

Add 3 drops of lavender and 1 drop of geranium to a medium- sized bowl of cool water. Mix well, then regularly use this to sponge over the affected skin. Also add 3 drops of geranium oil and 5 drops of lavender to a bath.

## SKIN CARE

Air travel, changes in climate and diet can take their toll on your skin. When travelling it is as important as ever that you maintain your cleansing routine but you may need a richer moisturiser than usual. See Chapter 9 for details of

essential oils for your skin type and how to prepare and use
your own facial oils, creams, aromatic waters, face masks
and exfoliating scrubs. A rich moisturiser can be made by
including 10 per cent avocado and 10 per cent jojoba
with your chosen base oil. Wheatgerm oil which is good
for burns and scarring is also very useful.

To keep you fresh in sunny climes lightly mist or wipe
your face and body with a floral water of your choice, or use the cooling
eau de Cologne recipe from Chapter 8. Orange flower (neroli) water is
refreshing and when combined with geranium uplifts your spirits and keeps
you going when trekking!

For a cooling and deodorising foot bath, add 2 drops of peppermint oil
to a large bowl of water, mix well then soak your feet for at least 10 minutes.
This also has the advantage of reviving your mind and keeping insects at
bay. Other effective deodorants are cypress and petitgrain oil.

For a nourishing after sun oil or cream, mix 10 drops of camomile oil
and 15 drops of lavender into a 50ml bottle containing 35ml of sweet
almond oil, 5ml of wheatgerm oil and 10ml of jojoba. Alternatively buy an
aqueous cream and add the same amount of essential oil as above but to
30ml (6 teaspoons) of the rich cream and mix very well before applying to
the skin.

## SPRAINS

To help relieve inflammation and pain, apply a cold compress to the *sprain
as soon as possible. Make this by adding 3 drops of camomile and 3 drops of
lavender oil to a bowl of ice-cold water. Then wrap the compress and an ice
pack around the affected joint. Repeat this treatment often and for gentle
support use a crêpe bandage. Rest the joint, apply ice using a compress
and elevate the injured limb – a method which is known as RICE.

## SUNBURN

To help cool and soothe inflammation add 5 drops of camomile and 5 drops of lavender oil to a cool bath. Alternatively, if the area is fairly small, apply a clean compress across the sunburn. Make it by adding 3 drops of camomile oil and 3 drops of lavender to a bowl of cool water. Afterwards apply the nourishing after sun oil or cream listed under Skin Care above. If the person cannot bear to be touched use the oil blend in a spray container and finely mist the sunburned area.

> *Never massage a sprain and always consult a doctor as a bone may have been fractured.*

## TRAVEL SICKNESS

If the nausea is experienced because of anxiety before travelling, mix 4 drops of lavender, 3 drops of neroli *or* rose and 5 drops of sandalwood oil into 25ml of base oil. Apply this blend to the stomach area in a clockwise direction and to the pulse points on the wrists and neck a few hours before your trip. For motion sickness, sprinkle 2 drops of peppermint oil onto a tissue and inhale deeply.

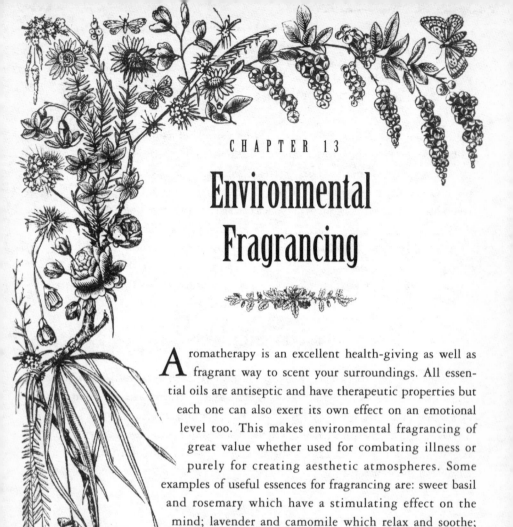

## CHAPTER 13

# Environmental Fragrancing

A romatherapy is an excellent health-giving as well as fragrant way to scent your surroundings. All essential oils are antiseptic and have therapeutic properties but each one can also exert its own effect on an emotional level too. This makes environmental fragrancing of great value whether used for combating illness or purely for creating aesthetic atmospheres. Some examples of useful essences for fragrancing are: sweet basil and rosemary which have a stimulating effect on the mind; lavender and camomile which relax and soothe; and bergamot and jasmine which uplift the spirits.

These days we are bombarded with a wide range of synthetically fragranced items, from cleaning products to toiletries, 'air fresheners' and less obviously fragranced objects like carpets and varnished or painted surfaces; the list is endless. All of these can contribute (some more subtly than others) to an unhealthy living environment. Some people have now developed allergies to many of the chemicals found in their environment – for example, people who spend lots of time in high-rise, air-conditioned buildings.

A friend of mine works in such a place. The windows are sealed and complications with the heating and ventilation system sometimes mean her environment is too hot or too cold. A year ago she began to suffer from irritation of her eyes and throat, she then contracted one virus after another which in time lead to feelings of depression. She discovered many of her colleagues were also suffering from similar complaints. It was then that she decided to take control of her corner of the office and try out some pure essential oils. I am pleased to say that many of her symptoms have disappeared and her body's natural defences are now able to combat viruses more effectively. She uses the following essences regularly depending on her mood: bergamot, basil, lavender and tea tree, and people often come to her desk just for a whiff of the pleasing aromas!

Since the 1980s, the commercial potential of environmental fragrancing has been recognised by some companies in the USA and Japan and these countries remain at the leading edge of this fast-developing market. But in recent years some UK hospitals and hospices have also used essences, reporting positive results for both patients and staff. Other countries are now exploring the possibilities of this type of fragrancing. Who knows, we may someday live in an 'essentially' fragranced world and wonder how we ever survived without the versatile qualities of aromatherapy!

## TREAT YOURSELF TO SOME HEALTHY SCENTS

Here is a brief guide to the different qualities of some essential oils. For further information on specific essential oils and a description of their aromas, see Chapter 3.

### Relaxing
Camomile, Atlas cedarwood, clary sage, frankincense, lavender, mandarin, sweet marjoram, neroli, rose, sandalwood, ylang-ylang.

## Uplifting
Bergamot, clary sage, geranium, grapefruit, jasmine, orange, rose, sandal-wood, ylang-ylang.

## Harmonising
Bergamot, cypress, geranium, grapefruit, myrtle, petitgrain, sandal-wood, ylang-ylang.

## Sensual
Clary sage, jasmine, myrtle, neroli, patchouli, rose, sandalwood, ylang-ylang.

## Energising
Sweet basil, juniper, lemon, peppermint, pine needle, rosemary.

## Purifying
Bergamot, eucalyptus, juniper, lavender, lemon, pine needle, tea tree.

## Mentally stimulating
Basil, lemon, rosemary.

## Insect repellents
Sweet basil, citronella, eucalyptus, lavender, lemon, lemon verbena, lemongrass, patchouli, peppermint.

## Essences for the festive season
*Clove, frankincense, mandarin, myrrh, orange, pine.

## Essences for parties
For adults choose from the above effects. For a children's party try: geranium, mandarin, ylang-ylang.

> *Clove oil can cause irritation when applied to sensitive skin, but when used in a room fragrancer it adds a spicy warmth. Use it sparingly or it could overpower the blend.*

# HOW TO CREATE YOUR OWN ROOM FRAGRANCERS

Depending upon your mood you can create various types of atmospheres, relaxing, uplifting, sensual, harmonising or mentally stimulating are just some of them. Aromatic fragrancers can be used in the home, at work, while travelling, for healing and for pleasure. Because essential oils are volatile (they evaporate easily), your environment and mood can be transformed within minutes with the help of citrus or woody aromas, exotic, floral or herbal fragrances. Choose one or a selection of essential oils according to the effect you desire and then use any of the following methods.

Depending on the size of the room or environment you'd like to fragrance, and the required strength of the aroma, use between 5 and 10 drops of essential oil.

### VAPORISER

Half fill the top of a vaporiser with water, add between 5 and 10 drops of essential oil then light the candle. As the candle warms the water the essential oil will begin to diffuse through the room After a while the water will need to be topped up. Many excellent electric vaporisers are now available and are much safer than traditional vaporisers as there is no naked flame involved.

### BOWL OF HOT WATER

Sprinkle between 5 and 10 drops of essential oil into a bowl of hot water and the aroma will quickly diffuse throughout the room. The humidity generated by this method is especially beneficial to dry coughs when used with purifying essences in a sick room.

### SPRAY CONTAINER

Fill a plant spray with approximately 100ml of water then, depending on the strength required, add up to 10 drops of essential oil and shake well before spraying. This method will leave your room subtly fragrant and is an ideal for repelling insects. However, if essential oil is

kept in plastic for any length of time it causes the plastic to deteriorate, so a ceramic spray would be a wiser investment.

> *When using any of these methods make sure they are put in a safe place out of children's reach and away from pets. Also some essences can stain, so keep away from expensive fabrics and polished wood surfaces.*

### INSECT REPELLENTS

Use any of the above methods – I find the spray container method most useful. Alternatively sprinkle a few drops of essential oil on to damp cotton wool or kitchen towel and fix or wipe these around door jambs, steps, window frames and the edges of your bed, etc. See the list above for useful essences.

### THE WORK PLACE

If you want to use environmental fragrancing at work ask your colleagues' opinions too. The aromas will also affect them and they may not have the same odour preferences as you or appreciate being relaxed when they need to concentrate! Get together and agree on the strength of the aroma and which essences are pleasing to everyone. A particular theraputic effect can often be acheived with a number of different essential oils, each with its own unique fragrance. For example, basil, rosemary and lemon are all mentally stimulating but smell completely different. Alternatively, a less invasive way of using essential oils for yourself is to sprinkle a few drops onto a tissue and inhale from it at regular intervals. A skin perfume can also be used, see Chapter 8 for details.

Countless different combinations can be made using essential oils as 1 drop more or less of a certain essence can change the whole aroma and effect of a blend. For tips on successfully blending essential oils see Chapter 5. You may also find it useful to refer to the perfume section in Chapter 8.

## CHAPTER 14

# How to Find an Aromatherapist

How do you find a qualified aromatherapist, and what should you expect from them? A good aromatherapist will be caring and empathetic, have skilful hands, a wealth of knowledge, respect confidentiality and much more besides! Contact the International Federation of Aromatherapists for details of a qualified aromatherapist local to your home.

However, I believe the best way to find a professional aromatherapist is by personal recommendation. This way you have the advantage of actually knowing someone who has visited her or him and can vouch for their professionalism. If this is not possible contact your local natural health centre, or an orthodox health-care professional. Many complementary therapists advertise or are known by your local doctor or healthfood shop proprietor.

The study of essential oils is a specialist area and I cannot stress enough the importance of consulting an aromatherapist who has completed a certified course lasting over a year. This will ensure that they have a thorough knowledge of essential oils, massage and may have studied other related subjects like touch for health, reflexology and basic counselling skills. This will give you the opportunity to experience a high-quality treatment at the hands of a true professional.

Once you have made contact, the aromatherapist should be glad to answer any questions you may have. It is quite common for an initial free

talk of 10 minutes or so to be arranged, so that you may meet and discuss whether aromatherapy is the appropriate therapy for your condition. It is important that you feel at ease with the aromatherapist as a treatment usually involves massage, so you need to feel comfortable with the person who is touching you. Many women prefer to consult another woman. This rarely proves to be a problem as at this time the majority of trained aromatherapists are women. Costs can vary depending upon the area and the aromatherapist. Some aromatherapists operate a sliding scale of charges where you pay for treatments according to your financial circumstances. Aromatherapists are often fairly flexible concerning the times of their treatments; many working patients need evening or weekend appointments and others prefer to be seen in the daytime.

Every aromatherapist works slightly differently so *do* ask questions at your first meeting, although the aromatherapist should explain in detail about the way they work, how long a treatment usually lasts and so on. It is impossible to say for sure how many treatments you may need for a specific condition until the aromatherapist has talked to or examined you, but they may be able to give you an approximate idea. Aromatherapists may refer you to another health professional like an osteopath, homeopath or herbalist if they feel that aromatherapy is not the best therapy for you at this time. The aromatherapist will also need to liaise closely with your doctor or other health professional if your condition or current medication makes it necessary. Most aromatherapists work from clinics, hospitals, health clubs or other reputable establishments or from their homes. Some will accept home visits but you will usually have to pay for travelling time and expenses. However, this can be very useful if, for whatever reason, you are unable to visit a natural health clinic. While some people prefer home treatments others do not and are pleased to have an opportunity to 'unwind' outside the home in a specially prepared, healing environment.

## WHAT TO EXPECT AT THE FIRST CONSULTATION

An holistic aromatherapist will treat you as a 'whole' person, considering the state and needs of your mind, body, emotions and spirit as well as environmental factors, etc. Expect to spend up to two hours with the aromatherapist at the first consultation.

In order to know which is the best form of treatment and which oils are appropriate for you the aromatherapist must first ask you some questions. This will involve taking notes about your medical history and asking other appropriate questions to help build up an overall picture of you and your lifestyle. Don't feel nervous; the aromatherapist should put you at ease and you will probably be talking in a treatment room already full of soothing aromas. Besides being asked some preliminary questions like your name, address, date of birth and family status, the aromatherapist will reassure you of confidentiality and then ask you the reason for your visit and perhaps how you came to hear of her or him.

The aromatherapist will ask some questions about the physical functioning of your various body systems like the digestive, circulatory and menstrual processes and details of any current medication or ailments. Some questions will also relate to your thoughts and emotions. Do you sleep well? Is there anything or anyone causing you to feel stressed at the moment? It may be a good idea to note down important details concerning you and your life before the consultation. Information about any accidents, operations, illnesses and their treatment since childhood will also be needed.

After many questions the aromatherapist will offer a selection of appropriate oils for you after considering your condition as a 'whole'. If the oils do not appeal to you *do* tell the aromatherapist otherwise you will find the usually delightful massage that follows the interview thoroughly unpleasant. If you are 'fighting' against aromas that are not pleasing to you there is little chance that you will

relax, even under the most skilled of hands. There is often a range of essential oils which can be used for the same condition giving you many potential essences to choose from and the aromatherapist will be used to adapting blends to a patient's individual requirements. Sometimes because of the combined effects of aromatherapy and massage, emotions as well as physical tensions can be released. This is quite natural but if the aromatherapist has not sensed this do tell her or him how you are feeling.

After the massage which usually lasts between one and one and a half hours, the aromatherapist will leave the room and let you rest on the couch for a while. This allows you to come back 'down to earth' again and gives you some time to get dressed. When you are ready the aromatherapist will, if appropriate, discuss another appointment and may give you a blend of essential oils to use at home in between treatments. You may feel deeply relaxed or invigorated depending upon the essential oils and massage techniques used. At its best an aromatherapy treatment can help restore health and harmony to body, mind and emotions.

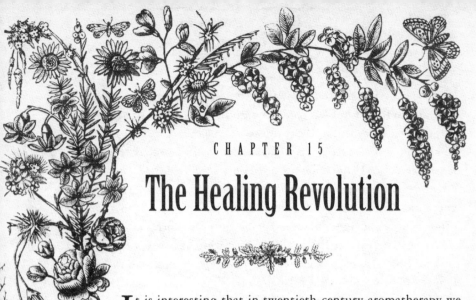

CHAPTER 15

# The Healing Revolution

It is interesting that in twentieth-century aromatherapy we still use some essential oils like black pepper, sandalwood and frankincense that were being used over 4,000 years ago. Sensual sandalwood oil was known by ancient civilisations for its aphrodisiac effects and is still used as such. Frankincense has been linked throughout history to spiritual ceremonies and its ability to create a meditative atmosphere is still used by the Catholic church today. Though other secrets have been lost in the mists of time those of essential oils have not.

From the earliest times essential oils seem to have been in constant use by peoples all over the world. This encouraged an exchange of knowledge which was handed down from one generation to the next. Essential oils were used for many different purposes throughout history – for healing, in rejuvenating cosmetics, incenses and even in the mummification process. And from ancient times the mind, body *and* 'spirit' of a sick person had been taken into consideration before prescribing treatment. However, in the early nineteenth century, chemists learned to isolate the active constituents of plants which had previously been used as a 'whole'. These new advances in drug therapy led to the decline of more traditional remedies and ways of healing.

# Useful Adresses

*AROMATHERAPY*

Essential Oil Trade
Association (EOTA)
*General Secretary*
*(Joe Sapsford)*
*61 Clinton Lane*
*Kennilworth*
*Warwickshire CV8 1AS*

International Federation of
Aromatherapists (IFA)
*Stamford House*
*2-4 Chiswick High Road*
*London W4 1TH*

*COMPLEMENTARY
HEALTH ASSOCIATIONS*

Bach Flower Remedies
*Dr Edward Bach Centre*
*Mount Vernon*
*Sotwell*
*Wallingford*
*Oxfordshire OX10 OPZ*

British Chiropractic
Association
*29 Whitley Street*
*Reading*
*Berkshire RG2 OEG*
General Council and

Register of Consultant
Herbalists
*Grosvenor House*
*40 Sea Way*
*Middleton -on-Sea*
*West Sussex PO22 7SA*

General Council and
Register of Osteopaths
*56 London Street*
*Reading*
*Berkshire RG1 4SQ*

British Homeopathic
Association
*27a Devonshire Street*
*London W1N 1RJ*

Institute of Complementary
Medicine
*PO Box 194*
*London SE16 1QZ*
*Tel: 071 237 5165*

Iyengar Yoga Institute
*223a Randolph Avenue*
*London W9 1NL*

London College of Massage
*5 Newman Passage*
*London W1P 3PF*

Reflexologists' Society
*General Secretary*
*44 Derby Hill*
*Forest Hill*
*London SE23 3YD*

Shiatsu Society
*Foxcote*
*Wokingham*
*Berkshire RG11 3PG*

Traditional Acupuncture
Society
*1 The Ridgeway*
*Stratford-upon-Avon*
*Warwickshire CV7 9JL*

*GENERAL HEALTH
ASSOCIATIONS*

Active Birth Centre
*55 Dartmouth Park Road*
*London NW5 1SL*

Arthritis and Rheumatism
Council
*Faraday House*
*8-10 Charing Cross Road*
*London WC2H 0HN*

British Association for
Counselling
*1 Regent Place*
*Rugby*
*Warwickshire CV21 2PJ*

Foresight –
Pre-Conceptual Care
*Woodhurst*
*Hydestile*
*Godalming*
*Surrey*

National Asthma Campaign
*Providence House*
*Providence Place*
*London N1 0NT*

National Eczema Society
*4 Tavistock Place*
*London WC1H 9RA*